IMAGES
of America

FLOYD COUNTY

ON THE COVER: Originally a mercantile store for Howard and Thomas Huff, the Horatio Howard Building has been the Farmers' Supply Store for almost 100 years. (Courtesy of Floyd County Historical Society Archives)

IMAGES *of America*

FLOYD COUNTY

Floyd County Historical Society, Inc.

ARCADIA PUBLISHING

ISBN 978-0-7385-9271-8

Published by Arcadia Publishing
Charleston, South Carolina

Printed in the United States of America

Library of Congress Control Number: 2012931243

For all general information, please contact Arcadia Publishing:
Telephone 843-853-2070
Fax 843-853-0044
E-mail sales@arcadiapublishing.com
For customer service and orders:
Toll-Free 1-888-313-2665

Visit us on the Internet at www.arcadiapublishing.com

To Effie King Brown, in recognition of all her hard work to preserve Floyd County history and help create the Floyd County Historical Society. Without her vision, this book would not have been possible.

Contents

Acknowledgments

Floyd County Historical Society (FCHS) would like to thank all of the volunteers on the book committee, the individuals who allowed us access to their photographs, and the people of Floyd County for their continued support.

Photographs are courtesy of: Nola Shelor Albert (NSA), Russell Akers (RA), Sue Williams Back (SWB), Winfred Beale (WB), Judith G. Blackwell (JGB), Sharon Custer-Boggess (SCB), Goldie Boyd (GB), Sue Snead Boyd (SSB), Sue Anne Boothe (SAB), Stewart Childress (SC), Danny Cockram (DC), Bill and Roy Cole (BRC), Ricky Cox (RC), Haydon Dickerson (HD), Fisk University (FU), Melissa McAlexander Goodson (MMG), John Graham (JG), Frances M. Harman (FMH), Bert Hatcher (BH), Margaret Hubbard (MH), Jack Hylton (JH), June Harmon Hylton (JHH), Janet Slusher Keith (JSK), Alma Mannon (AM), Burnett Marshall (BM), David R. Martin (DRM), Debra Phillips McAlexander (DPM), Connie Harris Mitchell (CHM), Old Church Gallery – The Floyd County Collection (OCG), Catherine Pauley (CP), Shirley Q. Phillips (SQP), Mary Poff (MP), Zelda Quesenberry (ZQ), Jean Thomas Schaeffer (JTS), Stewart Shank (SS), George Shelor (GS), Janice Shelor (JS), Warren Shelor (WS), Carolyn Shockley (CSA), the family of Basil Poff Simpson Sr. (BPS), Alice P. Slusher (APS), Maurice Slusher (MS), Margaret A. Smith (MAS), Rhonda Fleming Smith (RFS), Curtis Sowers (CS), Genevieve C. Starkey (GCS), Denise Dalton Stilwell (DDS), Bruce Sweeney (BS), Lois C. Thompson (LCT), Rebecca A. Weeks (RAW), and Gino Williams (GW). All photographs not identified with a contributor's name came from the Floyd County Historical Society archives.

Some large groups are identified, but there was not enough room in some captions to list everyone. Contact the FCHS for complete identifications of those in group photographs. If you can name an unidentified person, please let us know.

Names are sometimes spelled several different ways. We chose to have only one spelling in this book, usually the one the contributor used.

This is the first in a series of books to be compiled by FCHS. Please continue to share your photographs so they can be digitally scanned and preserved for future generations.

Floyd County Historical Society
P.O. Box 292
Floyd, VA 24091
www.floydhistoricalsociety.org

Introduction

The Kanawha Indians were drawn to the land that is now Floyd County by Buffalo Mountain, the summit of which resembles the buffalo sacred to them. Place names like Indian Ridge and Indian Valley remind us that Native Americans camped and hunted here long before white explorers arrived.

Beginning in the 18th century, the forested, rolling hills of the Blue Ridge, covered in the blooms of chestnut trees like snow in spring, beckoned newcomers of European descent. Some were first- or second-generation German and Scotch-Irish immigrants moving down the Shenandoah Valley from Pennsylvania. Other early arrivals, mostly of English and French lineage, had been in the colonies much longer. Some had become prosperous enough to purchase slaves as successive generations pressed westward toward the mountains from the Virginia Piedmont. Mountain gaps opening onto the Blue Ridge Plateau made Floyd a natural shortcut between the Carolina Road to the east and the Wilderness Road to the west. Many people passed through or stopped only briefly, but many others found what they were seeking.

Rain falling in the eastern end of Floyd County makes its way to the Atlantic Ocean. But the majority of the county, lying west of the Eastern Continental Divide, is drained by tributaries of the New River, whose waters eventually reach the Mississippi River. Headwater streams suitable for small gristmills and sawmills flow from the county in virtually every direction. As various groups settled along these streams and became neighbors, cultures mingled and were adapted to the new lands, establishing ways of life that seemed to hardly change for generations, yet were constantly modified. Churches, stores, one- and two-room schools, post offices, and mills were often unifying features of the communities around them, supplying both a name to a spot on the map and a sense of identity to the people nearby. The collection of photographs in this book represents daily life as lived in many of these places from the 1800s through 1960 and offers a glimpse into the area's roots and values.

The 19th century brought great change as Floyd County was caught up in national concerns, with citizens divided by the issues of slavery and secession, and many county natives moved on to westward lands. One of Levi Coffin's Underground Railroad routes ran through the southwestern corner of Floyd County. Local men served in several Confederate regiments, including the 24th, 42nd, and 54th Virginia Infantry Regiments, the 21st Virginia Cavalry, Stuart's Horse Artillery, the 4th Virginia Reserves, and various other units. While few photographs exist from the era, Floyd County's Civil War heritage is represented here by photographs of former slaves, sites known to Union general George C. Stoneman as his army took the surrender of Floyd in early April 1865, and of other leaders, including Robley D. Evans, who later became a rear admiral in the US navy and a hero of the Spanish American War.

World and national events continued to shape Floyd County in the 20th century. Floyd men stepped up to do their part in World War I. The Prohibition era led to a spike in crime rates as legal distilleries were replaced by illegal stills and bootlegging. NASCAR's origins trace back to drivers like Floyd County's Curtis Turner, who hauled moonshine over the curving county roads.

With Mabry Mill as a major attraction, more miles of the Blue Ridge Parkway run through Floyd County than any other county in Virginia. During the Depression, residents found work with federally funded programs such as the Civilian Conservation Corps (CCC), the Works Progress Administration (WPA), and the Emergency Relief Administration (ERA), as well as with private contractors building the parkway.

As men headed off to World War II, women once again took over farms and many went to work in factories. Throughout the first half of the century, more and more families left their farms for public work jobs. One-room schools were consolidated into four county elementary schools and returning veterans opened new businesses. With the advances of automobiles, electricity, and paved highways, more Floyd Countians began to travel beyond their home communities for work and pleasure.

Ministers and musicians, farmers and entrepreneurs, baseball players and storekeepers, plowmen and politicians, are all faces forming this portrait of Floyd County. We hope you enjoy the tour.

One

PLACES

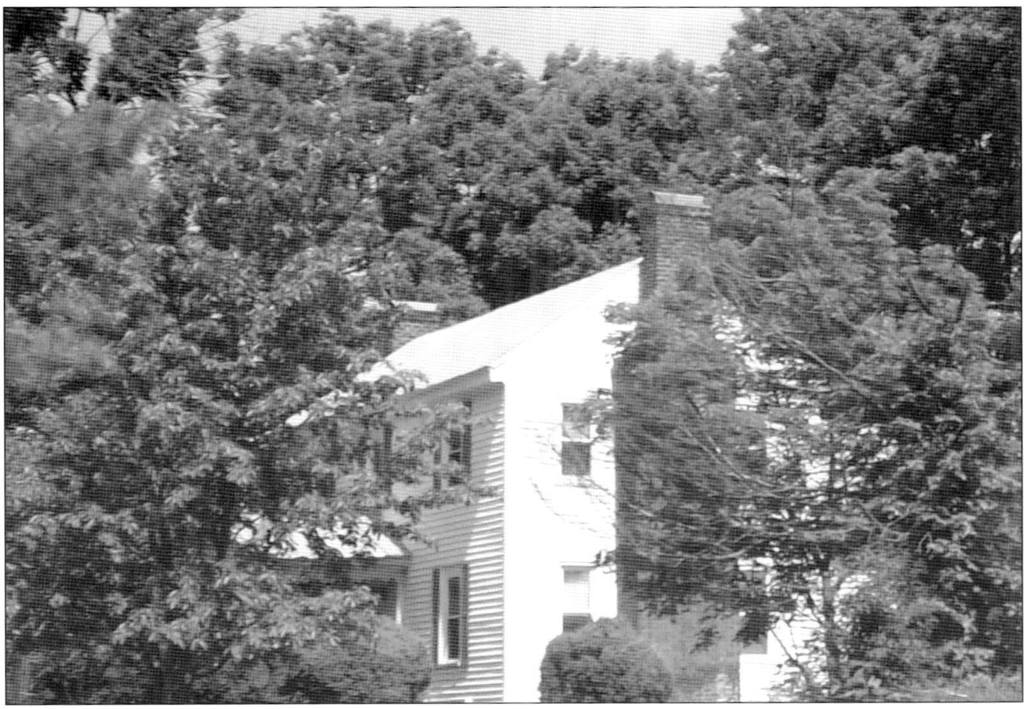

Rose Hill was the home of Col. Jacob Helms, who represented Floyd County in the House of Delegates when the county was formed. Tax records show him to be one of the county's largest slaveholders. The wealthy man served as "the bank" for early Floyd County and fought to locate the Floyd courthouse at Falling Branch near Rose Hill instead of at George Sowers's on Pine Creek. It was finally decided to split the distance from these two locations and place the courthouse where it is today. (DRM)

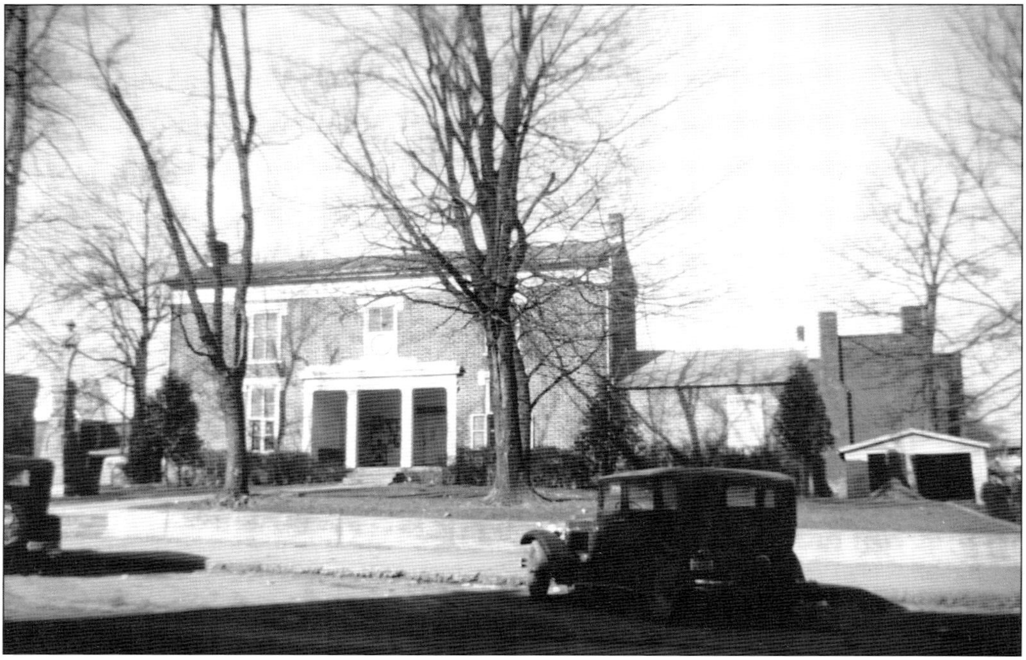

The second Floyd courthouse, shown here, replaced the original frame building constructed by James Toncray in 1832. The second courthouse remained in use for 100 years until it was replaced by the current building. The clock on the front of this building hangs in the courtroom of the current courthouse.

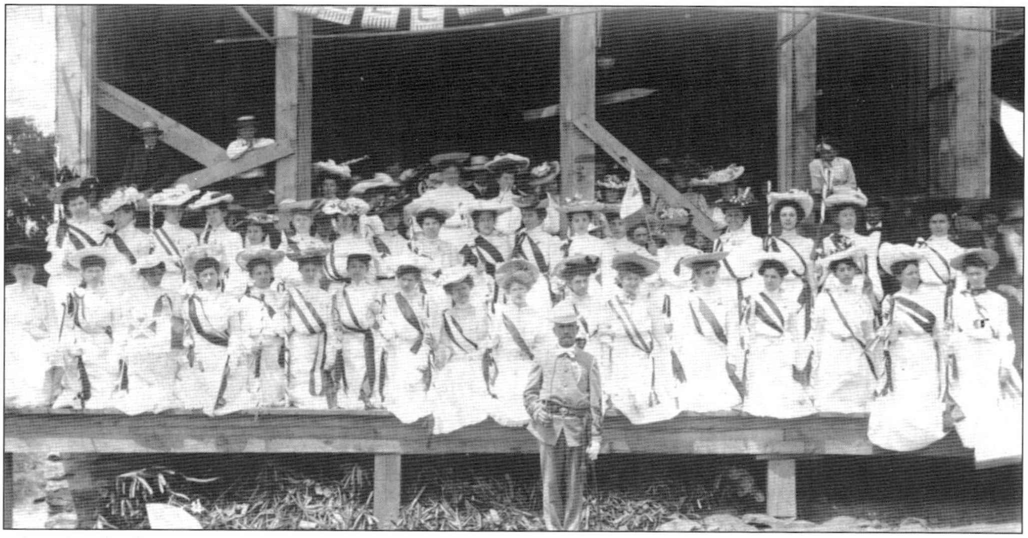

The Floyd Chapter 723 United Daughters of the Confederacy gathered on July 4, 1904, to dedicate the Confederate Monument on the grounds of the courthouse. It is thought that the man in the foreground is Dr. Callohill M. Stigleman, who gave the keynote address at the dedication. Dr. Stigleman was captain of the "Floyd Riflemen," Company A, 24th Virginia Infantry, and served as Floyd's first superintendent of schools and first mayor.

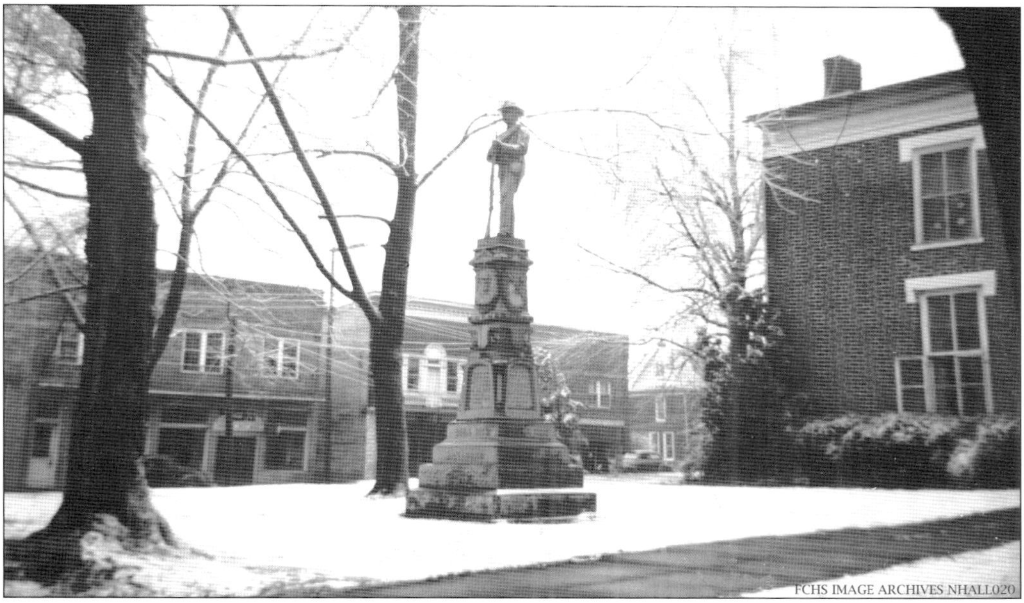

The Confederate Memorial stands guard in the snow in front of the second courthouse. It is believed the sculptor modeled the statue after himself, thus preserving his own likeness as well as memorializing Confederate soldiers on identical statues erected on courthouse lawns throughout the south.

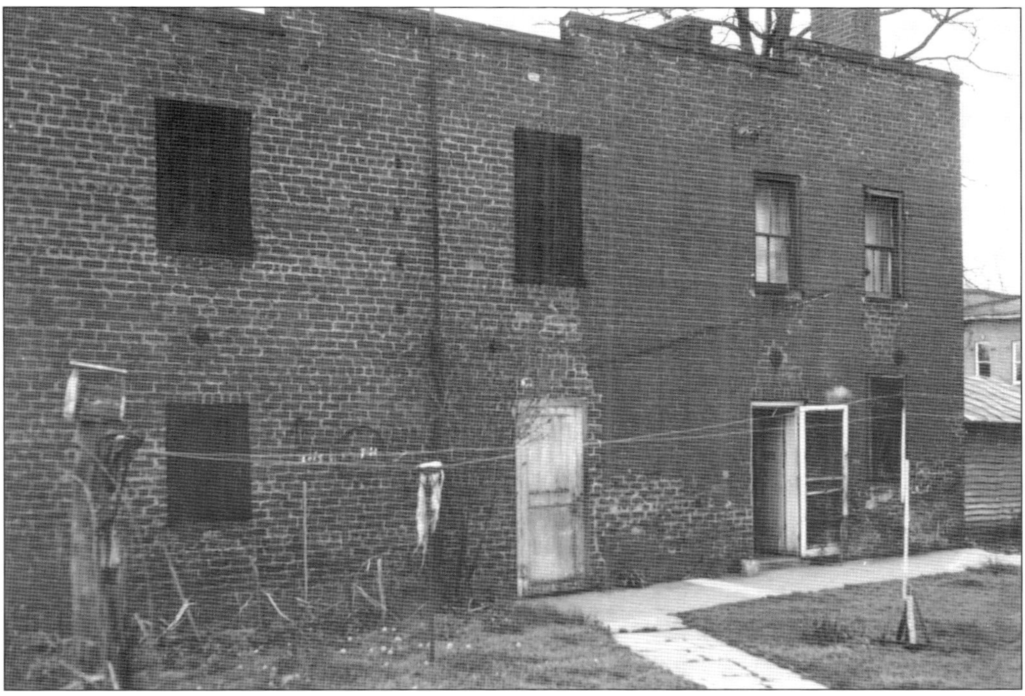

Floyd Jail, shown in rundown condition in the 1940s, was the main jail for Floyd County from about 1851 until it was replaced in the 1950s. It also acted as a federal transfer holding facility during the 1920s and 1930s. The jailers lived in the upper right portion of the jail. (AM)

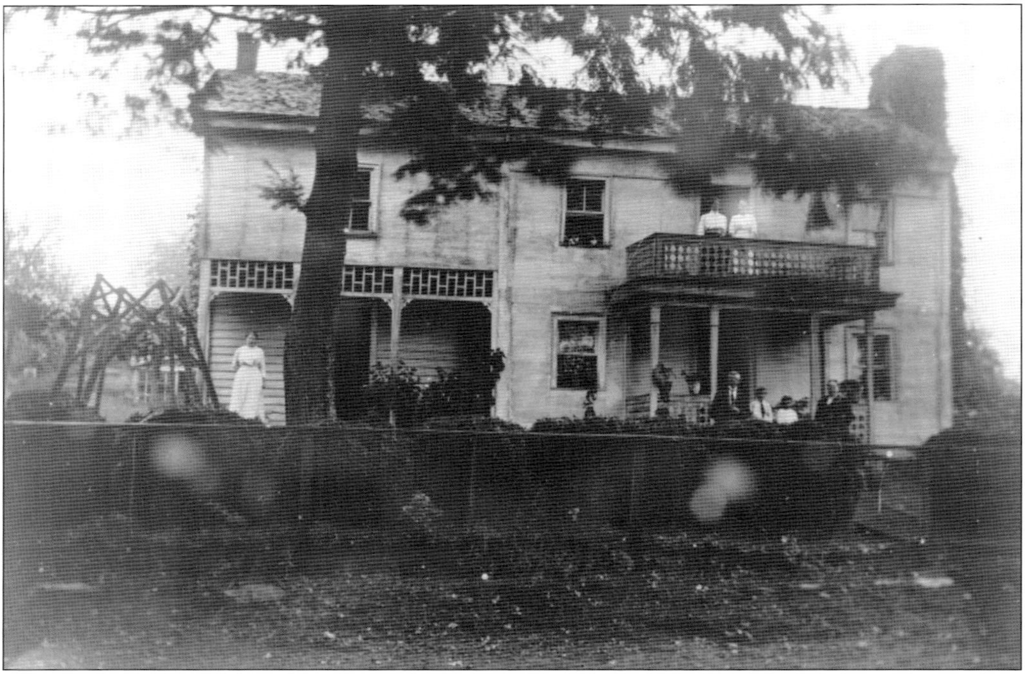

The George Phlegar house is north of the town of Floyd. A chimney inscription dates the original log section of the two-story, weather-boarded structure to 1816. The inscription on the chimney includes the letters "GP" for George Phlegar, one of many German-American settlers who arrived in the county after 1790. The two-story frame addition (left) was most likely constructed by his grandson, William S. Phlegar, shortly after 1900.

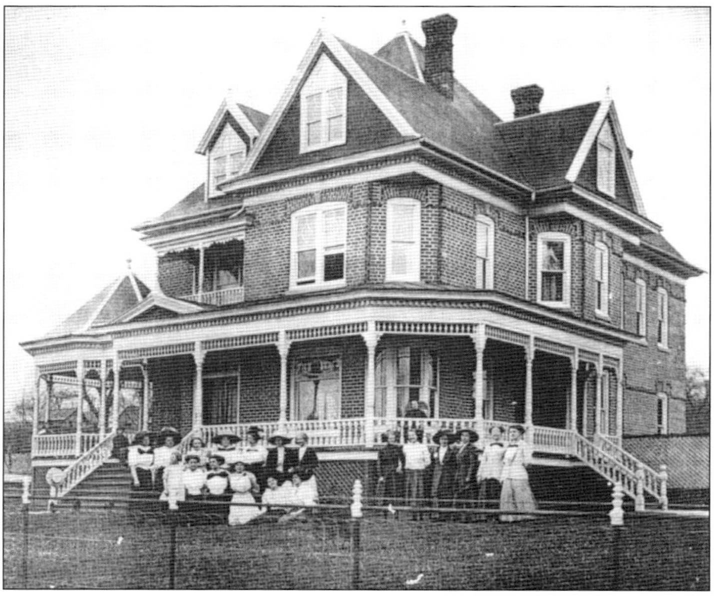

The Jabez Harman house, on Main Street, was the home of Dr. Jabez and Marcella Elgin Harman. The Queen Anne Victorian house was customized from a George Barber mail-order kit. Dr. Harman's medical practice was first conducted from a building in the backyard. The property remains in the Harman family. Dr. Harman's son, Christopher Columbus Harman Sr., was a beloved veterinarian in Floyd County.

Next to the Jabez Harman house was Dr. Harman's second office. This photograph shows the office with the Jacksonville (later Floyd) Methodist Church in the background. The dirt road in the front is Main Street. The office was built in 1904 to replace an 1897 office that was destroyed by fire.

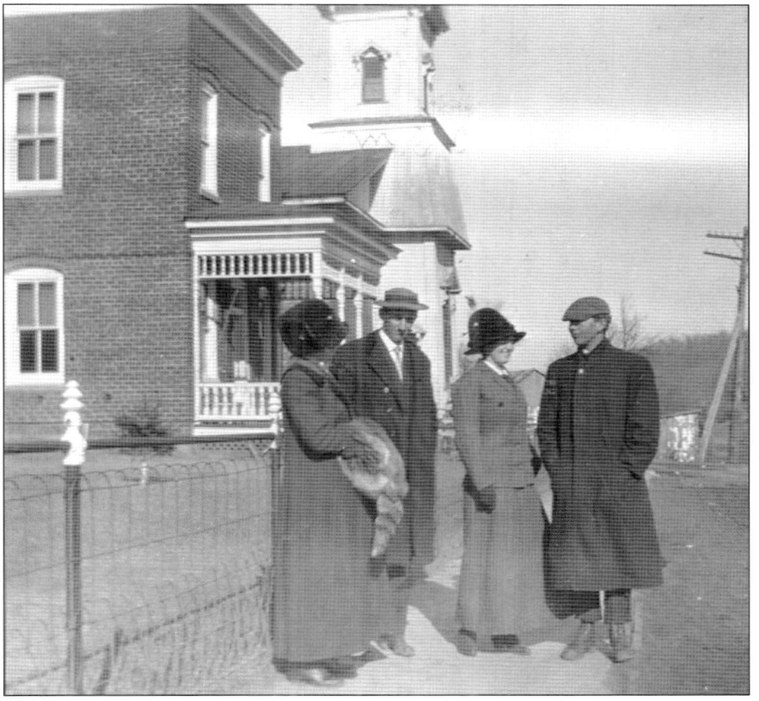

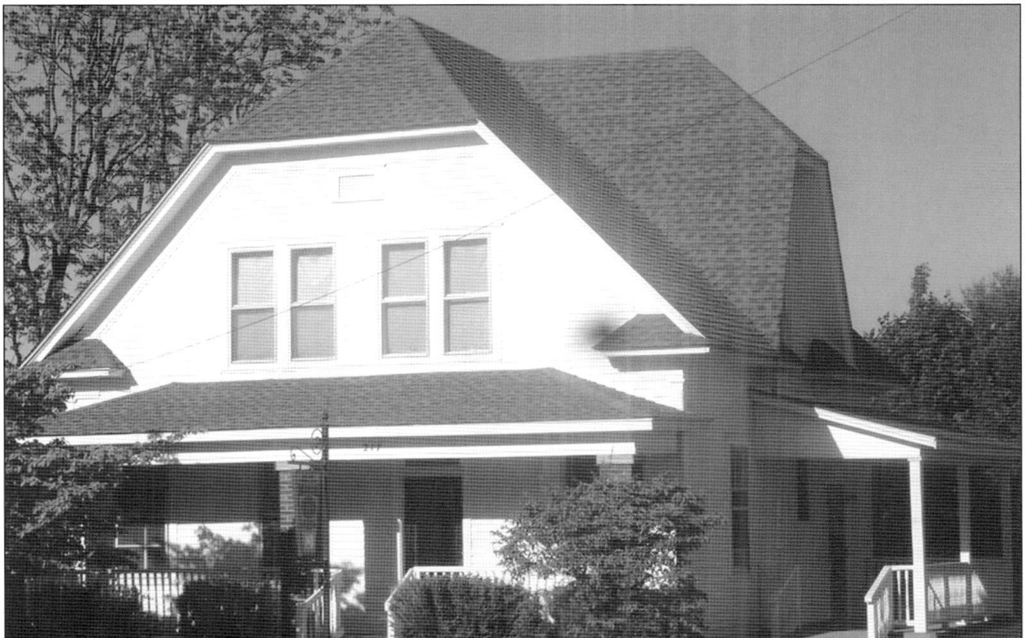

The Ridgemont was the first hospital in Floyd County. Built in 1913 by Lather Hylton for Dr. Martin Luther Dalton, the nine-bed hospital with a surgery room had the first x-ray machine in southwest Virginia and operated until 1923. In 2010, the Floyd County Historical Society opened a museum in the building, which had been the home of Marie Williams.

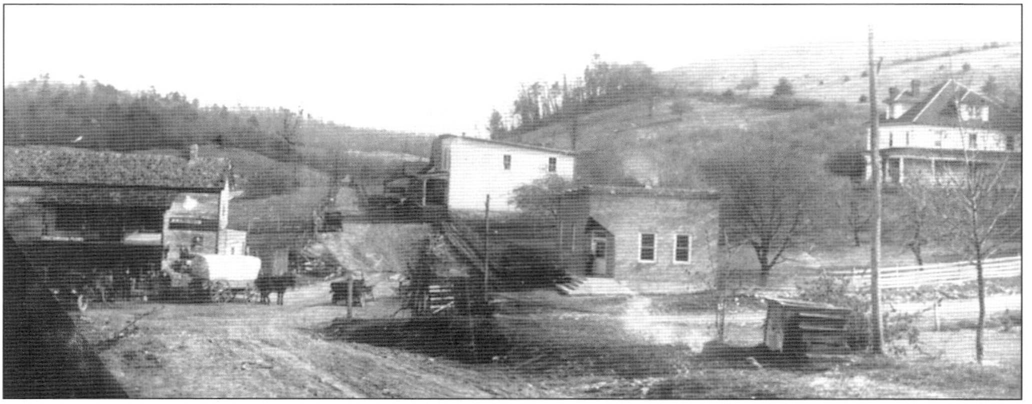

In this view of Check from around 1918, the road in the foreground ran from Simpsons to Graysville. The road crossing from left to right is the predecessor of Route 221 and the house in the upper right is the Horace Poff house. The State Bank of Check building, which was later the post office, is in the right foreground.

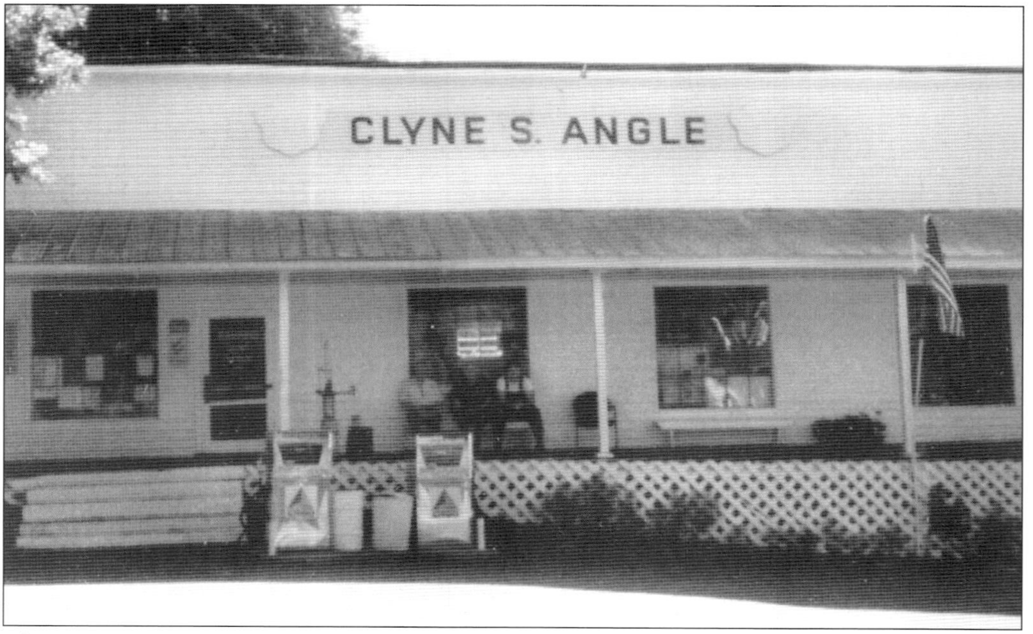

The Simpsons post office was in Clyne S. Angle's country store in Simpsons, a major crossroads in the early days of the area. The post office was established in 1823, eight years before Floyd County's formation. The post office was designated a Floyd County post office on June 9, 1832, and was operated until August 1979. (MS)

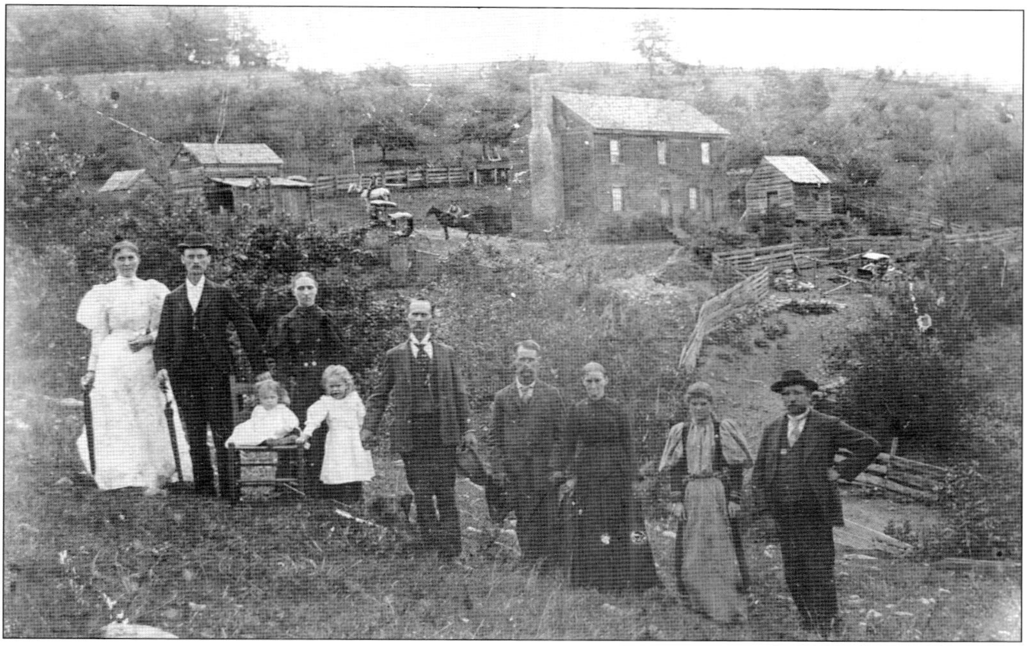

The Graysville post office was established on June 14, 1872, with Thomas K. Dewitt as the first postmaster. While serving as postmaster in 1879, Mark Custer used his residence as the post office location. Here, Custer stands with his wife, two daughters, and others with the Custer farm in the background. The post office was located southeast of Check, at various locations, from 1872 to November 1909. (SCB)

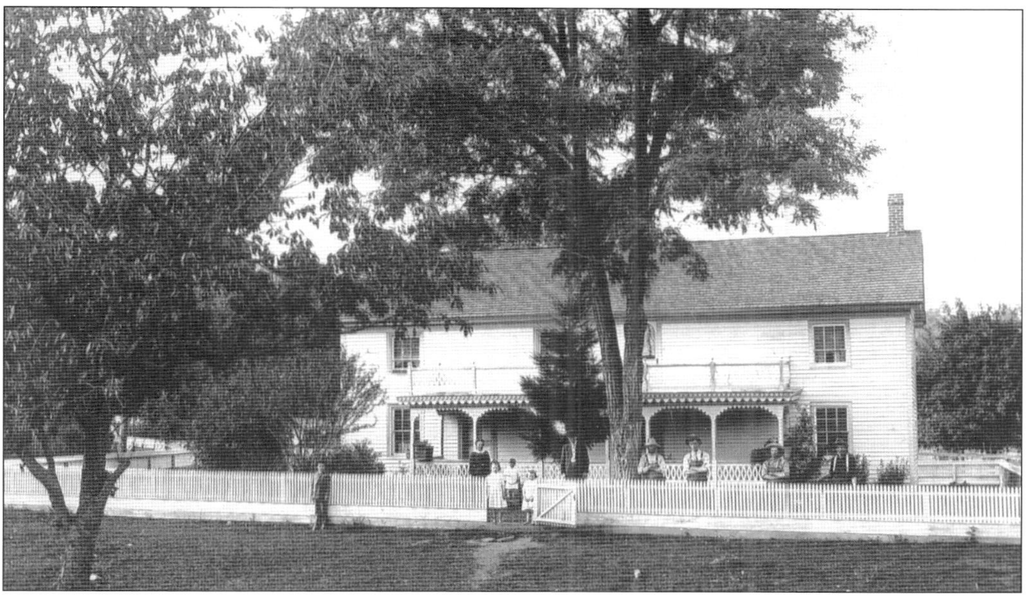

William M. Slaughter was the postmaster at the Santos post office when it opened on April 13, 1886. As with most small post offices, changes occurred often with both the postmasters and the office locations. Here, George W. Slusher, the Santos postmaster from 1900 until 1905, stands with his family in front of their home, which also served as the post office. (MS)

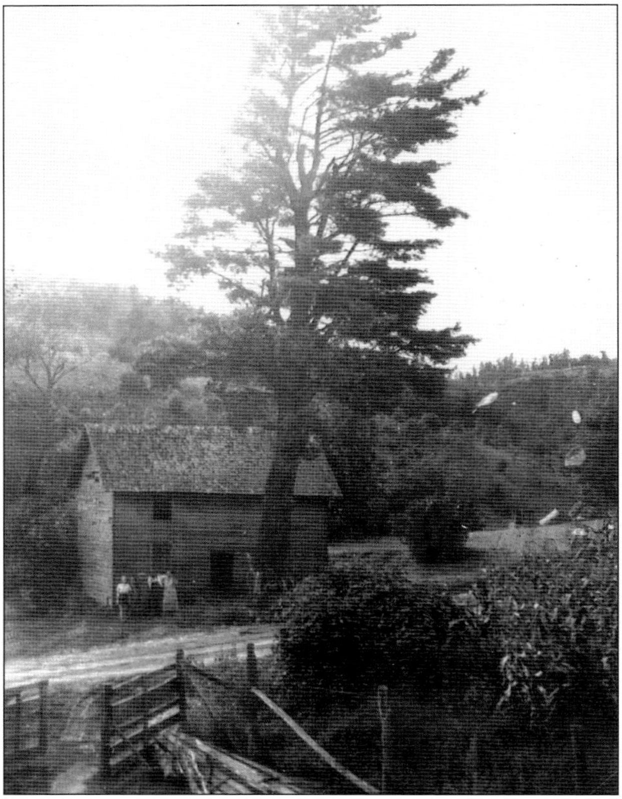

Postmaster Andrew Weddle and his family stand outside their home on Fairview Church Road (Route 720). The Weddle house doubled as the Weddle post office from 1890 until it closed in 1905. (MS)

James Andrew Simmons, his wife Bertha Simmons, and an unidentified person pose in front of the Sowers post office. Bertha Simmons served as the postmaster. The Sowers post office was located near the intersection of Sowers Mill Dam Road (Route 662) and Sowers Road (Route 705) near the Montgomery County line. (MS)

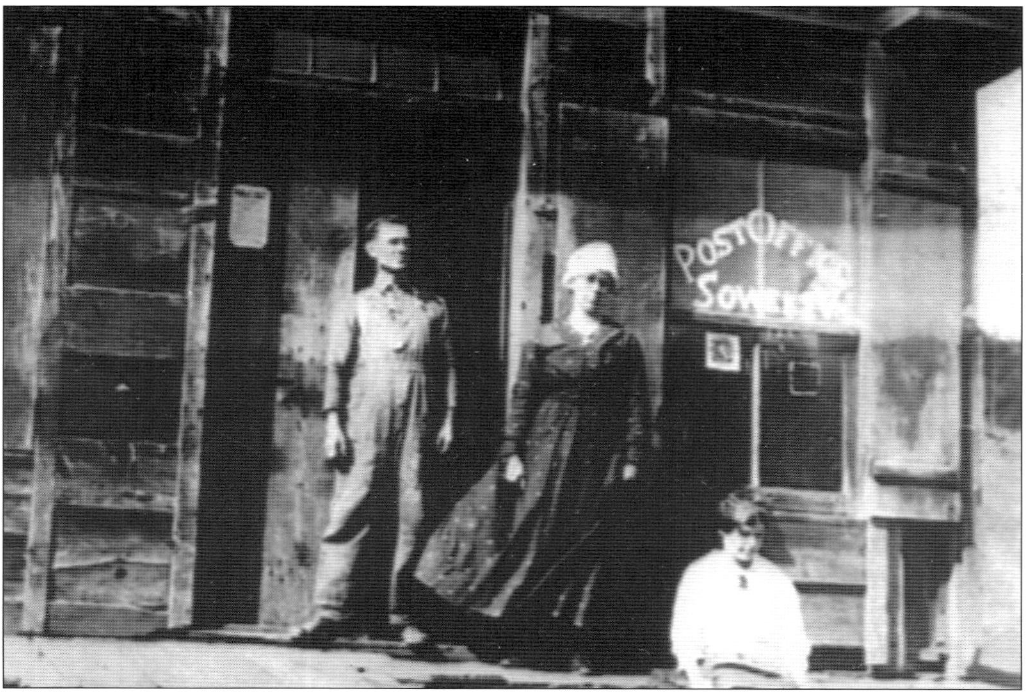

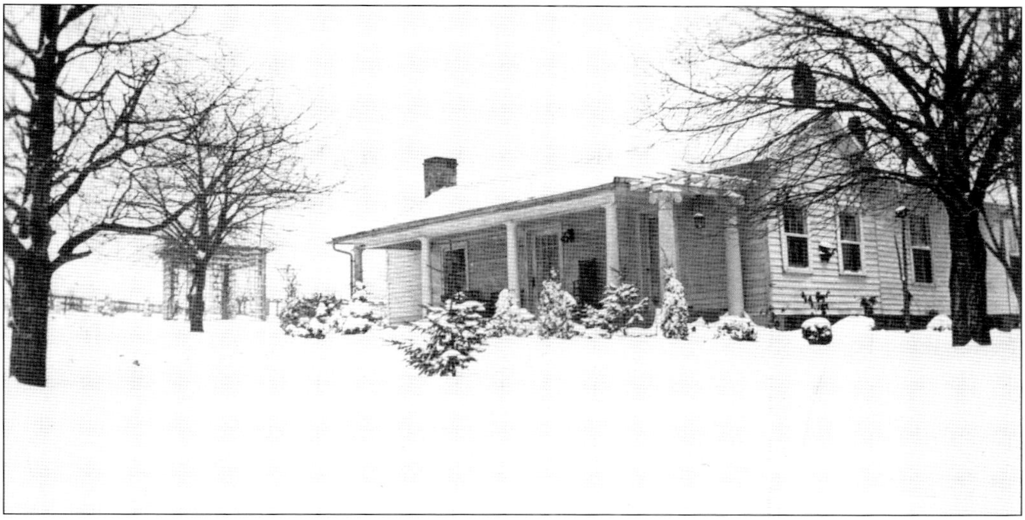

This is a winter scene at Summertime, the residence of Susan "Ma Sue" (Harris) Hall, which was on what is now Old Hensley Road and was then the main road to Stuart (Route 23).

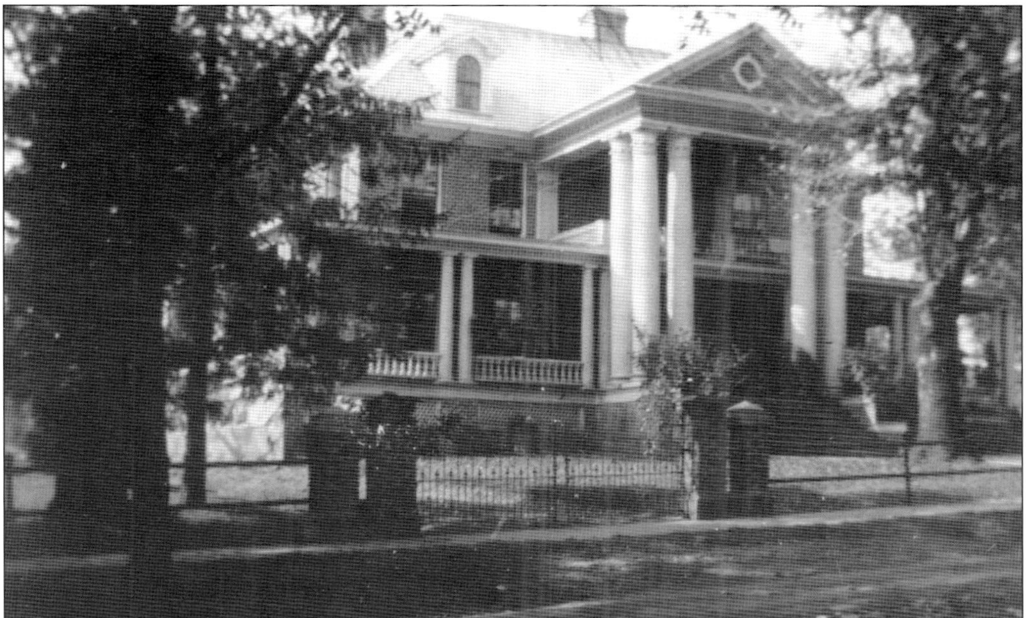

Nancy A. "Nannie" (Harman) Howard built this house in Floyd in 1913–1914. A two-story Georgian Revival brick structure, the house sits near the site of Aspen Hall, the boyhood home of Rear Admiral Robley D. "Fighting Bob" Evans. Sheriff John Brammer resided there as well as Hugh Rakes later on. The home reflects the prosperity of the community in the late 19th and early 20th centuries.

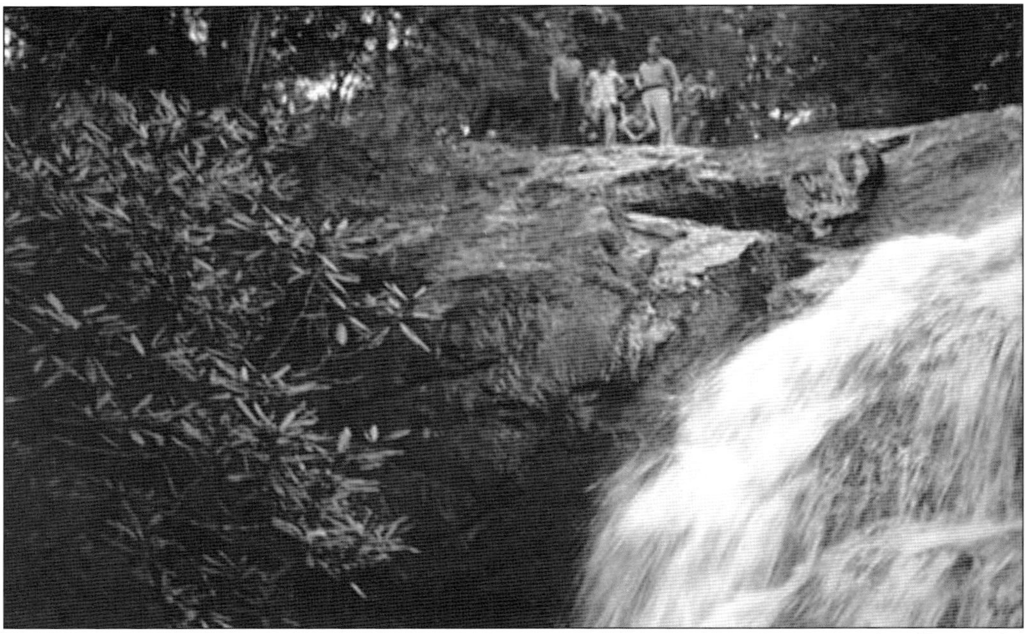

"The Falls" at Falling Branch was a popular destination for people of all ages until well into the 20th century. The area around the falls was used by school and church groups for picnics and other activities. A part of Gen. George C. Stoneman's Union cavalry camped near the falls in April 1865. The falls also supported an early electric power plant. (MAS)

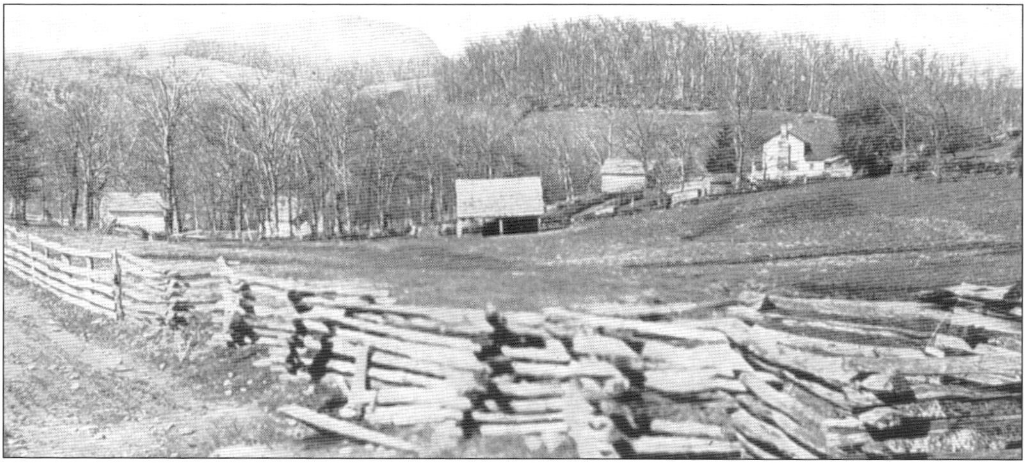

Buffalo Mountain overlooks the Keith farm at Union on Burks Fork Creek in this view from 1940. Prominent in the foreground are two types of chestnut rail fences. In 1922, the chestnut blight ended chestnuts being an important cash crop for many farm families. On the left is Union School, and beyond the trees is Burks Fork Church of the Brethren. The main road, Route 799, passed in front of the home. (CHM)

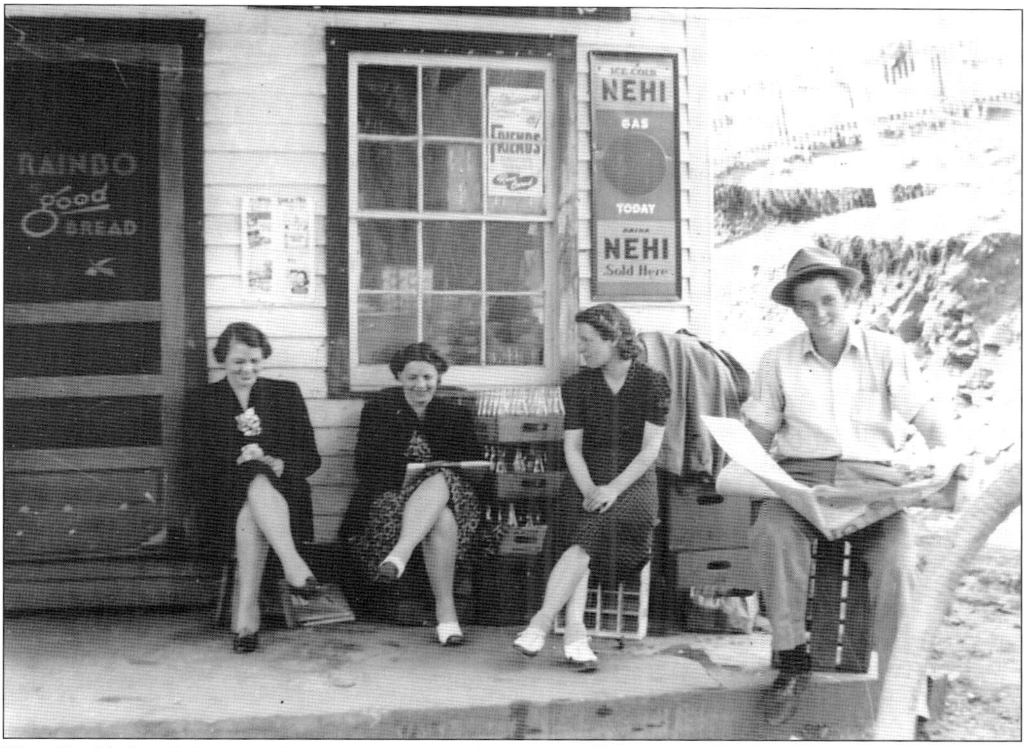

The Dodd Creek Service Station was one of many small community gasoline filling stations to appear in the 1950s. These small service stations carried a limited stock of grocery items for local convenience and often served as gathering points for local residents. From left to right in this image, Cora Yauman, Evelyn Clower, Elsie Ratliff, and Silas Ratliff check out the news. (RAW)

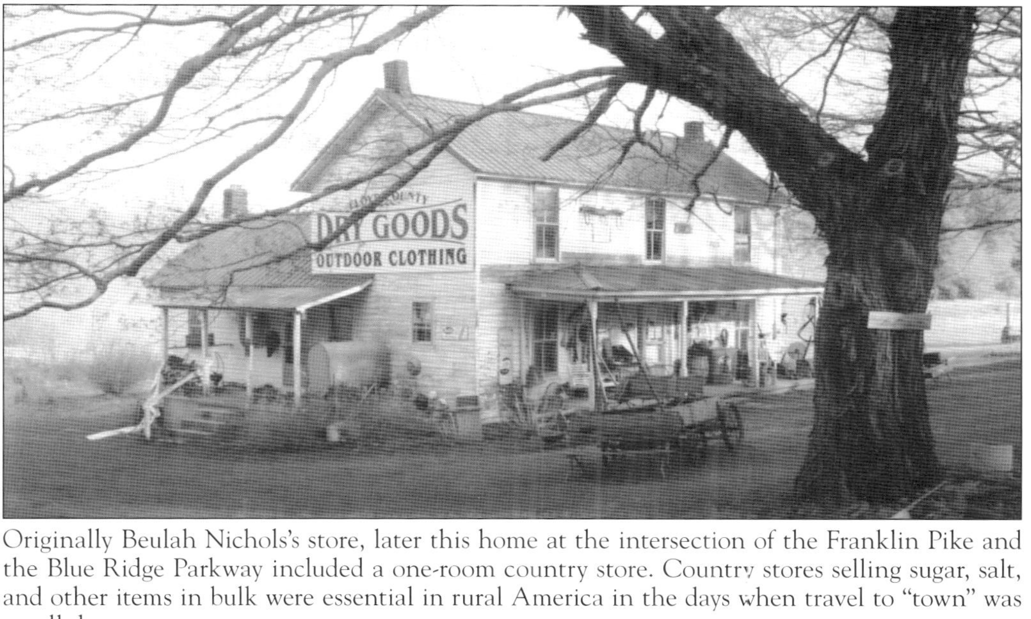

Originally Beulah Nichols's store, later this home at the intersection of the Franklin Pike and the Blue Ridge Parkway included a one-room country store. Country stores selling sugar, salt, and other items in bulk were essential in rural America in the days when travel to "town" was an all-day event.

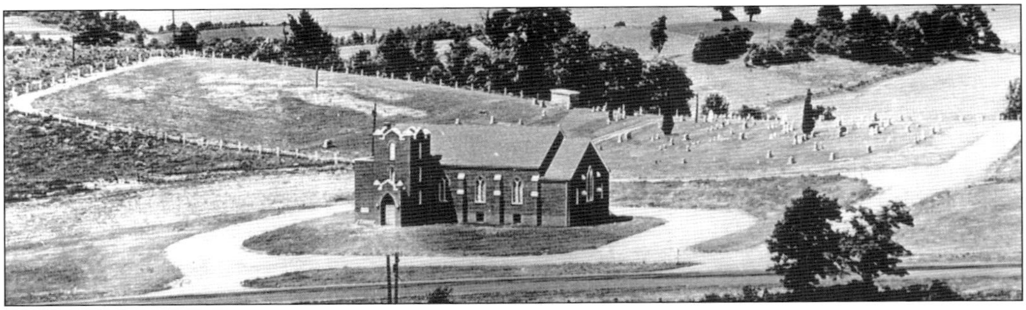

Topeco Cemetery on Route 221 between Floyd and Willis is seen here in the 1950s. Small cemeteries dot the county landscape, preserving the history of the people who settled in Floyd County. Without these well-kept cemeteries, much of the history of the community would have been lost. Genealogists and historians make use of cemeteries like this one to track individuals and families as they moved across the country. (JH)

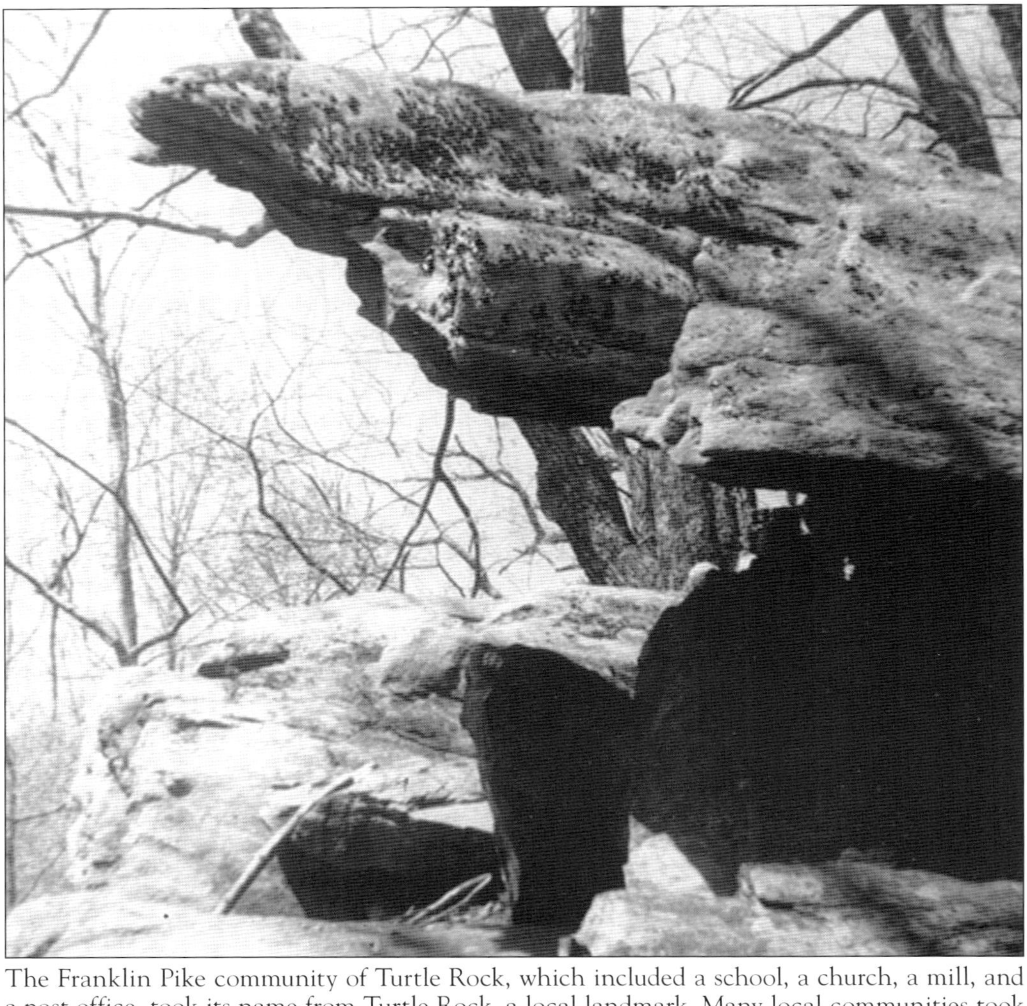

The Franklin Pike community of Turtle Rock, which included a school, a church, a mill, and a post office, took its name from Turtle Rock, a local landmark. Many local communities took their names from naturally occurring features and formations.

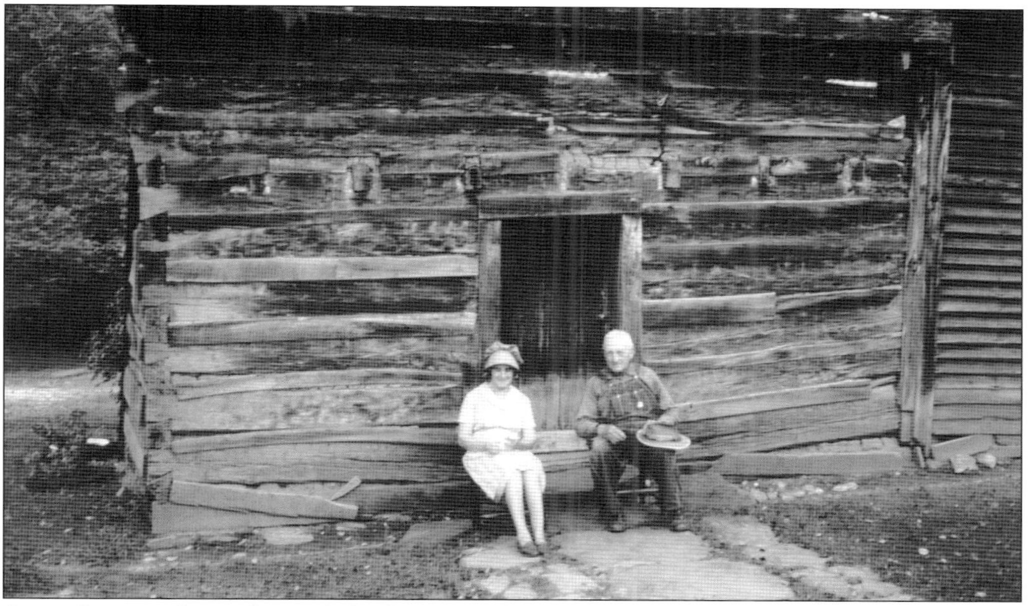

A couple sits in front of an early log home. With hand-hewn dovetailed corners—a Scotch-Irish technique—to strengthen and hold together the home, these small structures were the earliest homes in the area. This cabin would have had a wood shake shingled roof. Additional space was added to this cabin with more modern methods and a tin roof. Made from chestnut or oak, these residences were sturdy but cold and drafty.

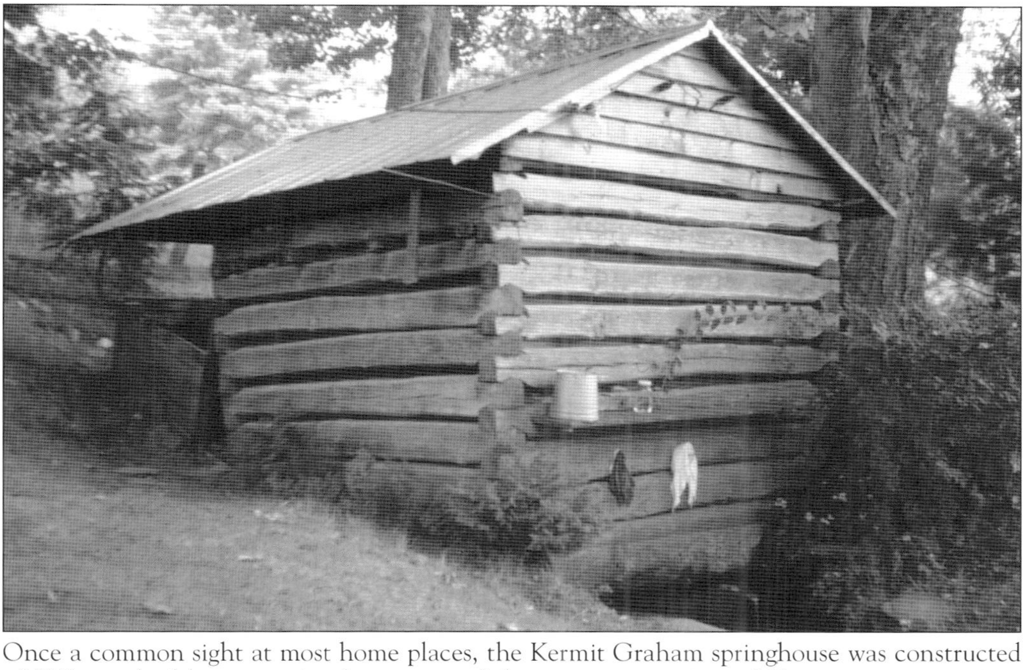

Once a common sight at most home places, the Kermit Graham springhouse was constructed of "V" notched logs seen in the corner of the structure, a sign of German construction. Springhouses were used to protect water supplies from animals and debris and as a rudimentary form of refrigeration.

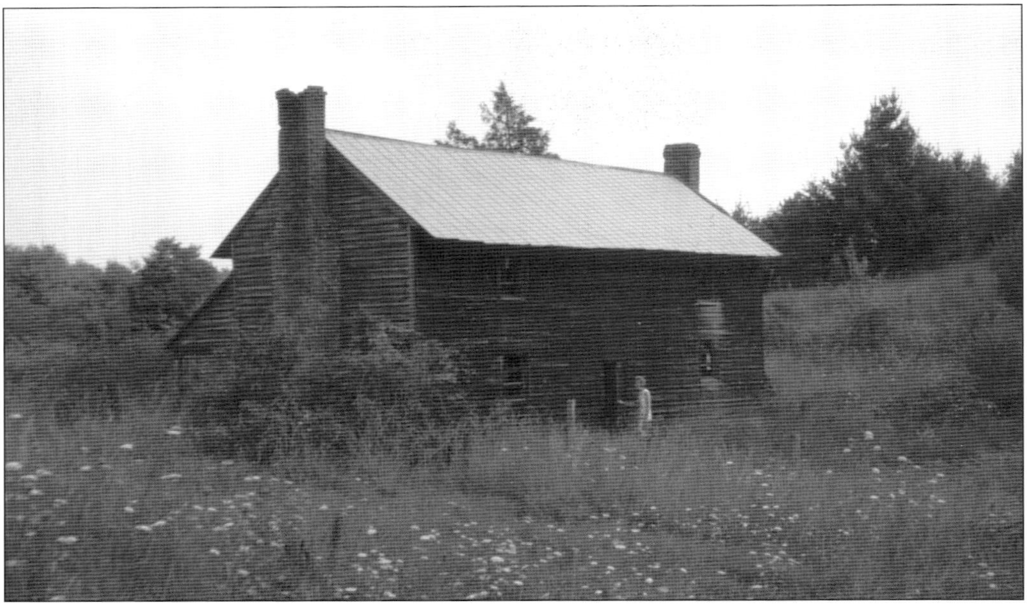

The Blanche Duncan house near Alum Ridge was a traditional rectangular frame farmhouse. Usually with four to eight rooms divided equally between first and second floors and heat provided by handmade-brick fireplaces, these houses had wooden roofs, which were later covered by tin. This style was popular throughout the county until at least the 1920s, with numerous examples remaining today.

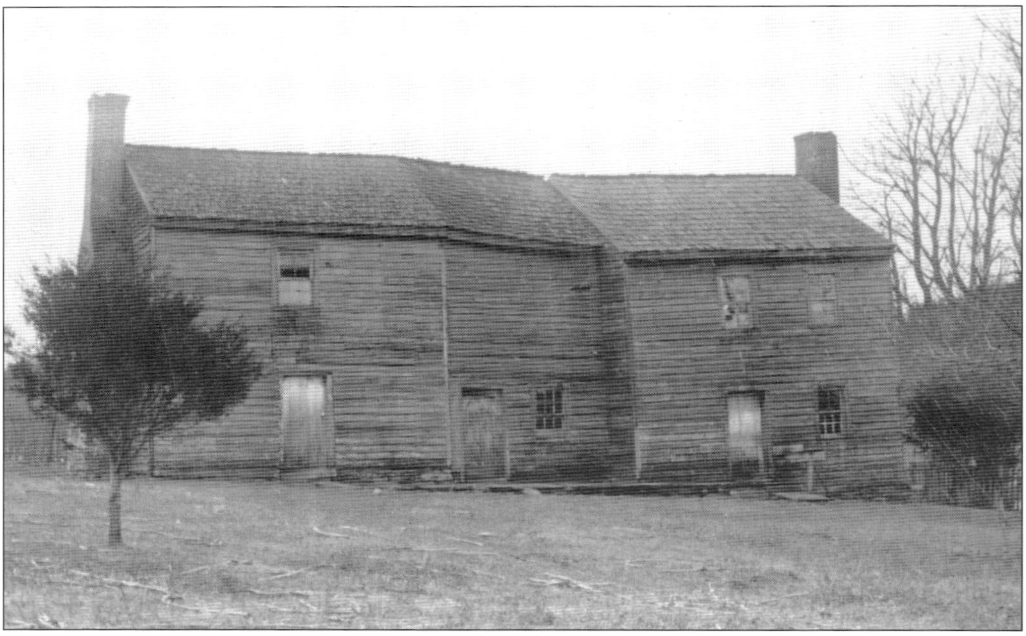

The Susan (Williams) Dickerson home shows how houses were altered to accommodate growing families. The original living space is to the right. The section to the left was probably the original cooking area, which was separate from the main quarters for fire protection. As cooking areas became safer and fire less of a threat, the two parts of the home were often joined.

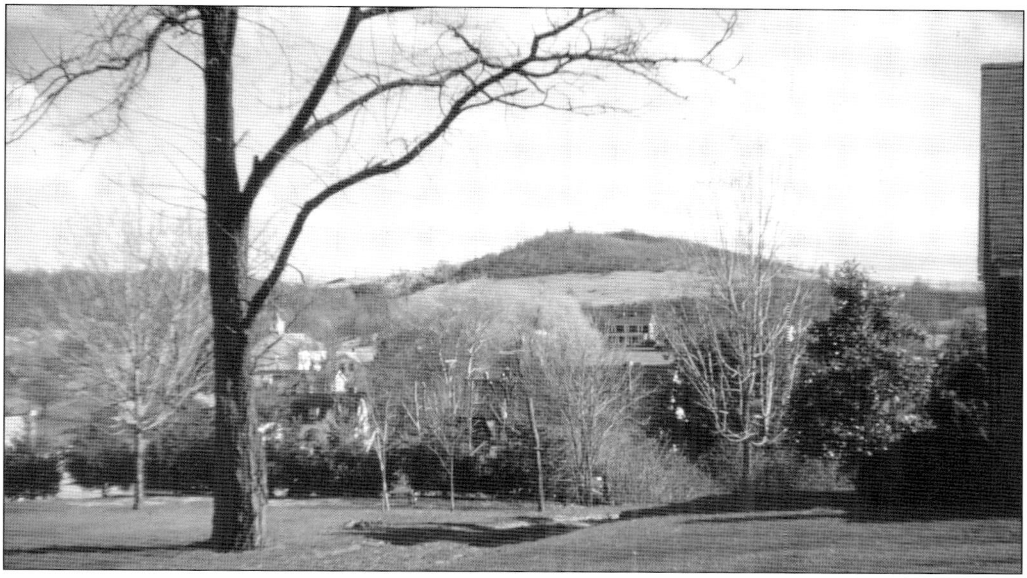

Rising over the town of Floyd is Stocker's Knob, reportedly named for an English deserter during the American Revolution. Through the years, the name has evolved to Storker's Knob, an example of how names change over time, whether due to an incorrect spelling or an innocent pronunciation error.

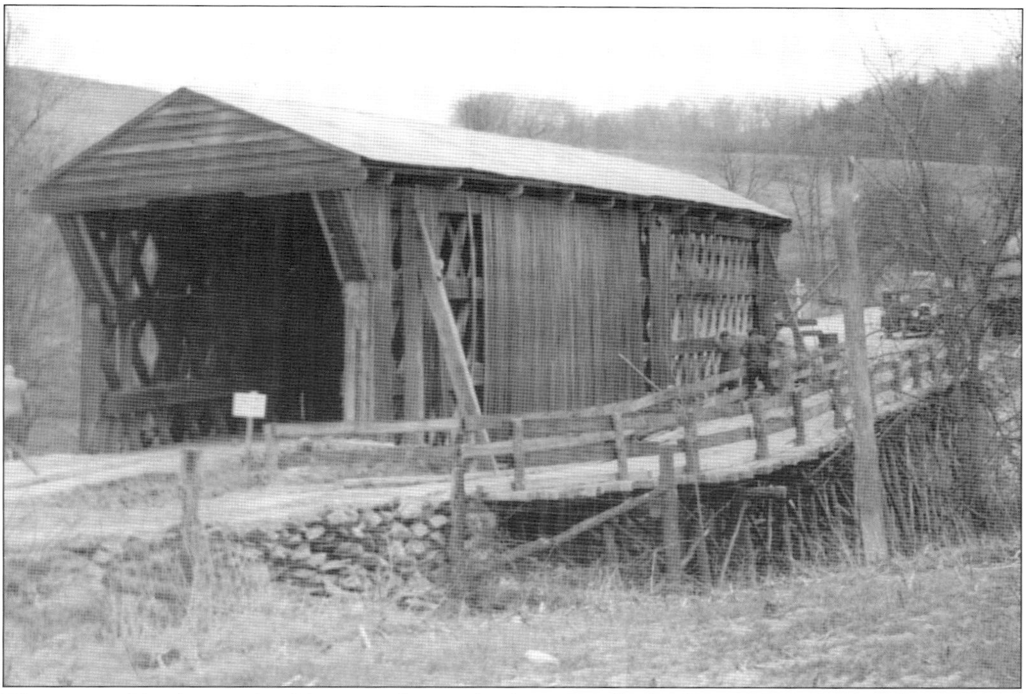

The covered bridge on the Christiansburg Pike (Route 615), the first of three bridges built on the site, was built to cut off two to three miles of travel to Christiansburg. The covered bridge saw travel from Confederate foot soldiers and Confederate and Union cavalry during the Civil War. After heavy use, the bridge was replaced by a steel-frame bridge in the 1930s. (AM)

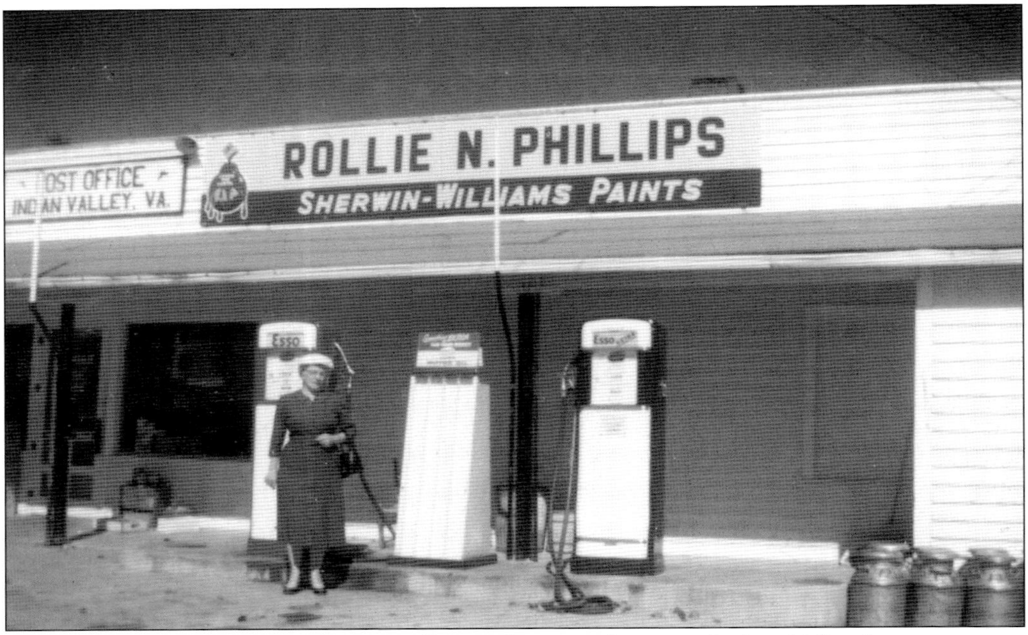

Rollie and Zula Phillips ran the post office and a general store in Indian Valley for many years. A famous prankster, Rollie Phillips was known to switch items on unwary customers and send them home with shoes or hats several sizes too large. The store closed in the 1960s, but the post office still operates a few hours each week. (MS)

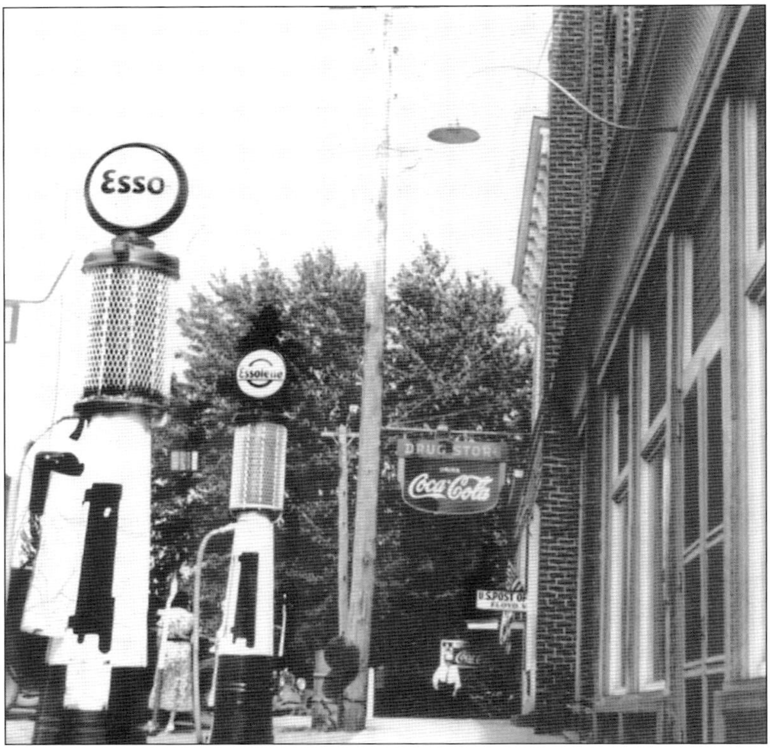

This 1930s view of Main Street in Floyd shows the Esso gas pumps in front of the Horatio Howard building. Originally a mercantile store of Howard and Thomas Huff, it has been the Farmers' Supply for almost 100 years.

This early photograph shows the A.T. Howard Building—the name is carved on the upper middle soapstone window block—decorated with bunting. The crowd and the decoration indicate a patriotic or civic event is about to take place. The Floyd post office was located in this building from 1915 to 1956.

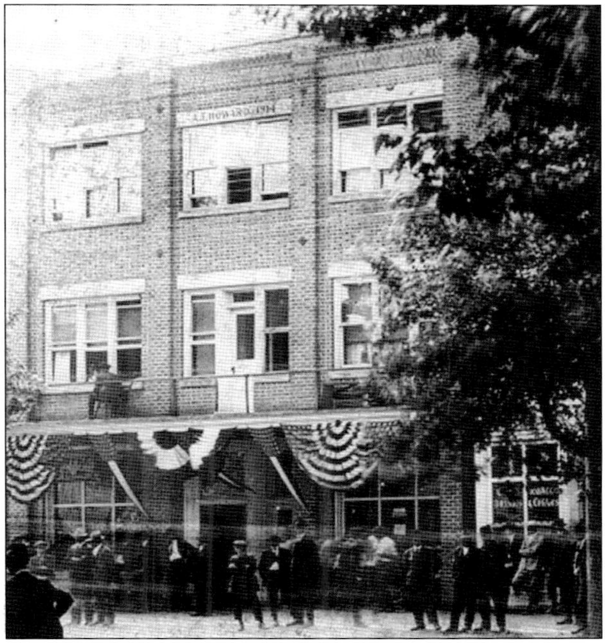

This view of a Huffville church and cemetery is from the Huffville post office. The buggy in the foreground was a luxury in early Floyd County, since most people walked or traveled by horse or buckboard wagon. The Huffville post office was on Huffville Road (Route 610) and operated from September 1857 to November 1919. (MS)

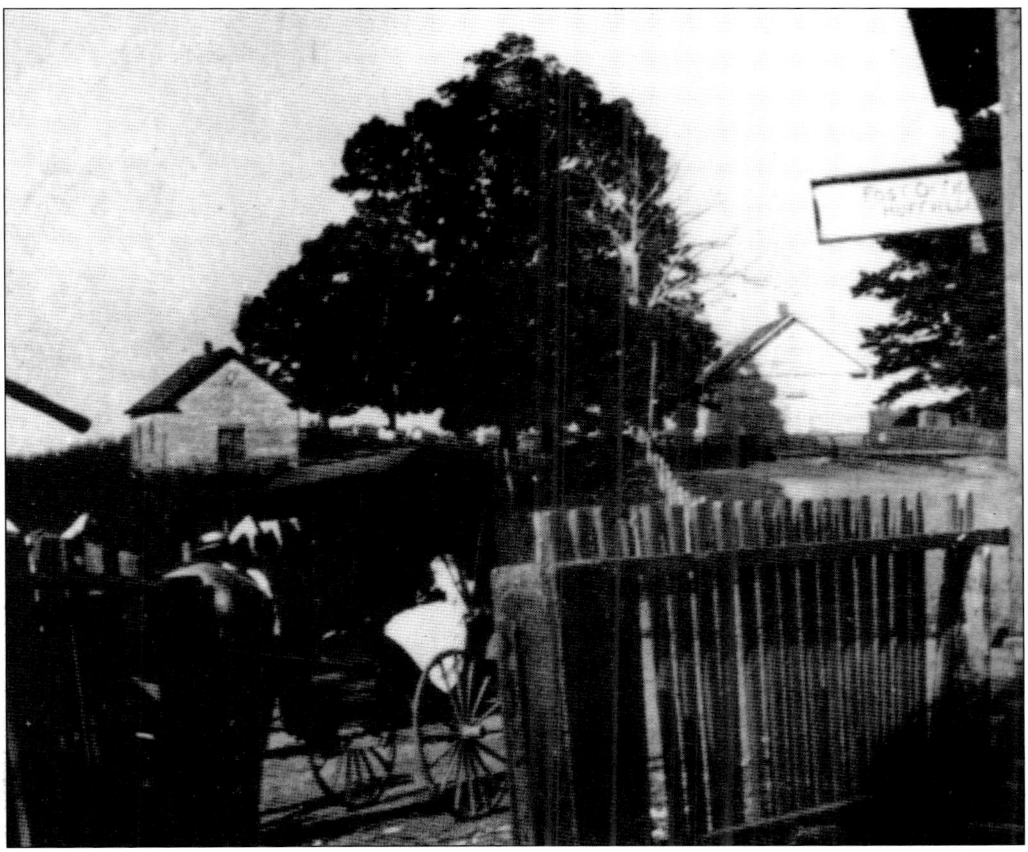

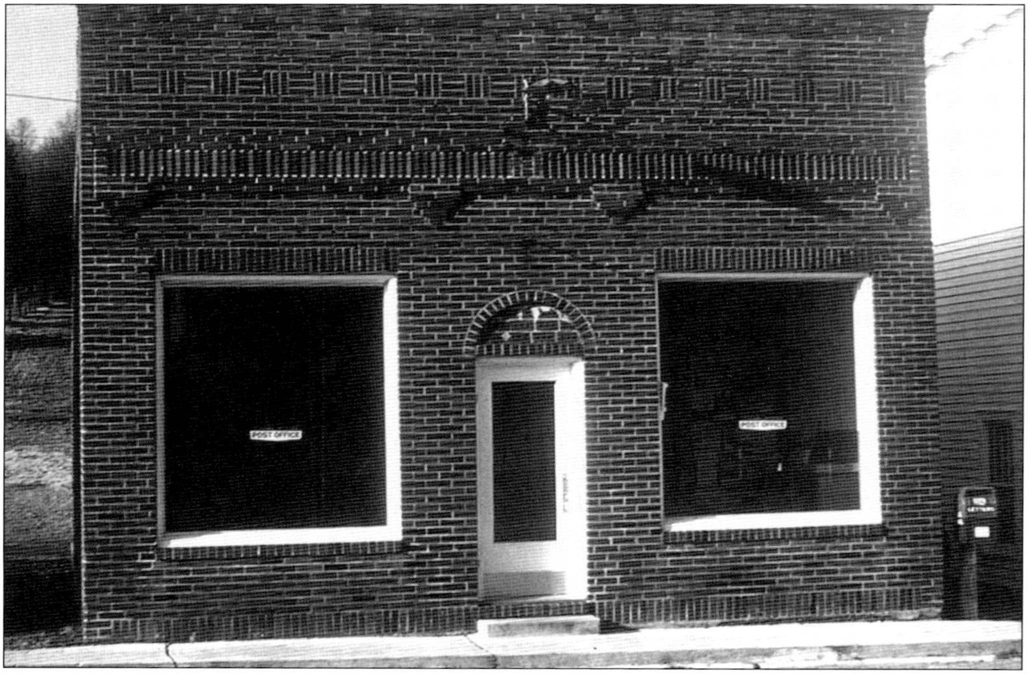

Opened on June 30, 1840, the Willis post office was originally named Greasy Creek. In 1880, the post office name was changed to Hylton. Confusion between Hylton and Hilton—in Scott County—resulted in a second name change to Willis on February 3, 1894. Hylton and Willis were prominent family names in the community. (MS)

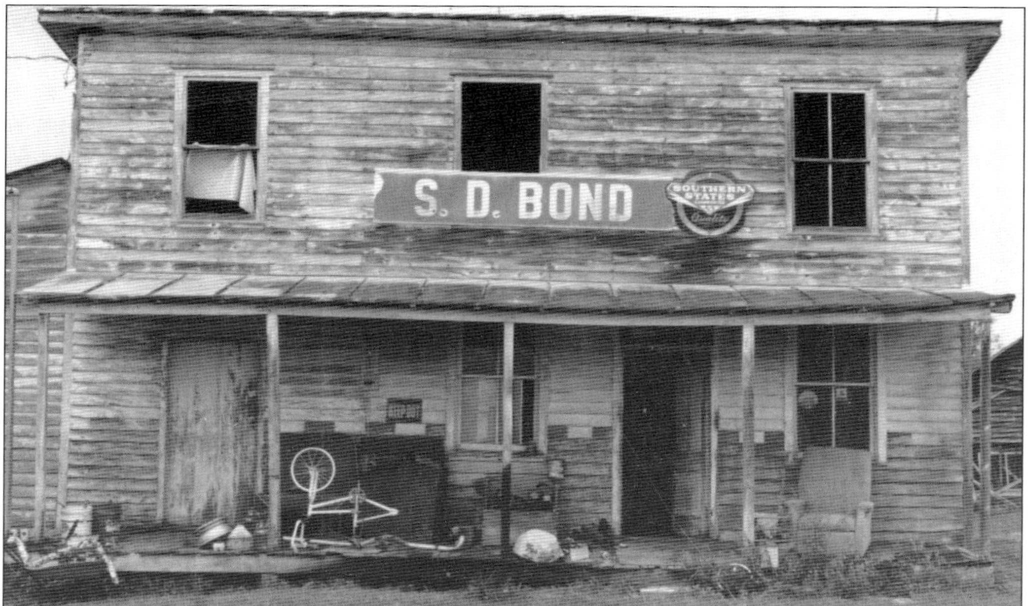

This photograph of the S.D. Bond store was taken after it had fallen into disuse. The store served as the Falcon post office, which operated from 1890 until 1903. Louisa T. Lester served as the first postmaster.

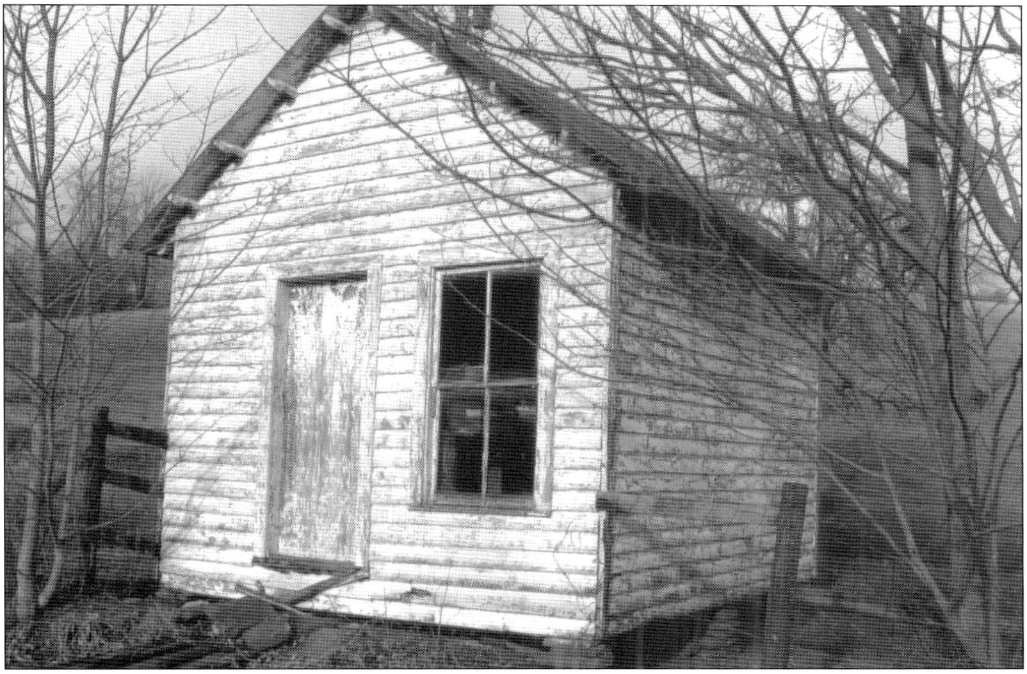

The Nasturtium post office was established in 1897 and used until 1905. James Earles was the first postmaster. (MS)

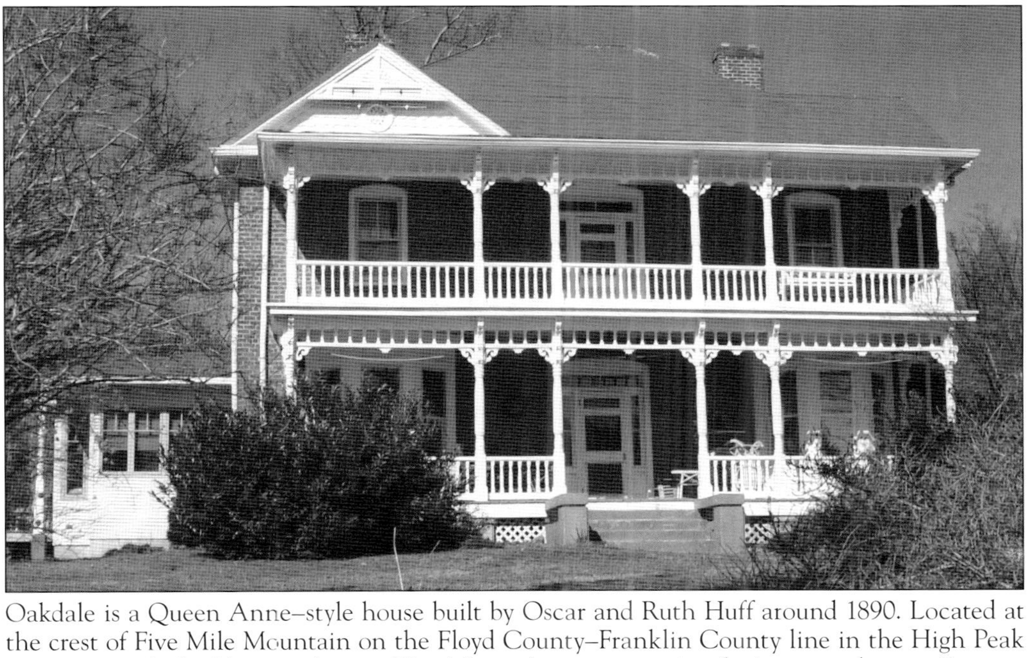

Oakdale is a Queen Anne–style house built by Oscar and Ruth Huff around 1890. Located at the crest of Five Mile Mountain on the Floyd County–Franklin County line in the High Peak community, the building made use of Eastlake-style ornamentation for its ornate beauty. Emmett Pate owned and lived in this house for many years. (DRM)

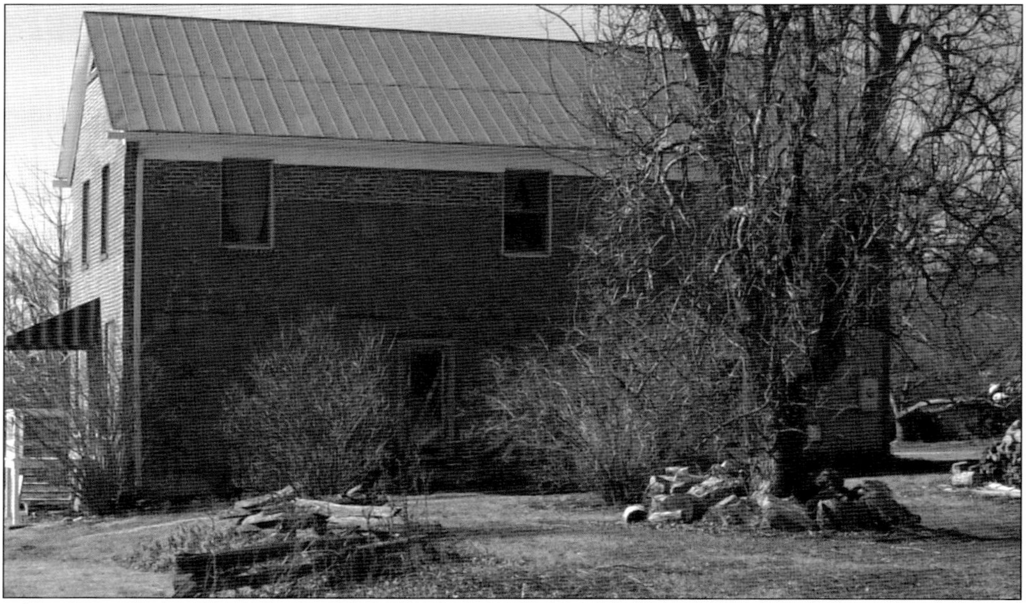

The Oscar Huff store is on Five Mile Mountain in front of the Huff house. The Huff store was the approximate halfway point between the town of Jacksonville (Floyd) and the train depot at Ferrum. (DRM)

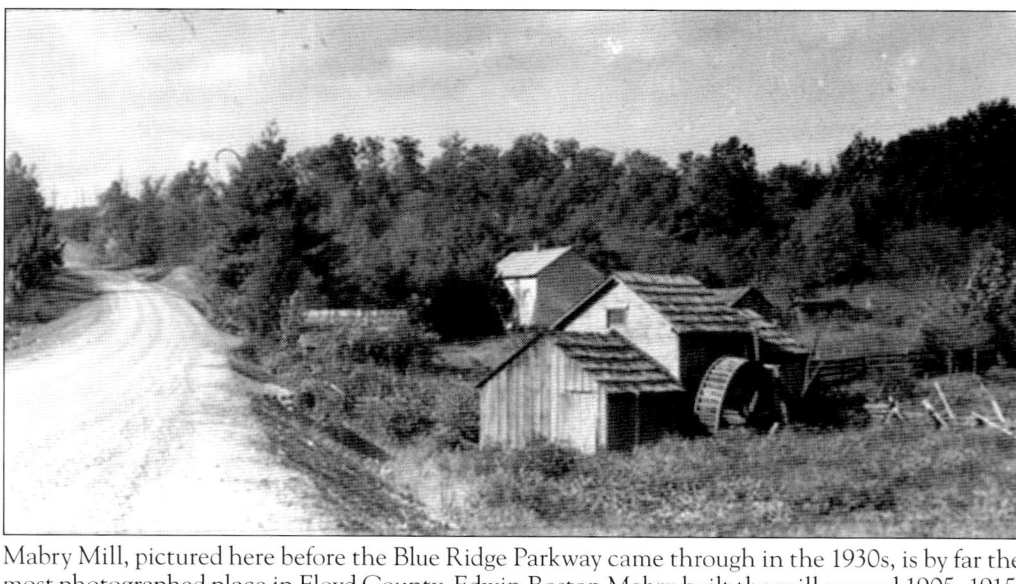

Mabry Mill, pictured here before the Blue Ridge Parkway came through in the 1930s, is by far the most photographed place in Floyd County. Edwin Boston Mabry built the mill around 1905–1915. It was restored in the 1940s and continues to be a popular tourist attraction.

Two

People

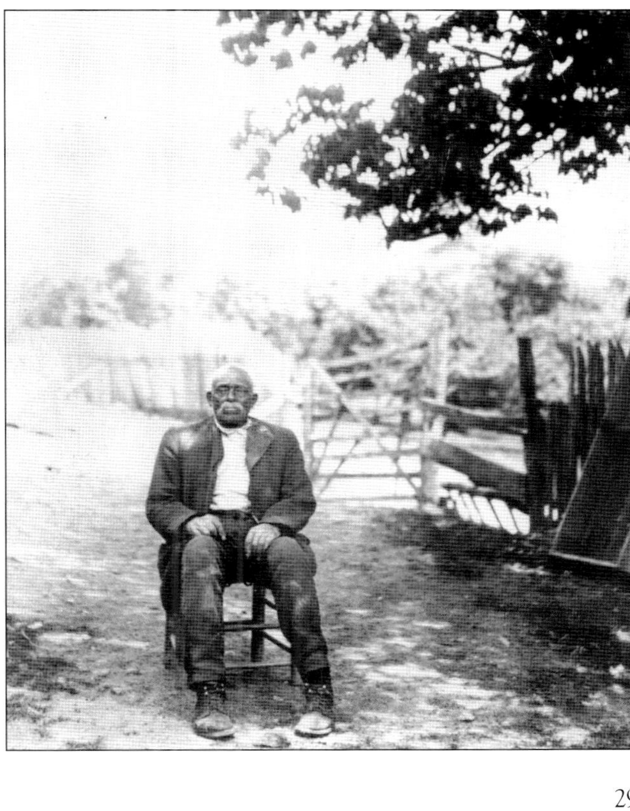

Thaddeus Palmer, who was 25 in 1866, was born into slavery in Richmond County. He was owned by David Goodykoontz, who lived on the family farm once known as Alkoontz Inn.

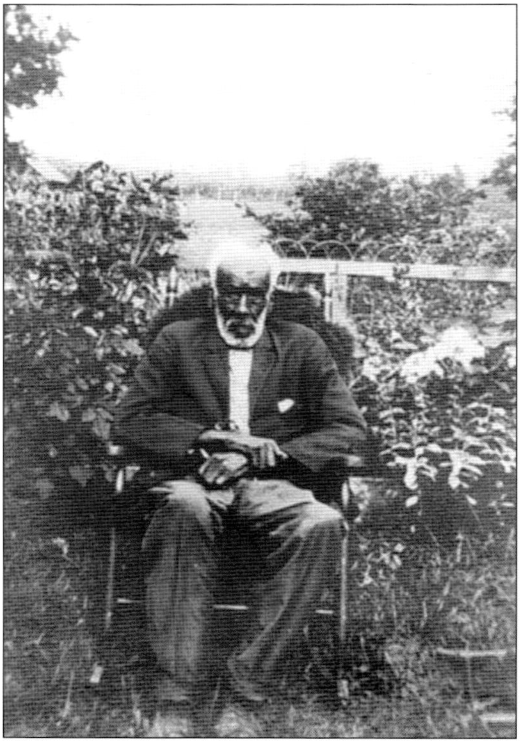

Creed Hylton was one of 20 Floyd County men listed on the February 16, 1863, list of slaves who were conscripted for use by the Confederate government. County authorities never delivered the slaves to Richmond. As a freedman after the war, he and his wife, Candace, continued working for the Archelaus Hylton family on the Hylton farm near Topeco and were probably buried in the Hylton Cemetery. (APS)

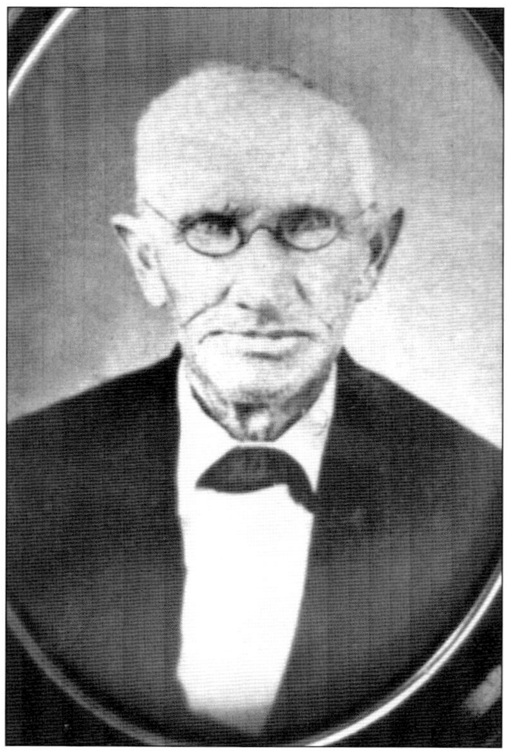

Irish immigrant Henry Dillon, a master builder and brick mason, built the Jacksonville Academy, known as "Old Brick," in 1846. He went on to build the 1851 Floyd County courthouse, the 1850 Presbyterian church, and several fine brick homes in town. (JS)

These local high school and elementary school teachers posing in front of the school are Principal Joe Poff, E.L. Lawson, Ruby (Bishop) West—who was later supervisor of all elementary school teachers—Mary (Winters) Dobyns, Katherine See, Nellie (Burke) Slusher, Elva (Smith) Keith, and Nellie Epperly.

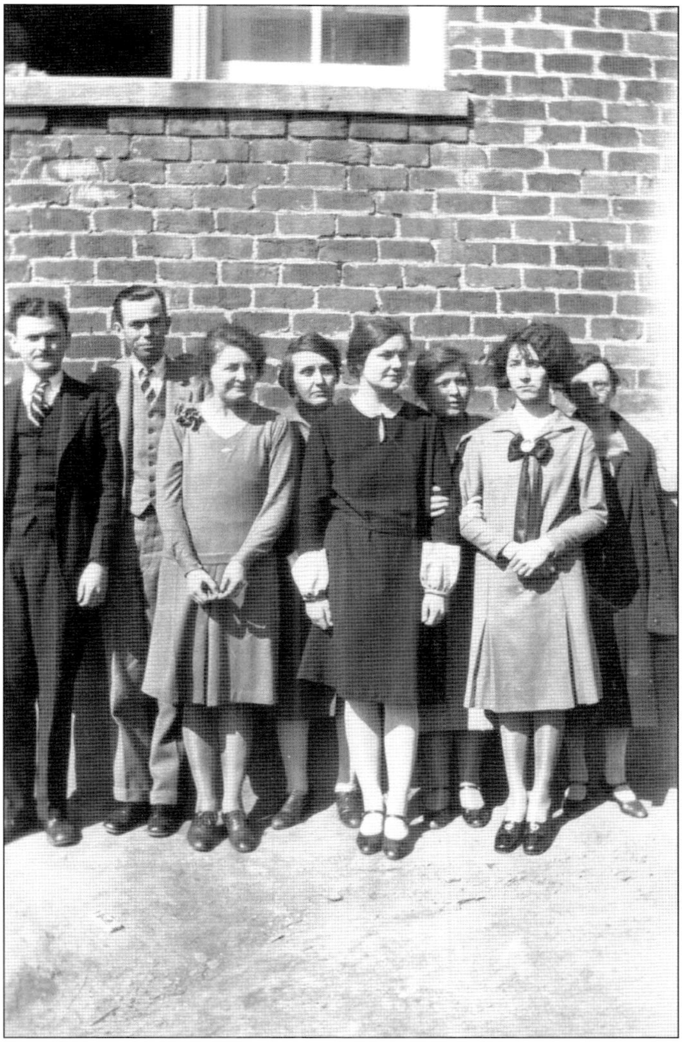

Floyd County home demonstration agents organized home demonstration clubs throughout Floyd County, including this group of black women in Floyd Courthouse. This was the only way black families could obtain group health insurance at the time. Shown from left to right are Josephine Beaver, Arlene Campbell, Annabelle Akers, Ada R. Vaughn, Octavia Akers, Clara Hayden, Mary Etta Taylor, Lillian Hayden, Katherine Sue Vaughn, Vivian Vaughn, Amelia Akers, and Fannie Mae Hairston. (AM)

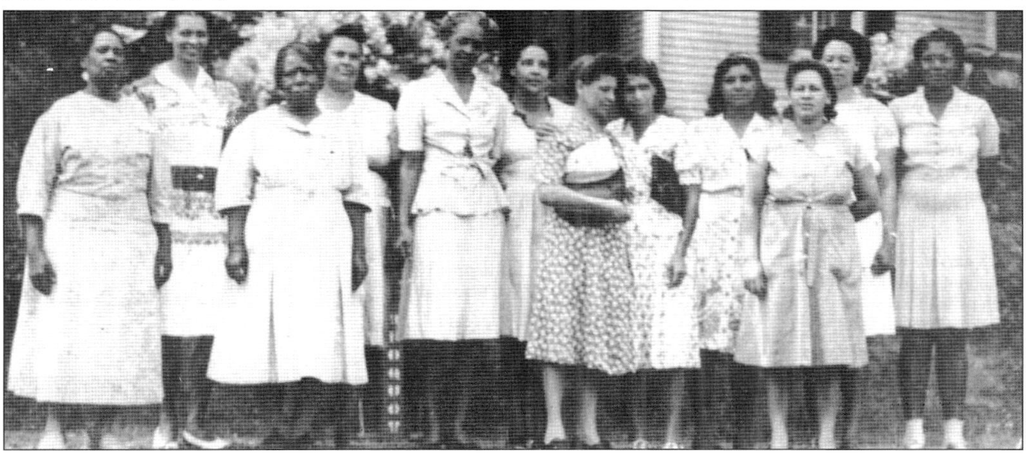

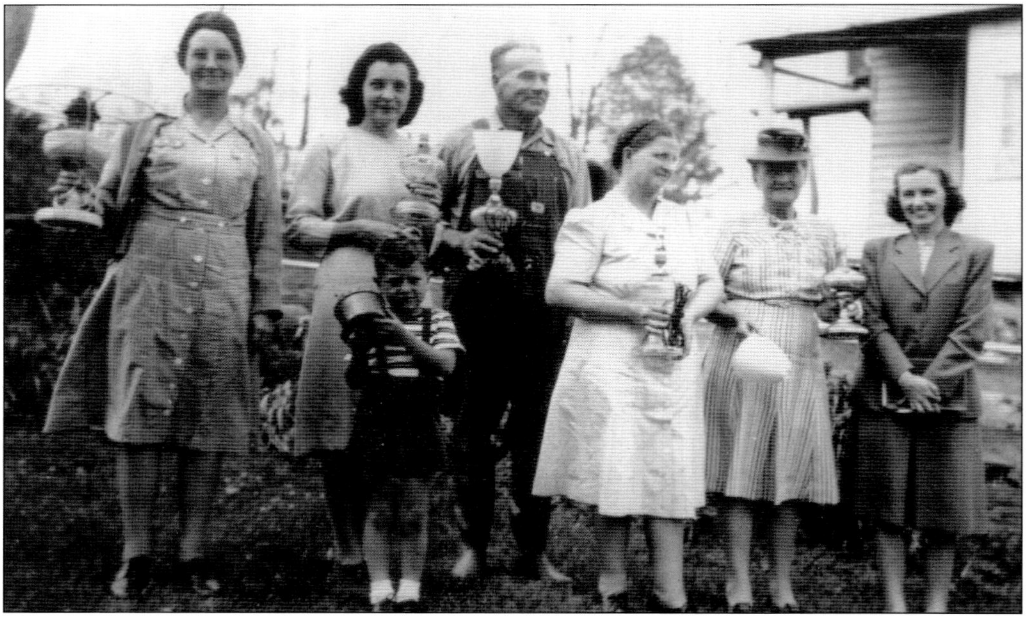

Home demonstration clubs, with guidance from extension agents from the Virginia Polytechnic Institute—Virginia Tech—held monthly meetings in members' homes. This club's members, meeting at Bettie Reed's home in Copper Valley in the late 1940s, learned how to convert oil lamps to electric lamps. These members include Bettie Reed, Senora Caldwell (with her son Joe), Lynch Duncan, Ocie Dehart, Ida Bishop, and extension agent Frances Graham. (RC)

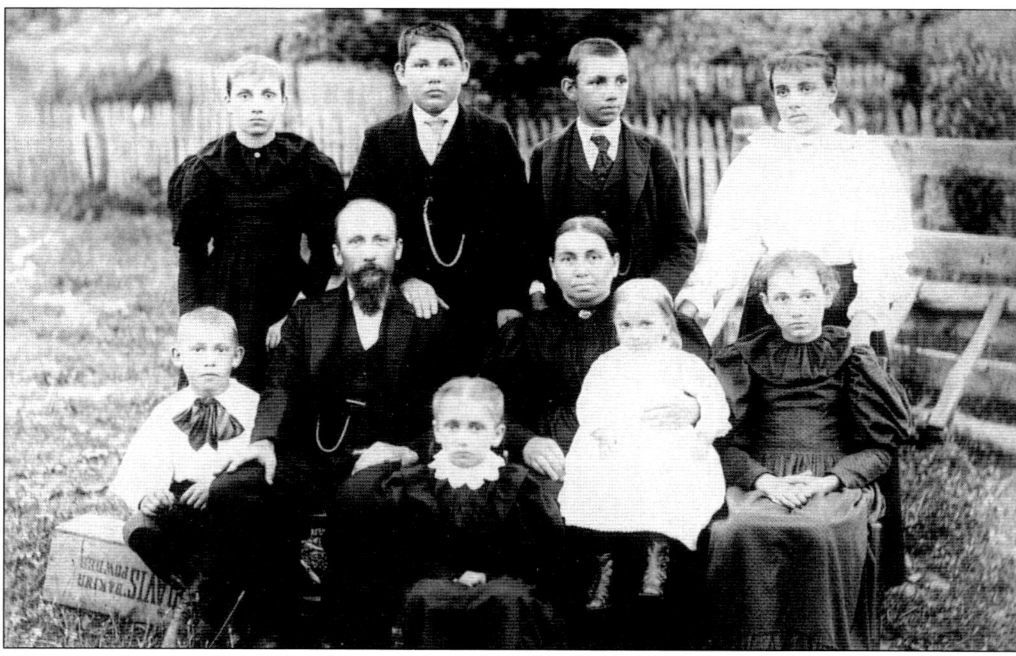

The James Peyton Phlegar family posed here for a family photograph. They are, from left to right, (first row) Frank, father James Peyton Phlegar, Blanche, mother Peradine (Lawrence) Phlegar, Josephine, and Pearl May; (second row) Annie Laura, Woody, Elbert O., and Cora A.

Pete Hallman interviews the Hon. Joseph Proffit, a member of the House of Delegates and a local attorney. Hallman was the son of Ella Ruth Sowers Hallman and the grandson of Aaron Sowers, who owned the *Floyd Press*. The newspaper was passed down to Ella Ruth, who passed it on to her son. (AM)

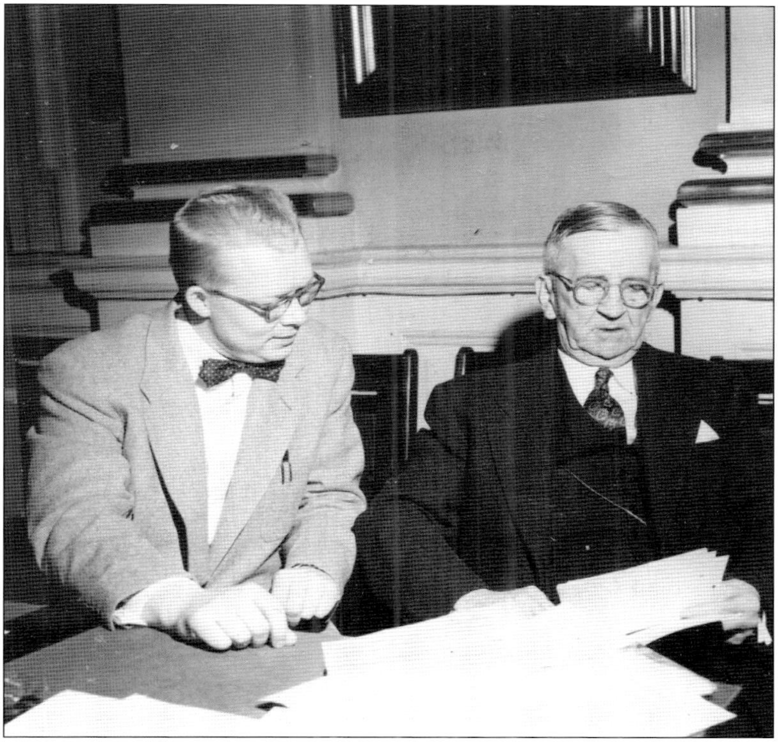

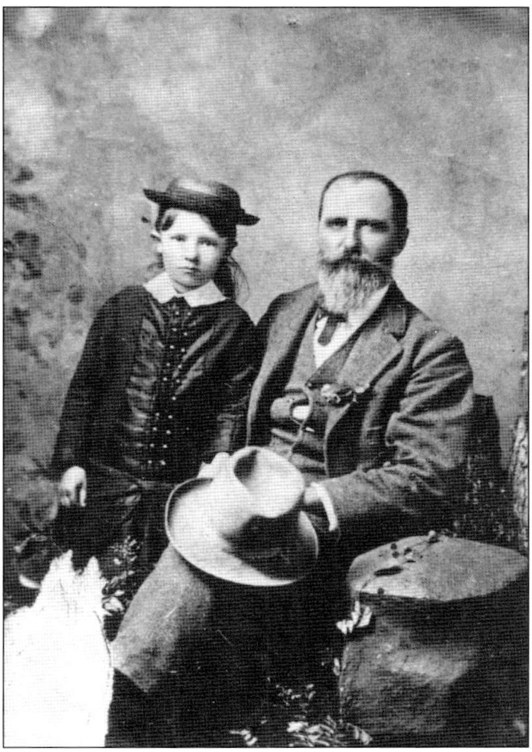

Ferdinand A. Winston, seen here with his niece, Irene Elliott, was a cabinetmaker and a head justice. Imprisoned in Richmond during the Civil War for being a Union sympathizer and a member of a pro-Union "Red String" organization, Winston was later elected sheriff of Floyd County. His white clapboard home on Main Street still stands and a chest signed and dated by Winston in 1853 remains in the county. Irene Elliott later married Homer Spencer.

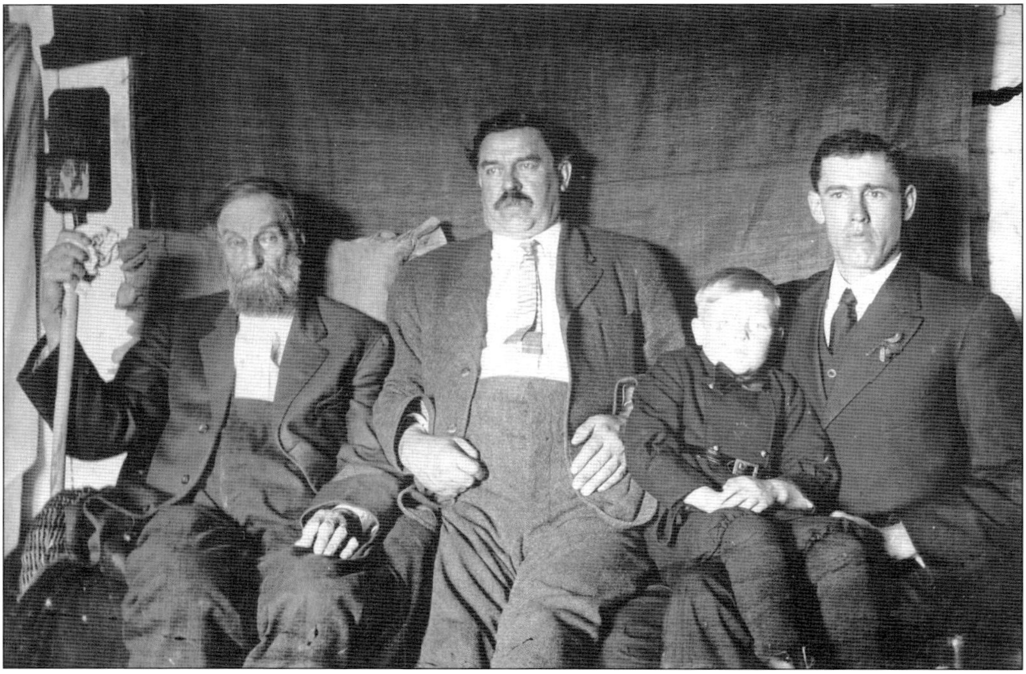

Four generations of the Shelor family pose for this photograph. From left to right, they are James "Jim" Shelor, George Shelor, Carl Shelor, and Ernest Shelor. (NSA)

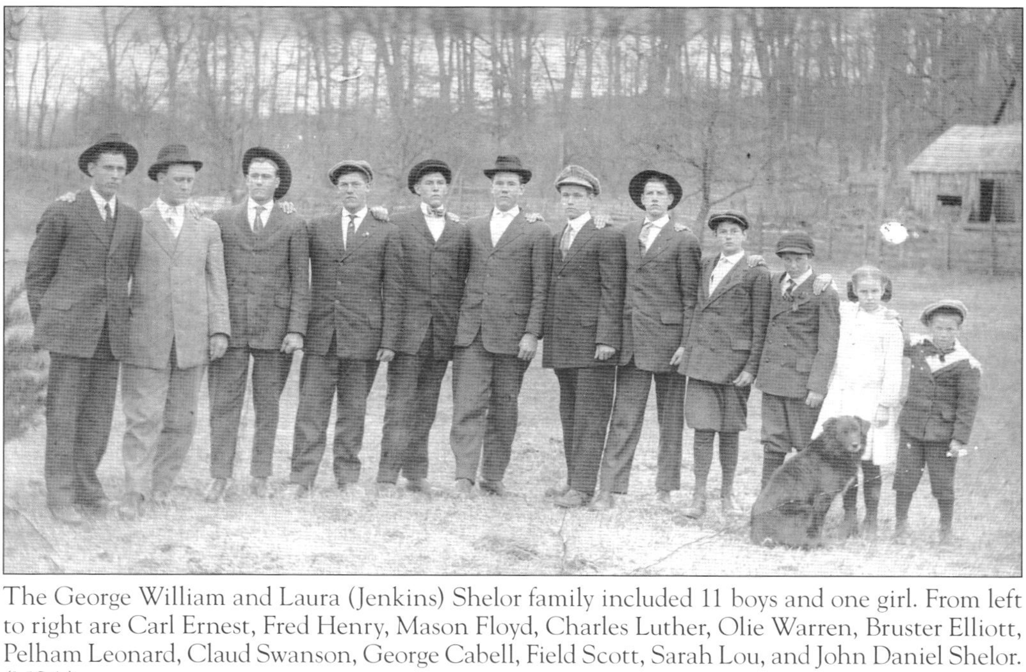

The George William and Laura (Jenkins) Shelor family included 11 boys and one girl. From left to right are Carl Ernest, Fred Henry, Mason Floyd, Charles Luther, Olie Warren, Bruster Elliott, Pelham Leonard, Claud Swanson, George Cabell, Field Scott, Sarah Lou, and John Daniel Shelor. (NSA)

Taswell and Ocie Hollandsworth are seen here around 1950 with their 11 girls and one boy. From left to right are (first row) Brenda Howell, Taswell, Wanda Grubb, Ocie, Martha Nester Bower (in her mother's lap), and Ren; (second row) Beulah Gallimore Quesenberry, Vada Cox, Anita Quesenberry, and Josephine Alderman; (third row) Winnie Dalton, Irene Gallimore, Lilas Higgs Webb, and Nina Browning. (RC)

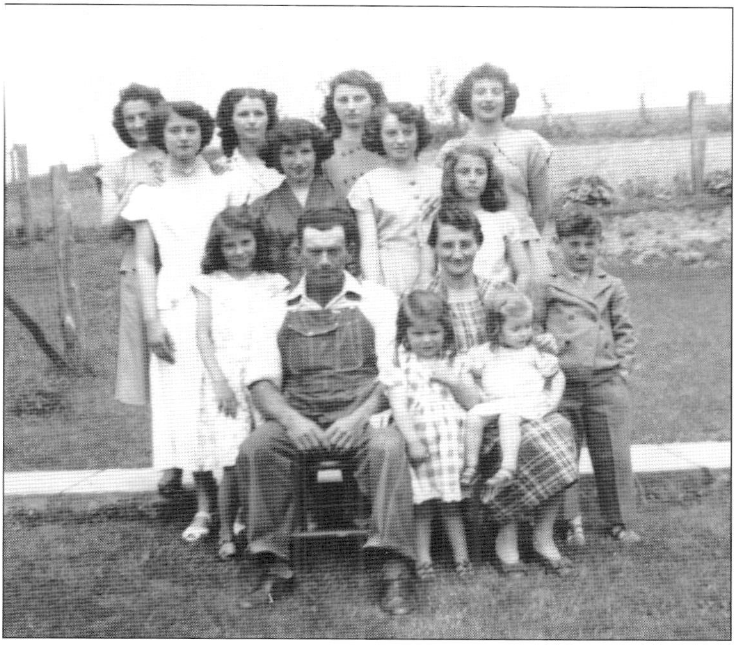

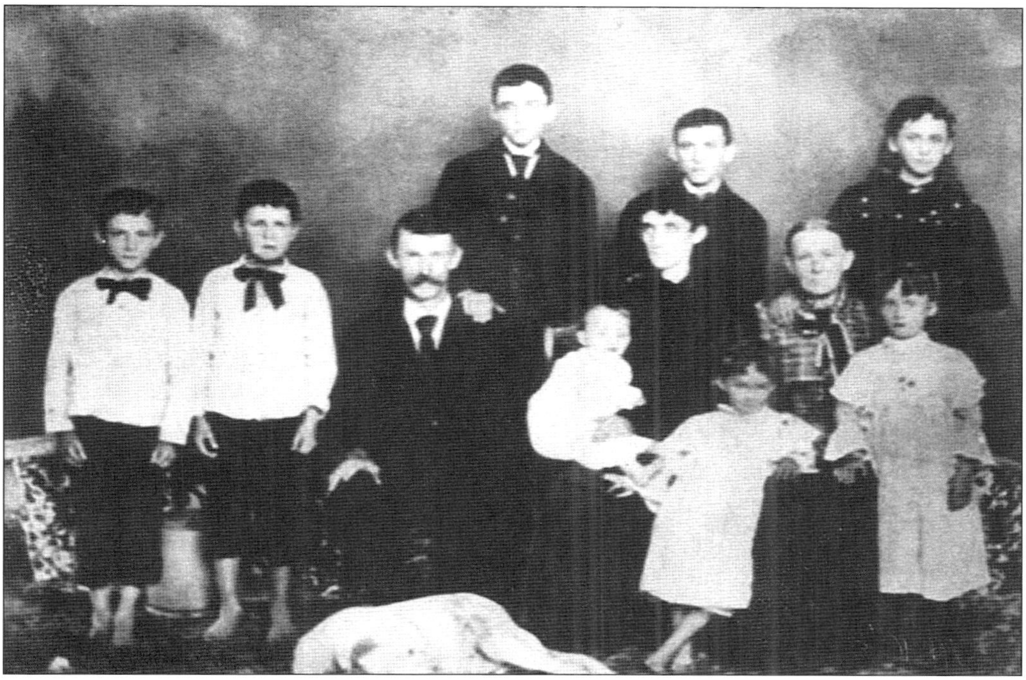

Members of the Thomas Matason Goodson family from Tindall pictured here in the 1890s are, from left to right, (first row) Ernest, Everett, Thomas, Sara (holding Vernon), Bessie, Julia, and Clara; (second row) Charles Ross, Russell, and Blanche. Moscow the dog is in the foreground. (MMG)

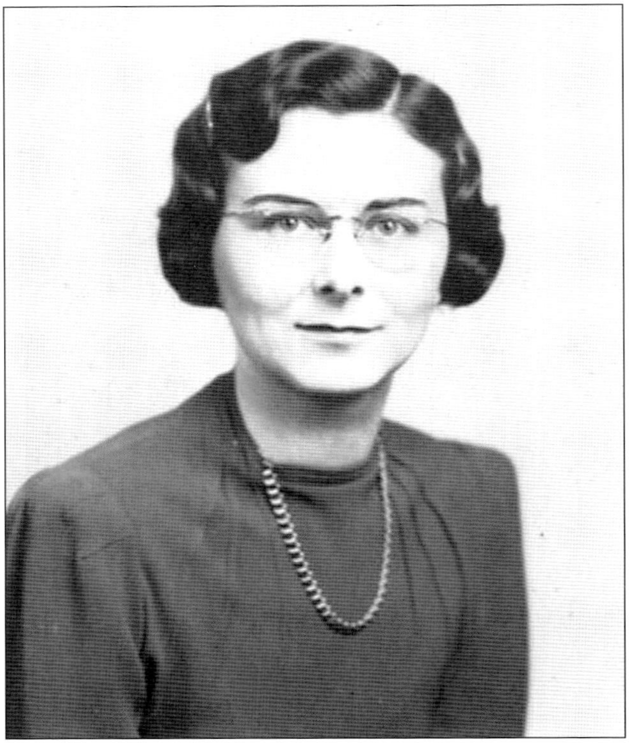

Marguerite Tise, the daughter of Rev. J. Marshall Tise and Alice Sheffey (Peterman) Tise, was educated in Floyd County schools and at Marion and Roanoke Colleges. She went on to become secretary to the US assistant secretary of state in Washington, DC, and traveled to the Potsdam Conference, the Geneva Summit, and the Paris Peace Summit with Pres. John F. Kennedy. She returned to Floyd to retire and became its unofficial genealogist and archivist.

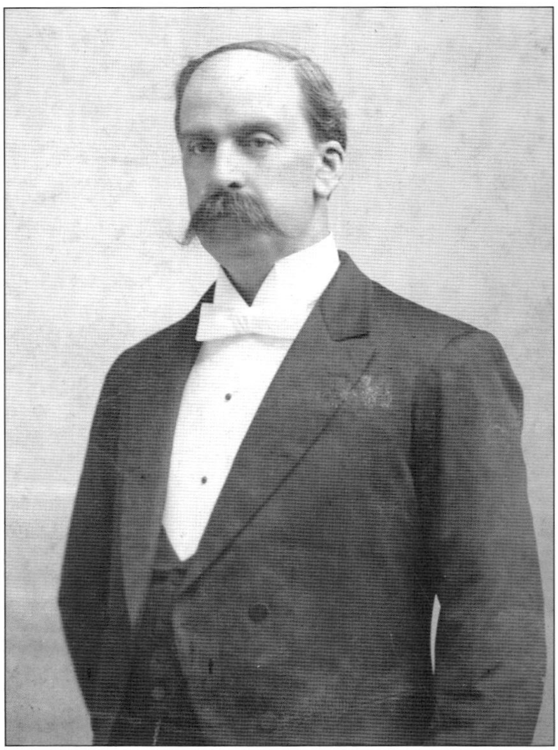

Elder Posey Green Lester, seen here in 1850, entered the Primitive Baptist ministry at age 25. He preached in 21 states and in Ontario, Canada, pastored in churches in Kentucky and Virginia, and served as moderator for the New River District and editor of *Zion's Landmark*. A two-term congressman from Virginia's fifth district, Lester lived with his wife, Emmette (Harris) Lester, in the Locust Street home that was later the office of attorney Warren Lineberry.

Two small children sit in a handwoven "butt" basket used to carry eggs and other farm produce to market on horseback. An unusual quilt pattern is used as a backdrop. (AM)

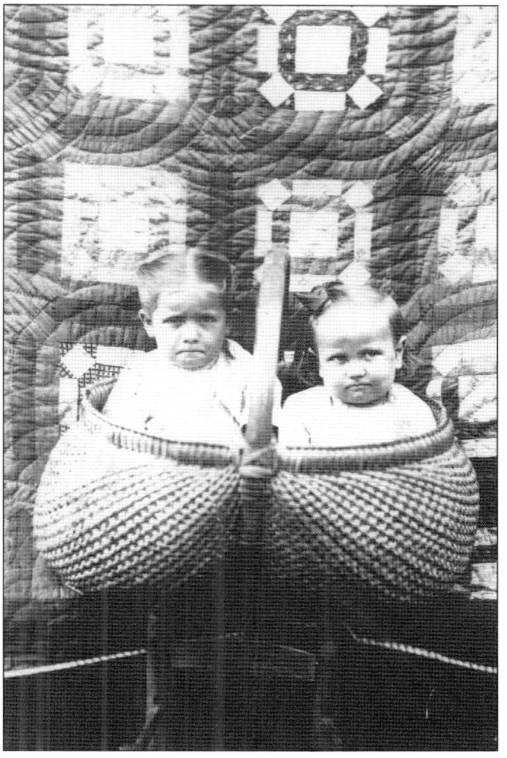

This celebration of Libby Hylton and Charlie Weddle's marriage in 1910 was at the home of her parents, Granville and Mary Terry Hylton, who are seated at far right. Many of the celebrants are from the Weddle, Slusher, Hylton, Harman, and Cannaday families. Libby and Charlie are in the doorway with the minister, Abie Hylton, just to the left of them. (JHH)

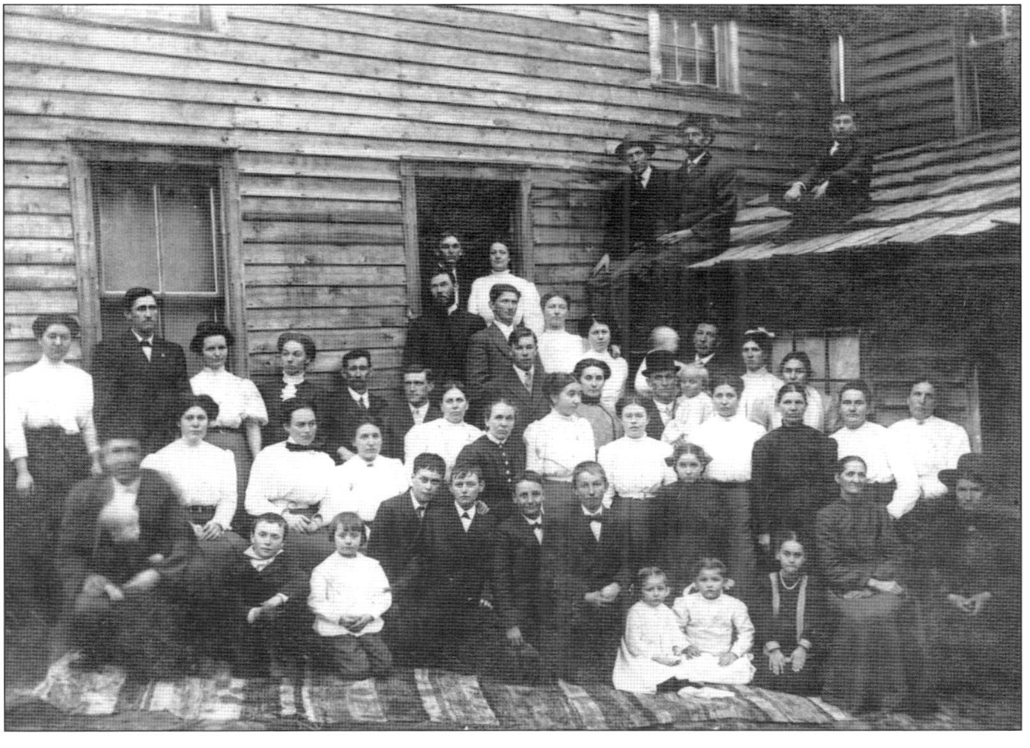

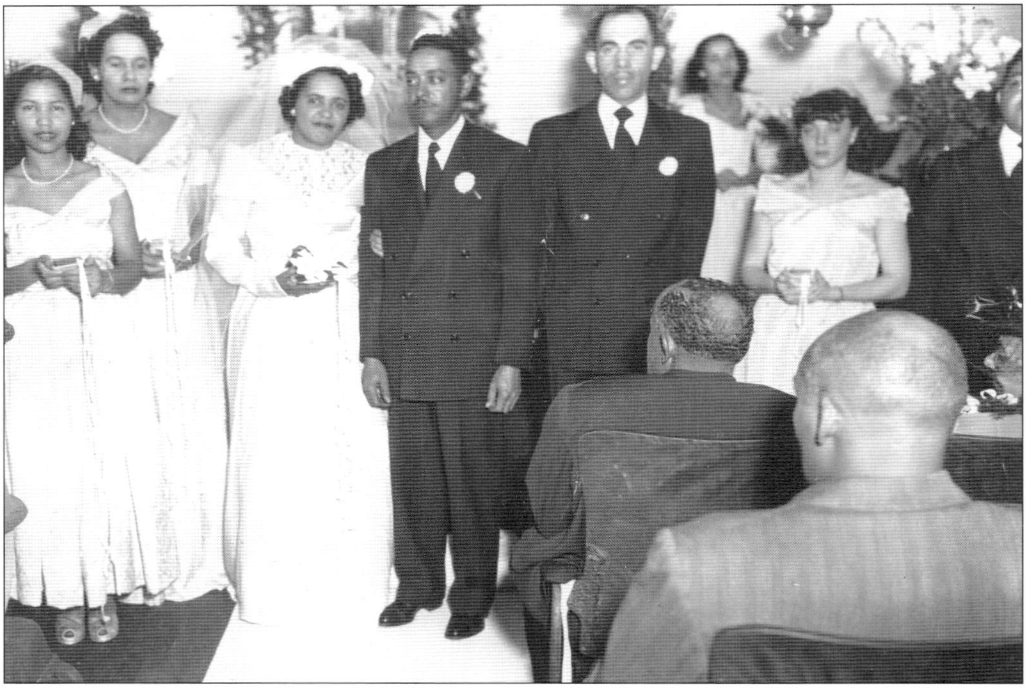

From left to right, Iva Spencer, Audrey Spencer, bride Eva (Spencer) Claytor, groom William Andrew Claytor, and Winfred H. Beale pose at their wedding on December 23, 1950. (WB)

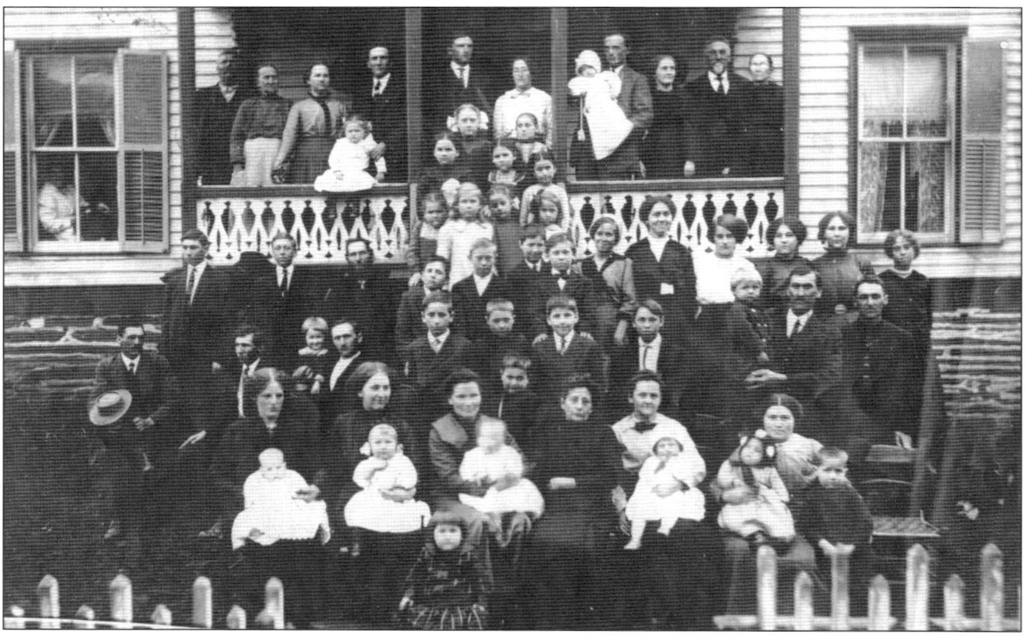

John William and Rosetta Essie (Weeks) Hylton (next to each other on the porch at far right) host their family at their home around 1913. Surnames in this photograph are Vaughn, Barringer, Hylton, Slusher, Manuels, Weddle, Helms, Donnelly, Conner, Slaughter, Farmer, Starr, Weeks, and Harman. (JH)

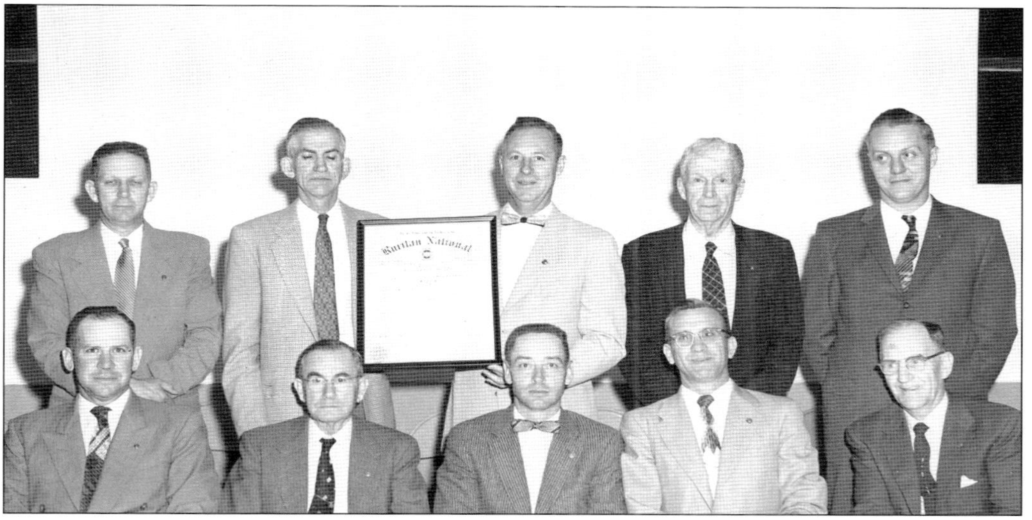

Members of the Floyd Ruritan Club gather around 1958. Their mission is dedicated to improving communities through fellowship, goodwill, and community service. These members are, from left to right, (first row) Allen Altizer, W.A. Compton, Edward Slusher, H.P. Jennings, and E.T. Barnett; (second row) state trooper Walter W. Moore, Willard Clower, Vernon Harris, Rev. R. Gamble See, and David Vest. (CHM)

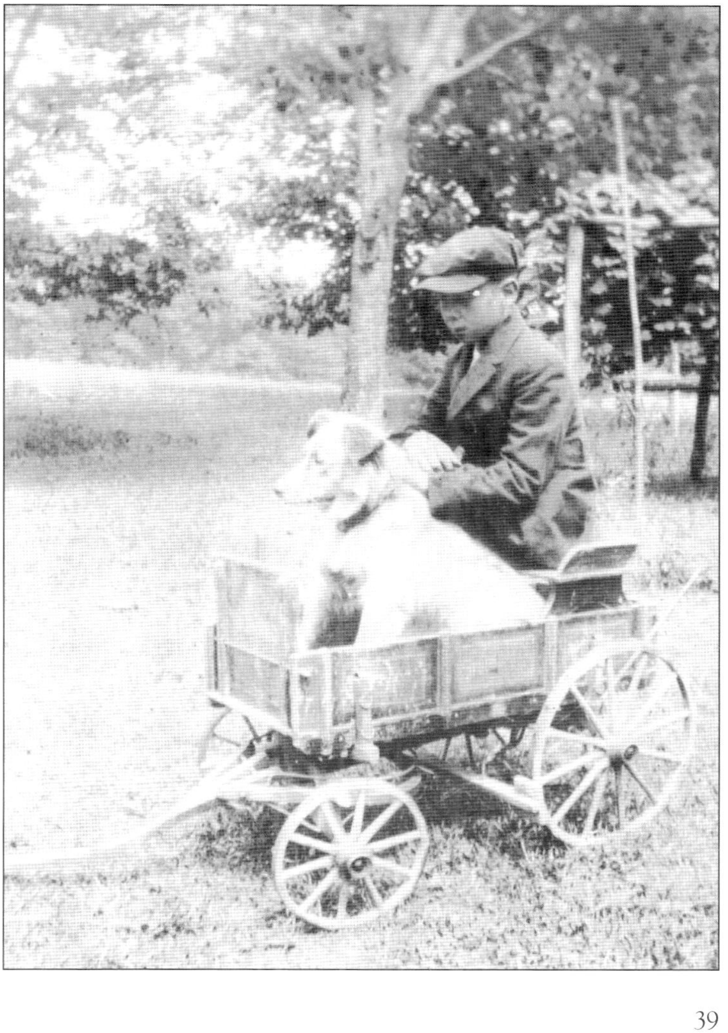

Guy Williams rides in his Studebaker wagon with his dog, Ring, at Piney Fork, the Williams family farm on Franklin Turnpike. His sister, Marie Williams, is the former owner of Ridgemont. (MAS)

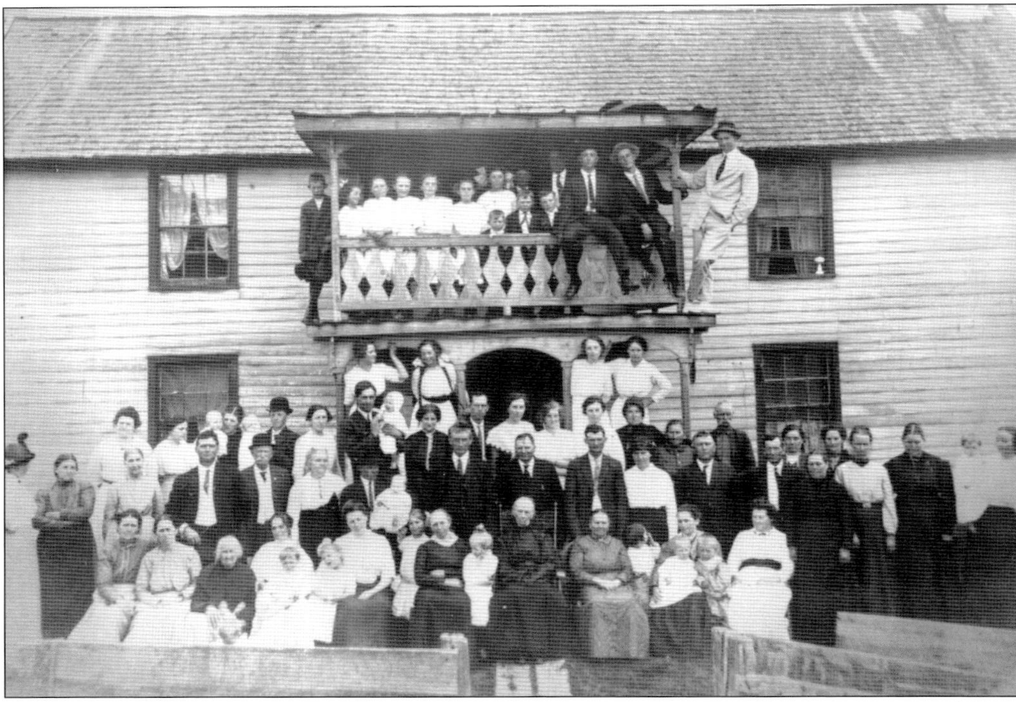

Family and friends gathered at the Helms family home on Black Ridge around 1912 to celebrate the birthday of Malissa (Earls) Helms (front row center), the widow of Joseph Helms. (JSK)

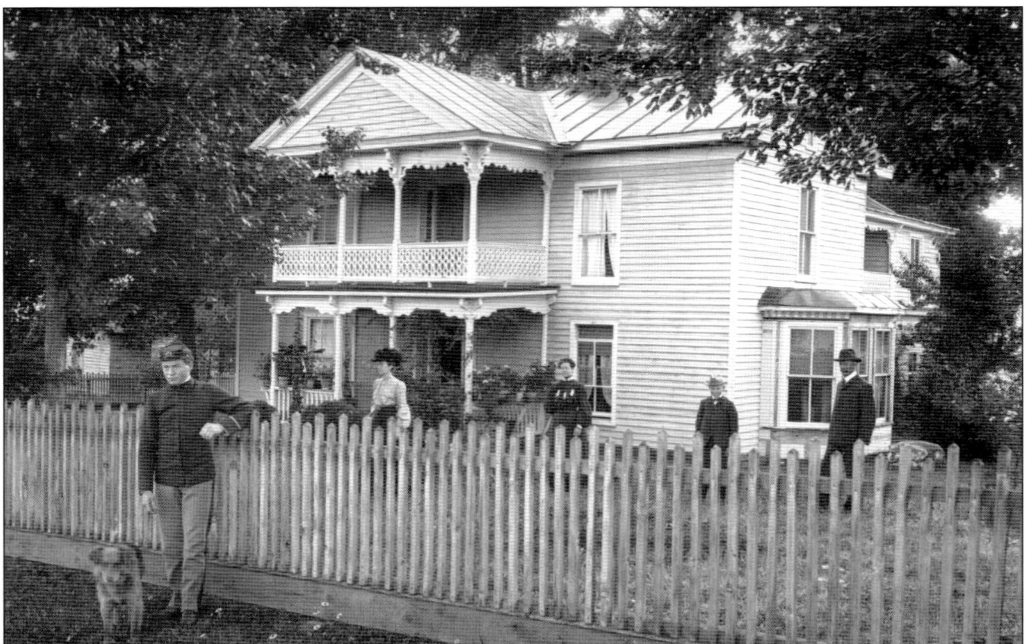

This young man leaning on the fence at the Henry Willis home in Willis wears a cadet uniform from the early 1900s.

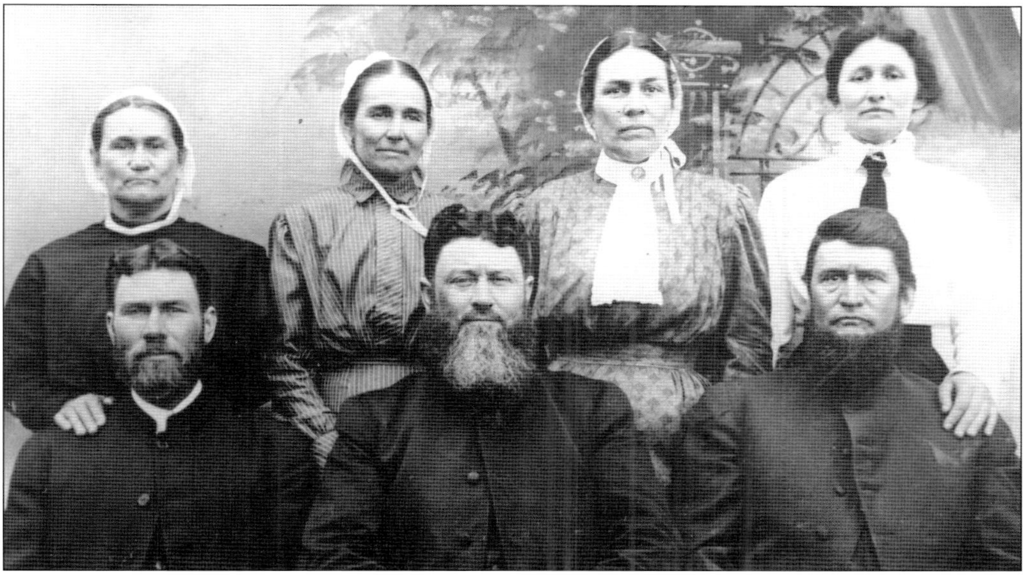

Elijah and Hannah (Bowman) Hylton's children wear clothing typical of Dunkards (German Baptist Brethren). They are, from left to right, (first row) Abram Hylton, who married Maggie Slusher; Joseph B. Hylton, who married Belle Collins; Granville Hylton, who married Mary Terry; (second row) Isabel Hylton, who married Levi Marshall; Roena Hylton, who married Alfred Marshall; Eliza Hylton, who married J.A.L. Sutphin; and Cassie Hylton, who married Pinkney R. Aldridge. Another son, Daniel Hylton, is not in the photograph because he had moved to Missouri.

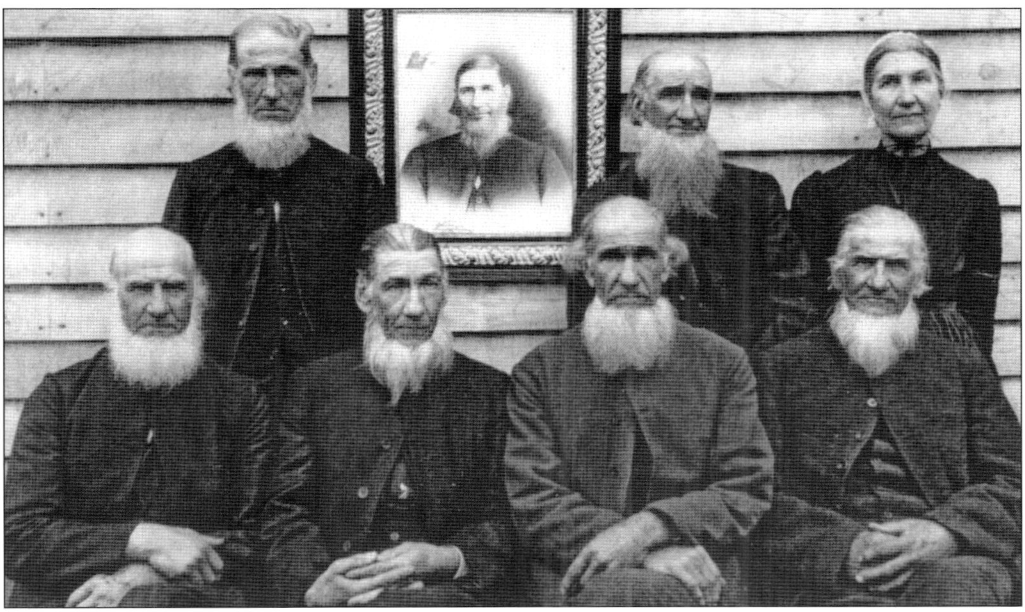

The children of Levi and Catherine (Harter) Weddle are seen here in the 1920s. They are, from left to right, (first row) Andrew Jackson, Calvin, Samuel, and Joel; (second row) Elkanah, Harvey (in portrait), Francis, and Elizabeth. Levi was the grandson of Benjamin and Mary (Eiler) Weddle, who settled eight miles west of Floyd in 1790. The congregation of the Church of the Brethren held their first communion in Benjamin's cabin around 1800. (JSK)

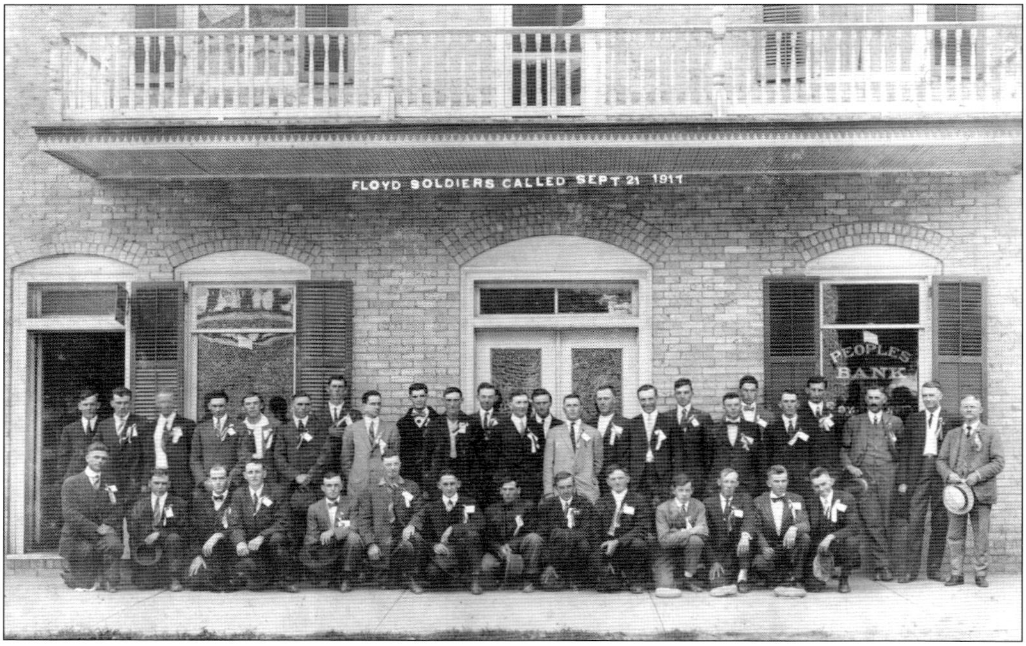

Floyd men departing for World War I stand in front of People's Bank on September 21, 1917.

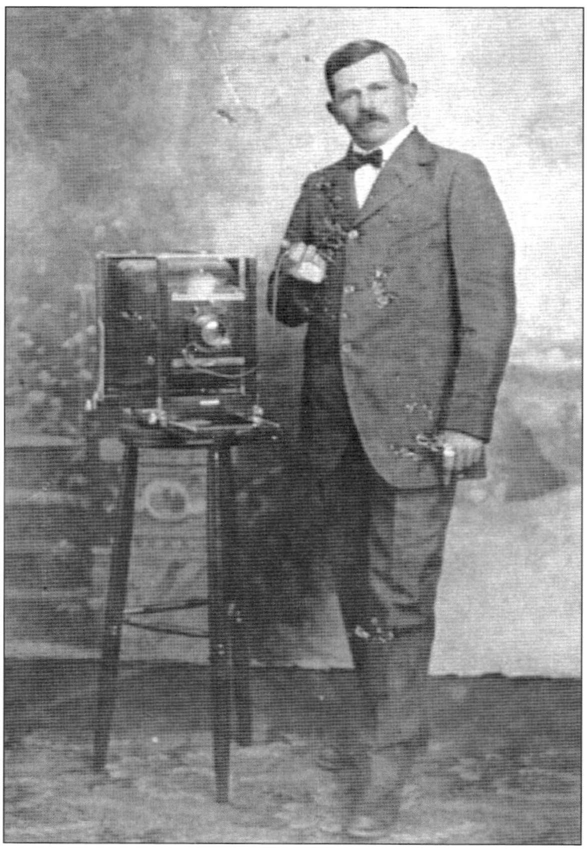

Dallas Cole was a professional photographer in the early 1900s with an office in an upper level of the old *Floyd Press* building on Locust Street. The photographs he took of World War I soldiers reporting for duty and school students graduating are still in the community today. He married French Altizer and they had four children: Douglas, Harman, Irvin, and Claudine. (BRC)

Rear Admiral Robley Dunglison "Fighting Bob" Evans was born in Floyd County on August 18, 1846, the son of Dr. Samuel Andrew Jackson Evans. He was educated in Floyd schools and was 10 years old when his father died. On September 15, 1860, Evans reported as a midshipman to the US Naval Academy in Annapolis, Maryland. He was ordered to active duty in 1863 and had a 40-year career in the US Navy. (GW)

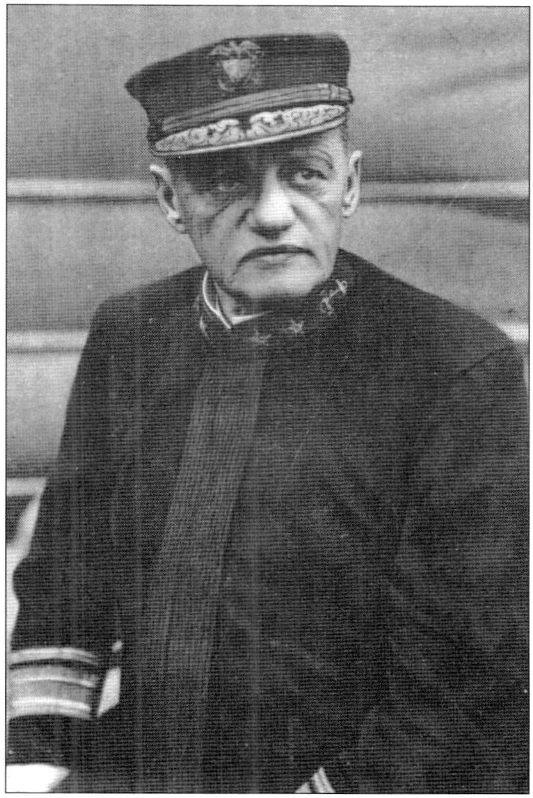

The family of Robert E. Lee, a former mayor of Floyd, included, from left to right, (first row) Irene Lee, a physical education teacher at Floyd High School; Robert E. Lee; his wife, Sallie Maude Lee; and Gerene (Lee) Williams, an elementary school teacher who married Al Williams; (second row) Bernard Lee, the owner of Floyd's first Esso station; Ed Lee; and Arthur Lee, the co-owner of the Esso station. (SWB)

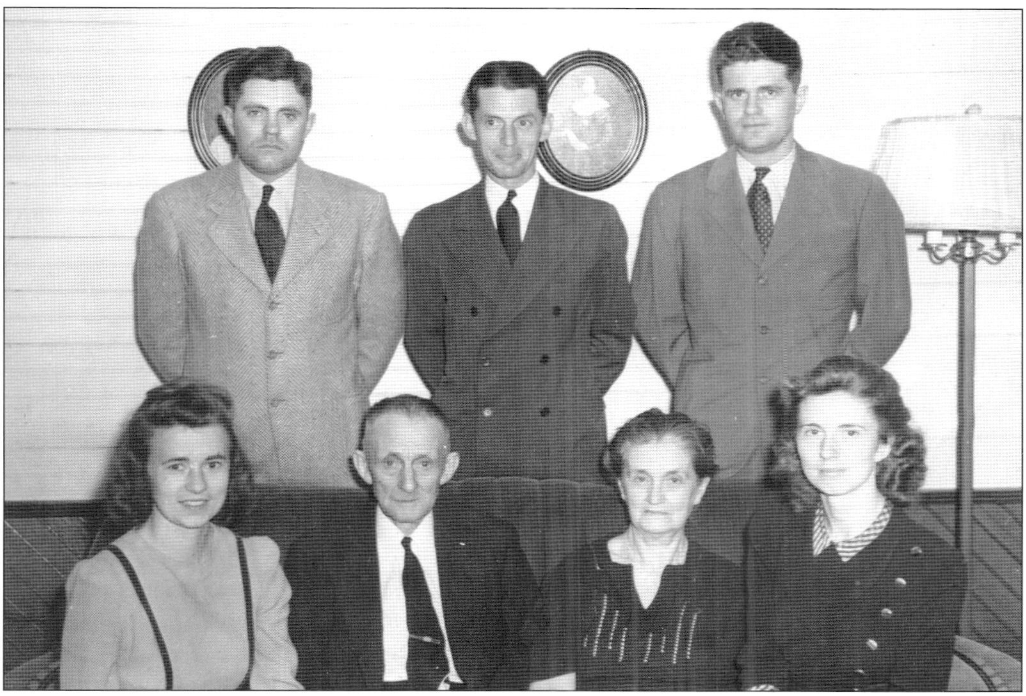

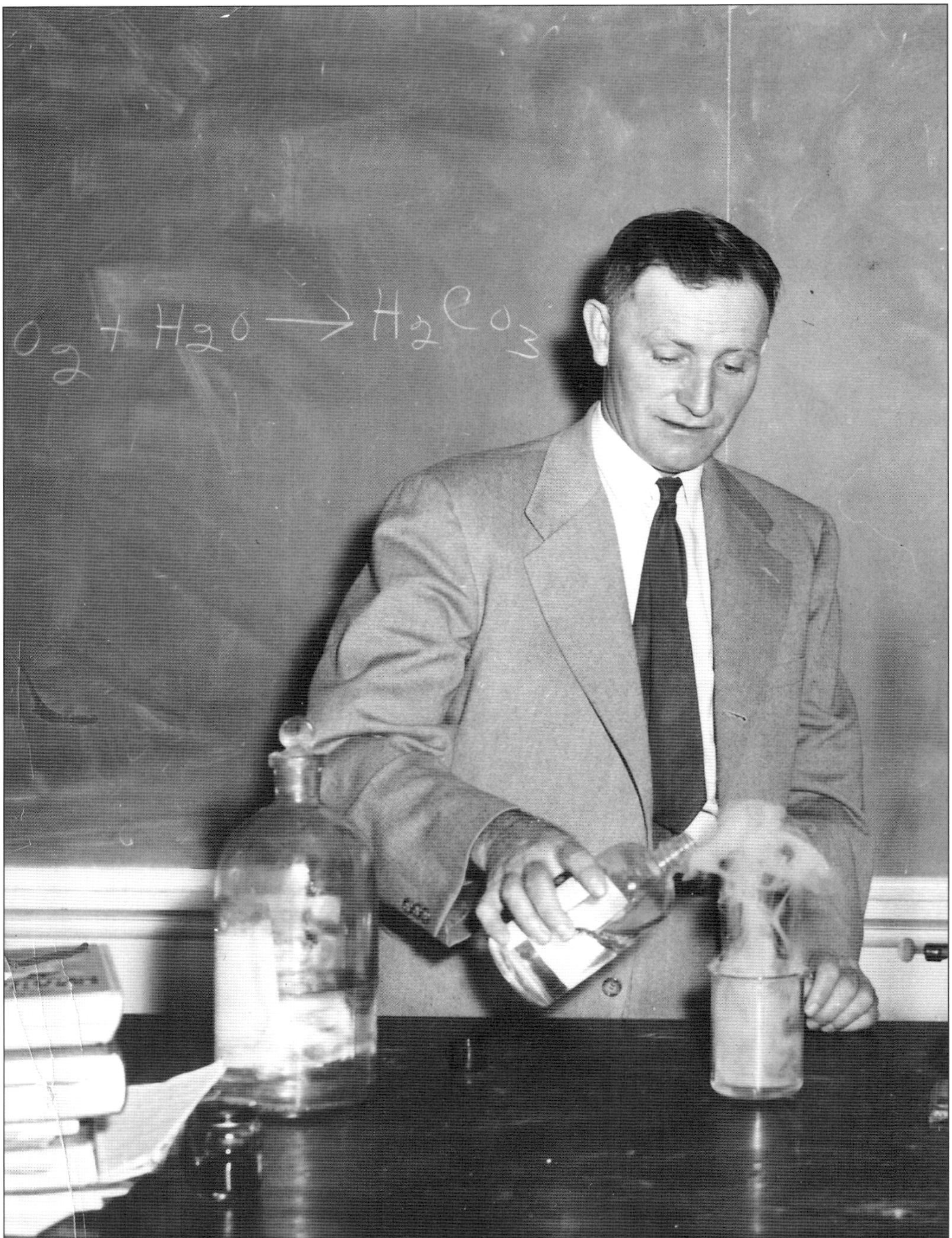

Max Thomas was a high school science teacher in Floyd County as well as a farmer and the author of *Walnut Knob* and *This Pleasant Land*. His wife, Clara (Turner) Thomas, was also a teacher, as were his daughters, Jean Schaeffer, who was president of the Floyd County Historical Society, and Janet Coiner. (JTS)

Susan "Ma Sue" (Harris) Hall, who was profiled in *Notable Women of Southwest Virginia*, was the daughter of Rev. John Kellogg Harris and Chloe (Bigelow) Harris. She was the executive secretary of the Red Cross in Floyd County, a reporter for the *Floyd Press* and *The Roanoke Times*, an office manager for US Steel in New York, the owner of Brame Hotel, and an unofficial social worker.

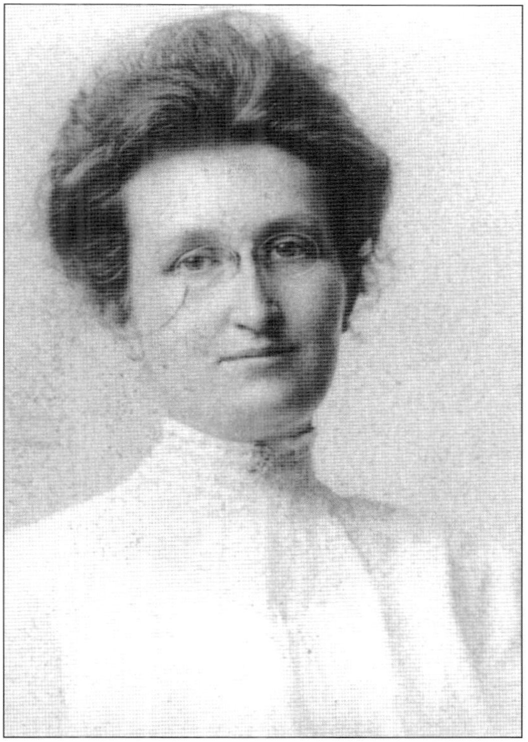

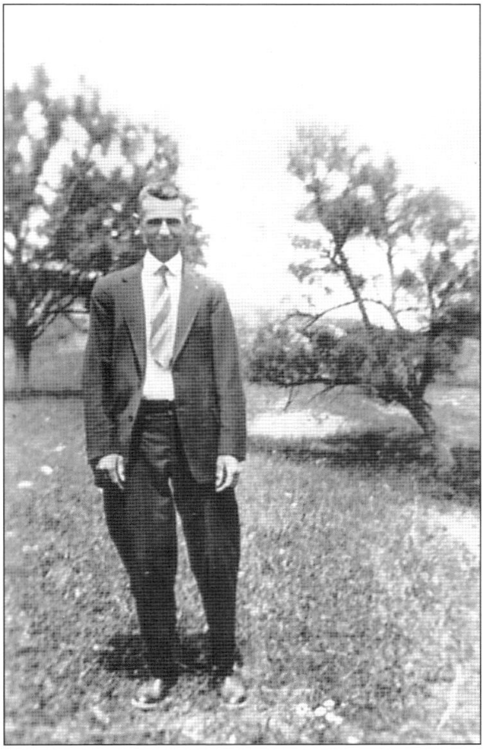

Arnton Perry Snead Sr. began his professional career as a carpenter with Lather Hylton. He built the Dr. F. Clyde Bedsaul house (1936), the Green Profitt house (1938), the Clarence Maberry house (1936), the Bill and Nancy Shelor house, Wood Funeral Home (1939), the Floyd County courthouse (1950), and the Bank of Floyd (1952), as well as more than 100 other buildings and homes in Floyd County. (SSB)

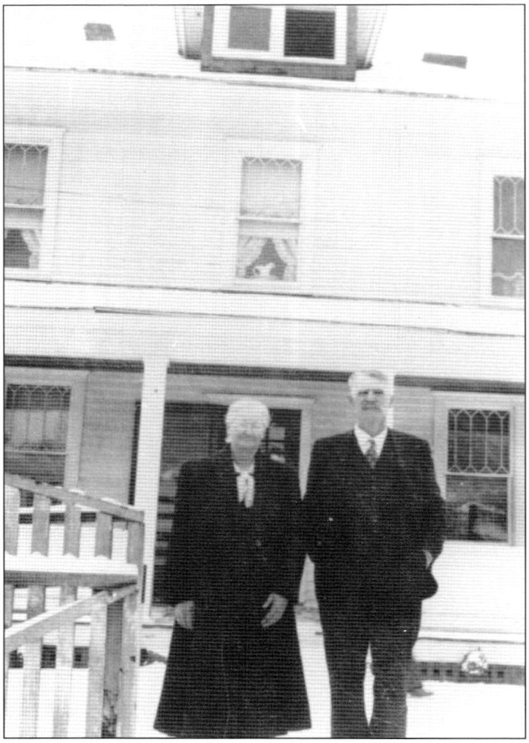

James Monroe Compton and Lucy Laura Dehart Compton built this home on Canning Factory Road near Route 8. Their original home place in the Rocky Knob area was given up for the building of the Blue Ridge Parkway. This house is presently the home of their grandson, Kyle Lee, and his wife, Frances Weddle Lee. (LCT)

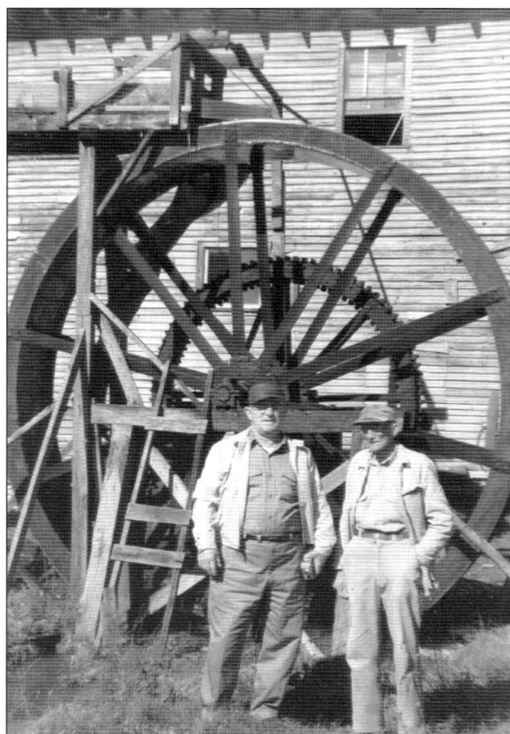

Noted photographer Earl Palmer (left) and Homer Roberson pose in front of the overshot water wheel at the Roberson Mill on Roberson Mill Road.

Three

Churches and Schools

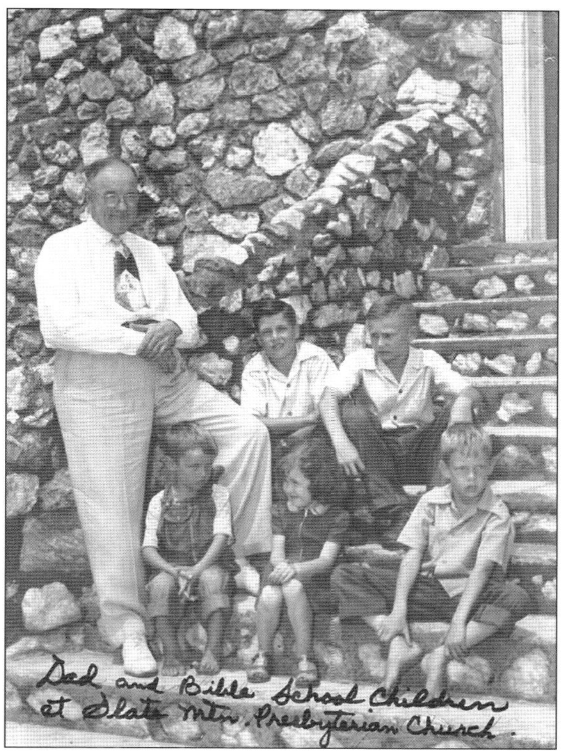

Of the six rock churches built by Rev. Robert Childress, two are in Floyd County. In 1932, the congregation hauled rocks by wagonloads to build Slate Mountain Presbyterian Church on Rock Church Road, on land donated by Guy and Dovie Underwood. Because Reverend Childress was pastor of so many churches, Sunday school and preaching were held on Sunday nights until about 1954, when he was forced to quit due to poor health. The roads were so poor that he was sometimes late for services but he told Luther Wood, the song leader, to keep singing until he got there. Reverend Childress is seen here with some of the boys of the congregation. The other rock church is in Willis. (SC)

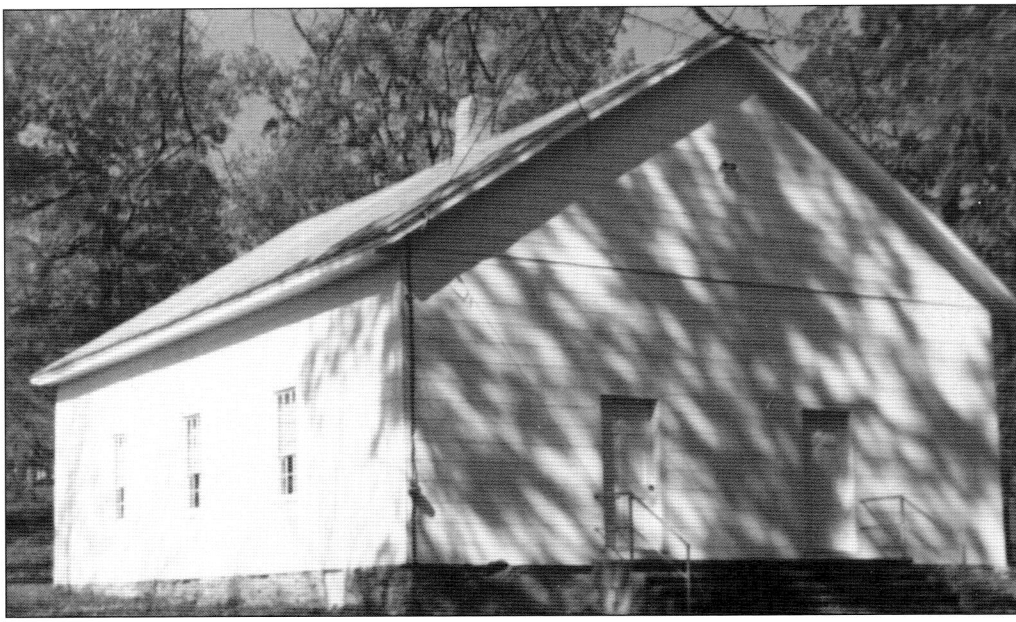

The Salem, or Head of the River, Primitive Baptist Church was established in 1784 by Elder William Howard and built on land deeded to the church by Daniel I. Conner. On the north side of the ridge, water flows into the Roanoke River and on the south side it flows into Little River, thus explaining its name. It is on Route 221 about 15 miles north of Floyd. The second church building is seen here. (MP)

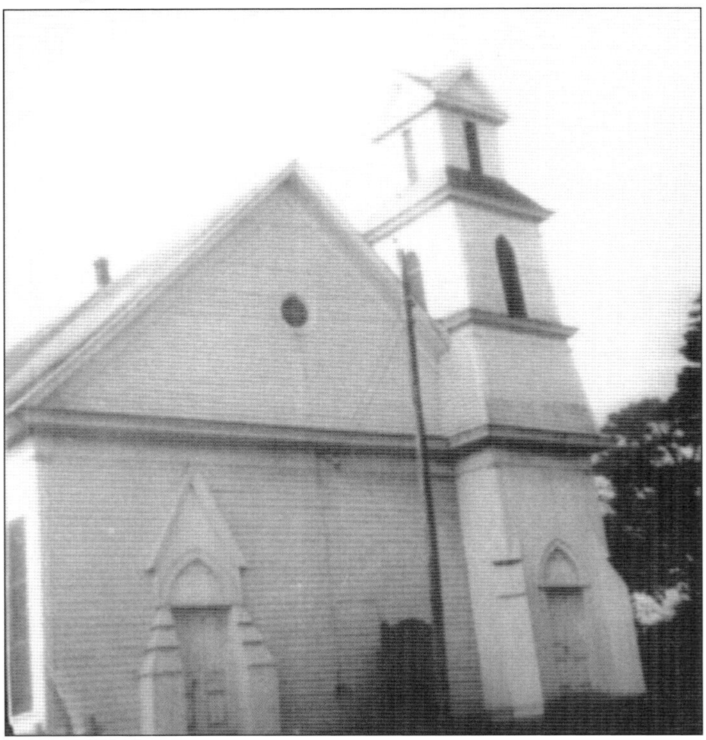

Floyd Baptist Church was organized in 1876. Prior to that time, it had been the Jacksonville Baptist Church (organized in 1845), the New Haven Baptist Church (when it moved to a nearby community in 1857), and finally in 1876 the Jacksonville Baptist Church. When the town of Jacksonville changed its name to Floyd, so did the church. The church now occupies a place of prominence in the center of town and includes a sanctuary, two educational buildings, and a fellowship hall. This photograph shows one of the older buildings.

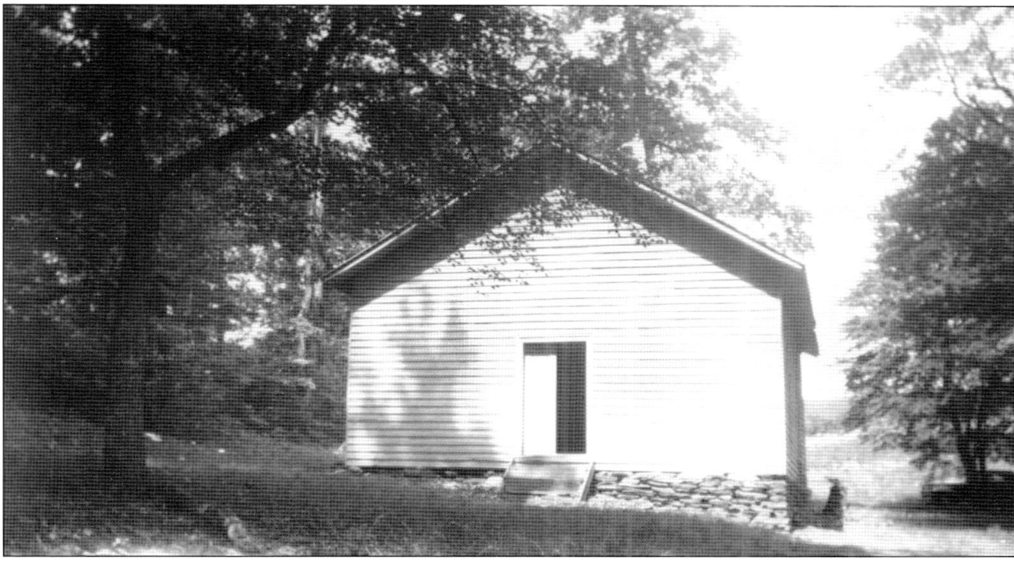

Pine Creek Primitive Baptist Church, on Spangler's Mill Road, was organized in 1790 by members of Salem Church. Elder Peter Howard was the first pastor, followed by Michael Howery, Thomas I. Roberson, Wilson H. Dodd, Amos Dickerson, H.V. Cole, and J.M. Dickerson. Eight Revolutionary War soldiers and several Civil War soldiers are buried in the cemetery adjoining the church.

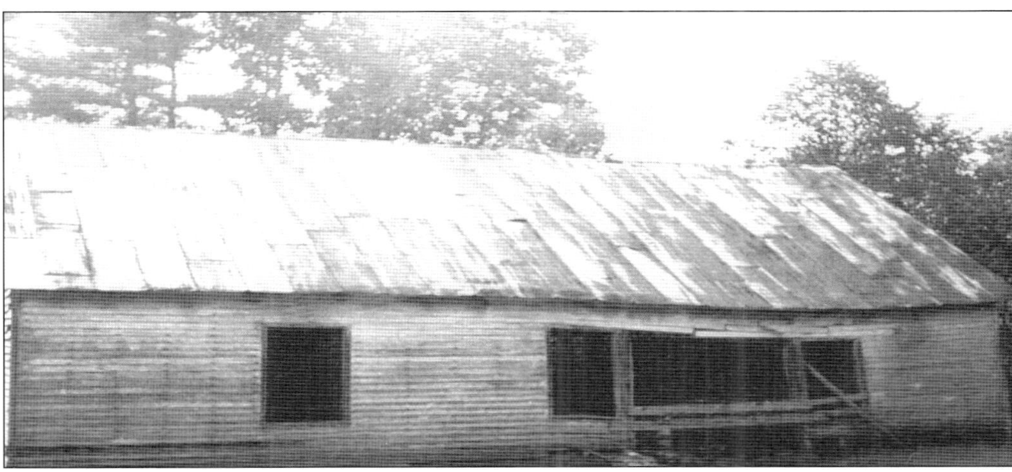

"Uncle" Billy Thompson began preaching in the home of Lewis Weeks. When his group outgrew the home around 1860, they built Weeks Chapel on Conner's Grove Road. In the mid-1930s, they joined the Methodist congregation in Willis.

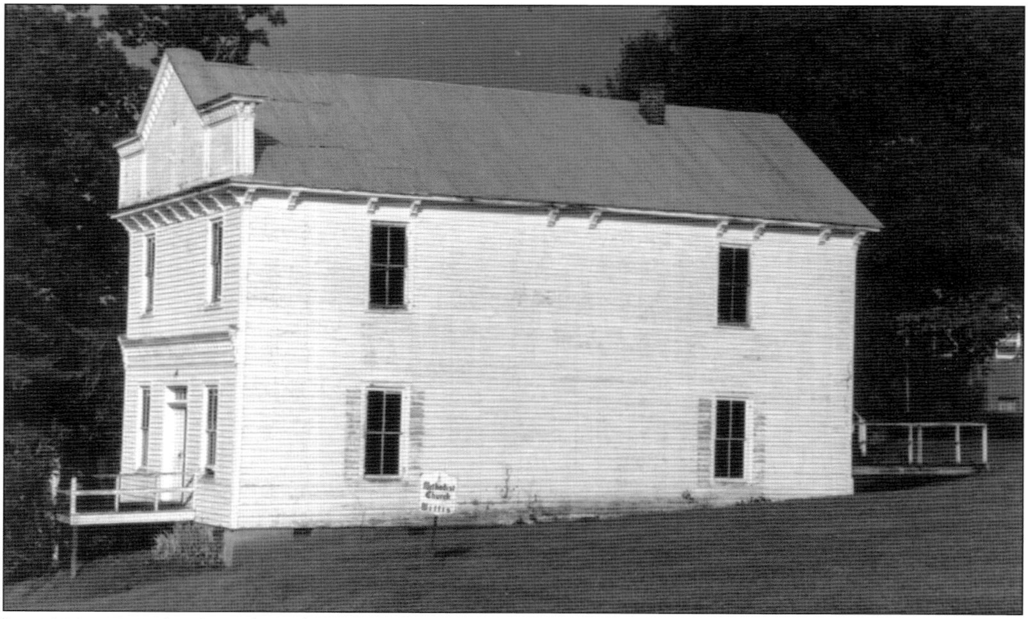

In 1893, a Methodist church was established in Hylton (later Willis) within the boundary of Holston Conference. It remained until this church was built in the 1930s by the Hylton Masonic Lodge 153, the Methodists, and the Baptists. The Baptists deeded their part to the Methodists in the 1960s. The Hylton Masonic Lodge 153 combined with the Floyd Lodge 329 in 1996 and deeded their part to the Methodists. (CSA)

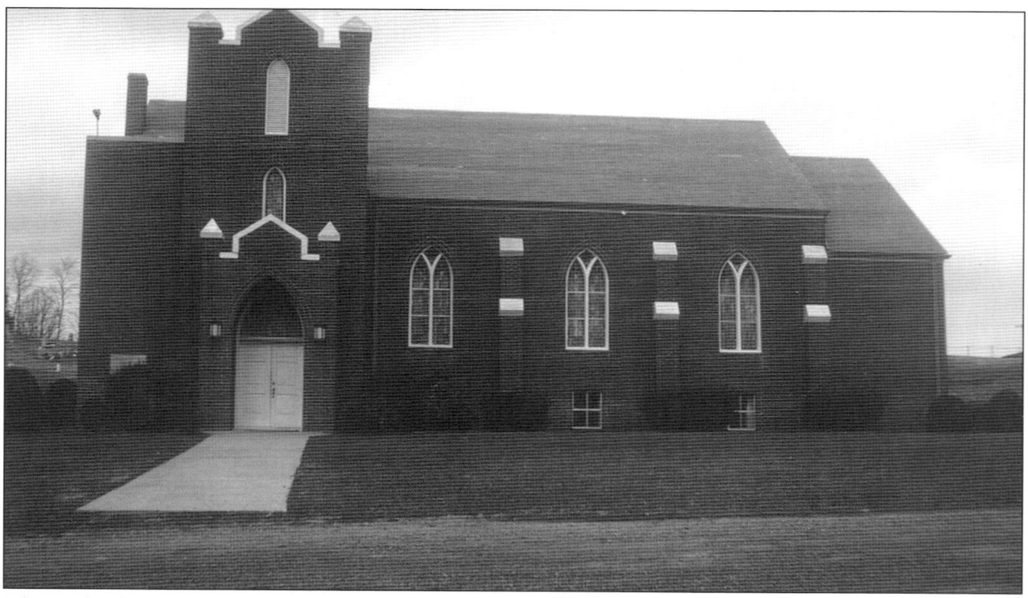

Through the efforts of William Smith, the Church of the Brethren was introduced in Floyd County when it was still Montgomery County, around 1800. Services were held in homes, barns, and groves. In 1857, the brick church was built at a cost of $1,300. The name changed to Topeco Church of the Brethren in 1896 when the brick church was replaced by a frame building. The present brick church was built in 1951.

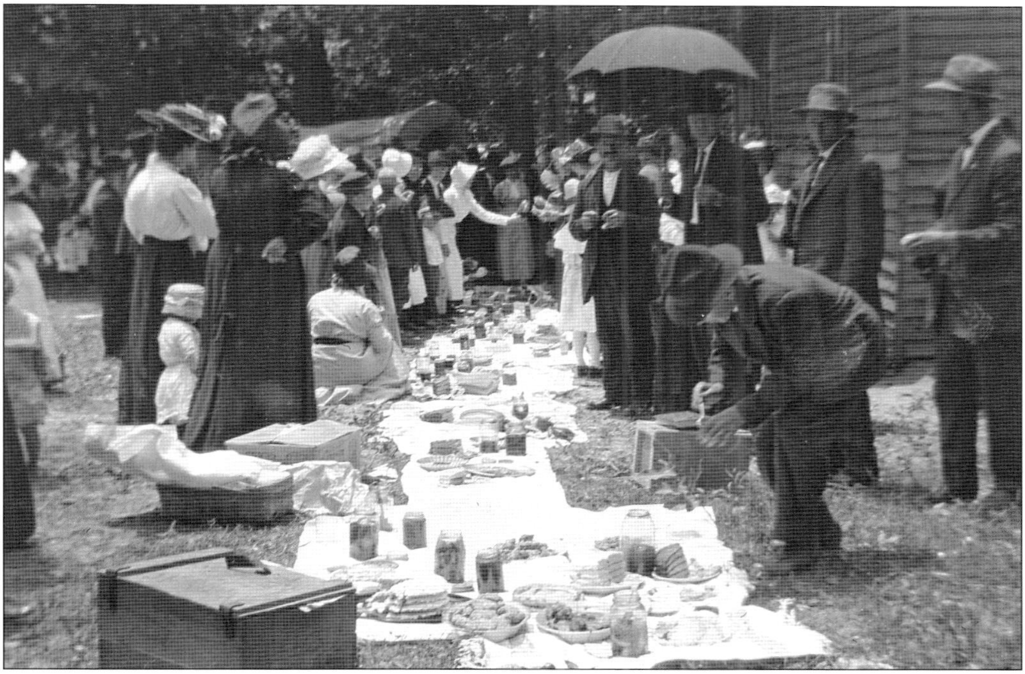

This scene calls to mind the familiar phrase, "All day preaching with dinner on the grounds." This particular meal may have followed a 1910s baptizing, also photographed by Richard Shank, shown on page 52. Note the many jars of pickles and multilayered cakes. (SS)

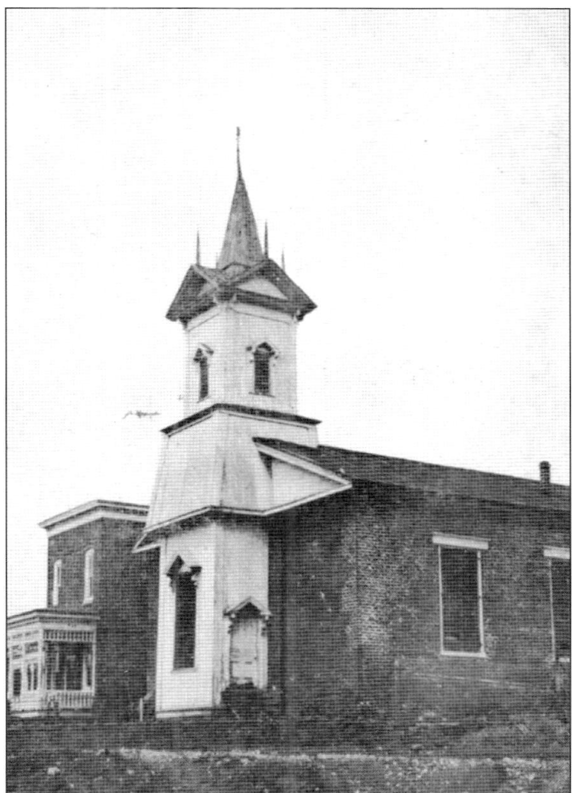

Floyd Methodist Church was completed around 1870. In 1873, it was placed in the Holston Conference with Reverend Barnes appointed as the first pastor. Final services were held on July 24, 1966. A marker sits on East Main Street diagonally across from the present-day church. (GW)

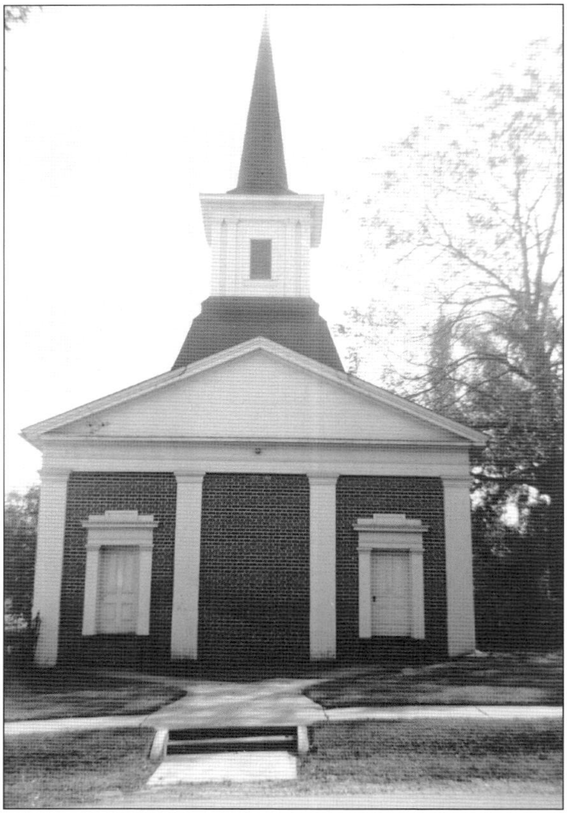

Built in 1850 by Henry Dillon, the original Jacksonville (Floyd) Presbyterian Church is on Main Street. The bell was crafted in Troy, New York, and brought on a train to Christiansburg and then by wagon to Floyd, which took three days. When the new church was built nearby in 1974, the bell was taken along. Among others, Rev. John Kellogg Harris and Dr. Robert Gamble See were pastors here.

This photograph of a baptismal service was taken by Richard Shank in the 1910s. Shank lived in the Stonewall-Cannaday School area, but the exact location of this event is unknown. (SS)

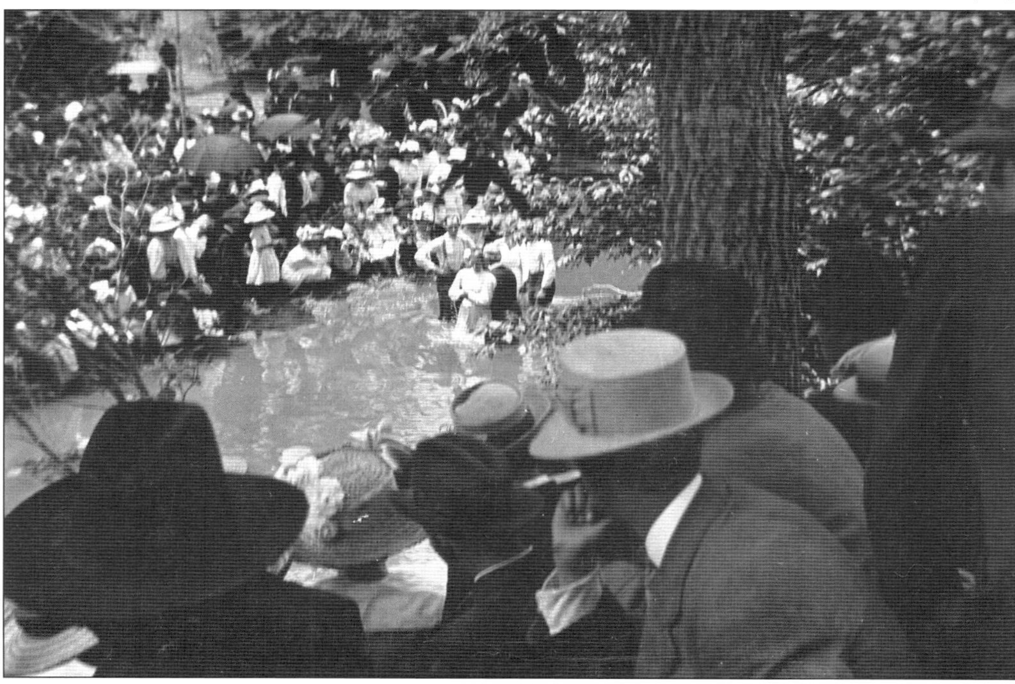

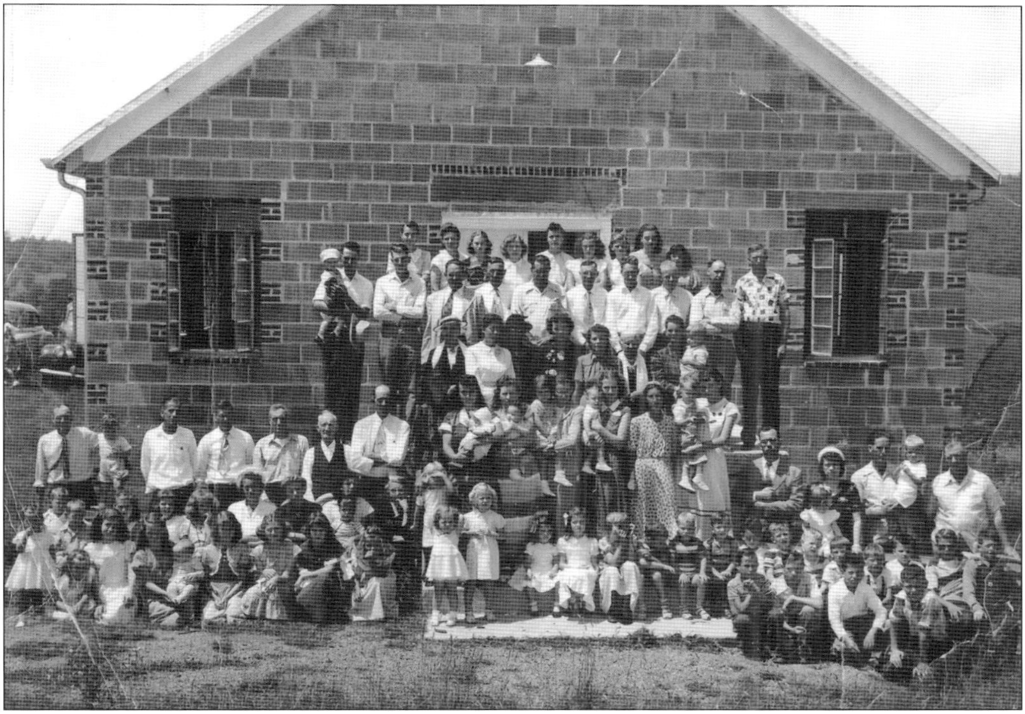

Indian Valley Church of God is seen here in 1952. The church, on Macks Mountain Road, was led at the time by the Rev. Dorsie Phillips. The church still stands at this location but is barely recognizable after two major renovations. (SQP)

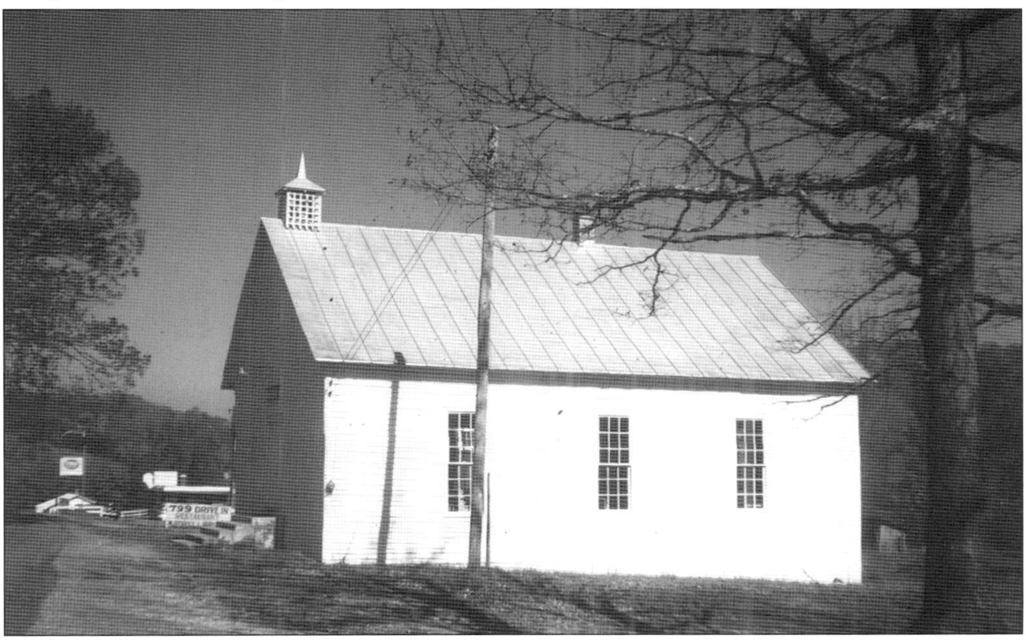

Harris Chapel Church on Conner's Grove Road is still used every Sunday. Rufus Harris donated the land and his sons Eck, Walter, Croff, Jim, and Frank built the church in 1915.

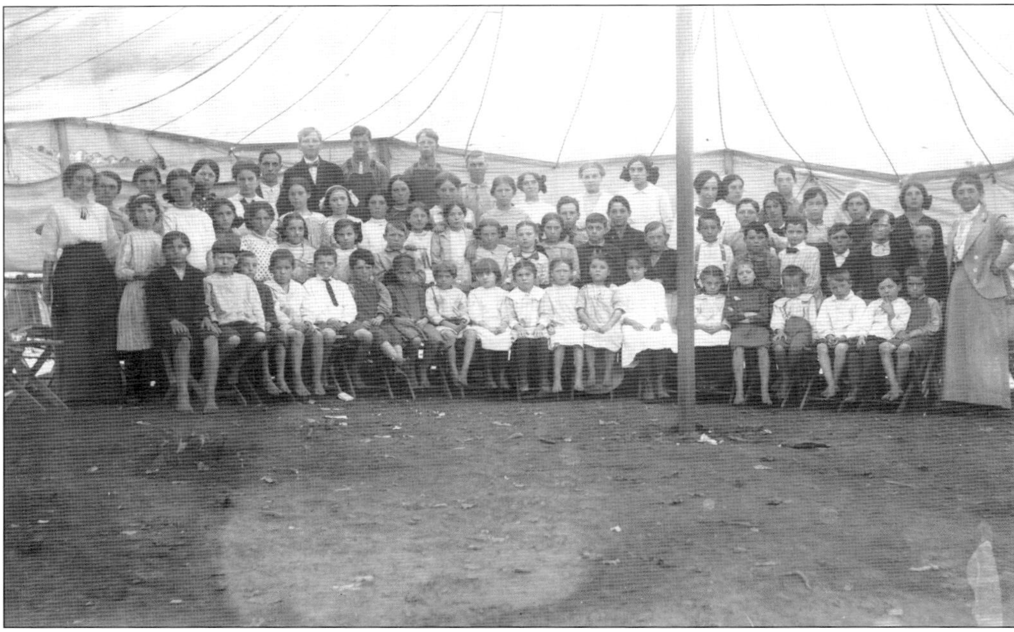

The students at Harris Cannaday School, on Cannady School Road, first sat on logs outdoors before the tent pictured above was erected. The tent was used until the school was completed in 1915. One grade per year was added and the first graduating class was in 1926. The school, a Harris Mountain Mission school, closed in 1938, but the church there remained active until 1967, when it and other small churches joined the Church of Floyd Presbyterian. Pictured below is the Harris Cannaday School and Church.

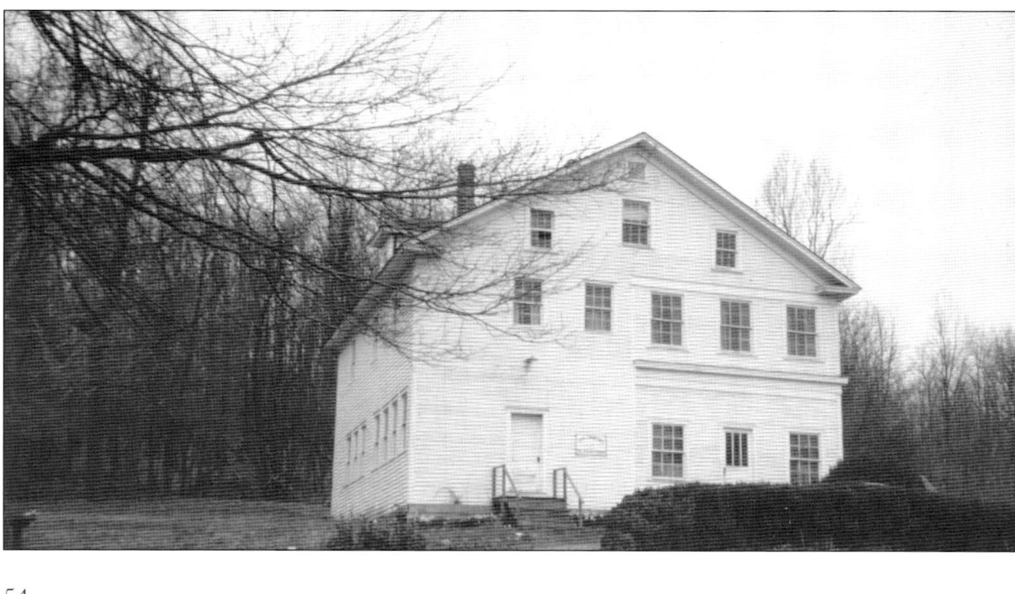

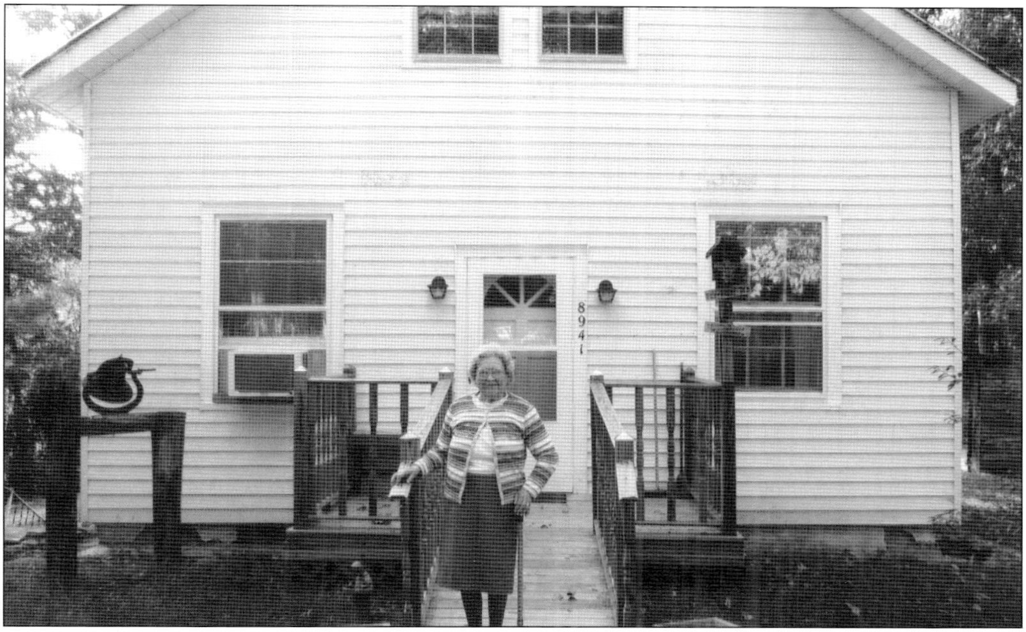

Effie (King) Brown is seen here at Piney Forest School, where she taught as a young lady. Brown was a schoolteacher, principal, and community historian all her life. She spearheaded the campaign to start the Floyd County Historical Society in 1976 and held several offices in the society, from president to parliamentarian, ending with her death on May 5, 2012. (MAS)

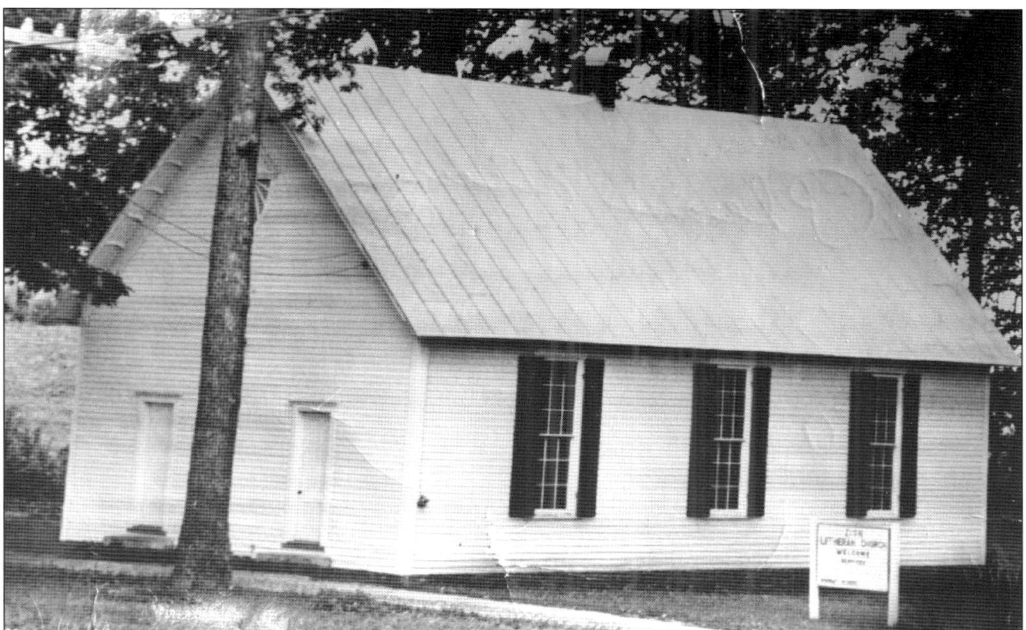

In 1791, the first wave of German-American pioneer settlers moved into the Floyd area from Frederick County, Maryland. This group formed the nucleus of the German Lutheran congregation, which was formally organized in 1813, and became Zion Lutheran.

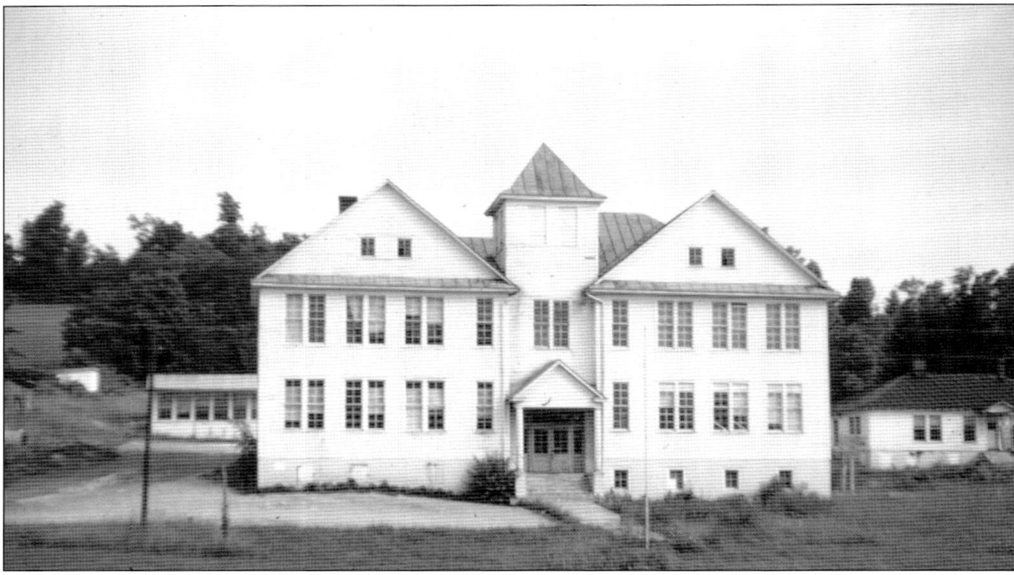

Willis High School, built by Lather Hylton in 1917, was used until 1962, when the three county high schools, Willis, Check, and Floyd, consolidated into the new Floyd County High School.

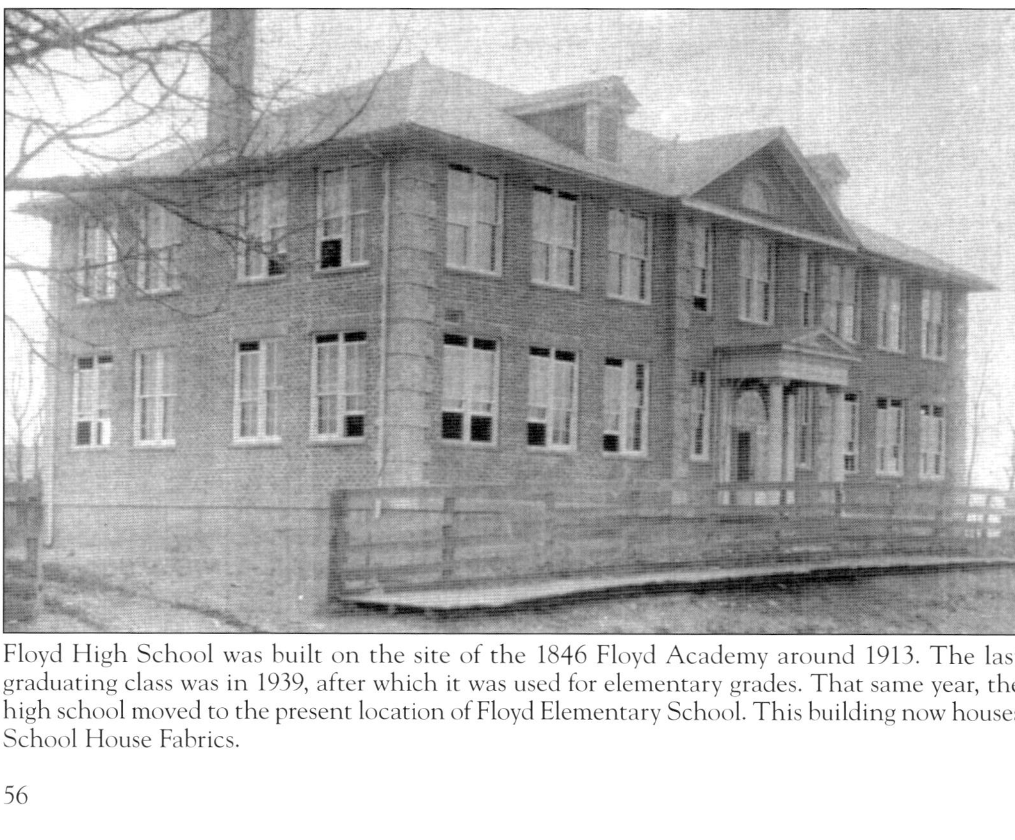

Floyd High School was built on the site of the 1846 Floyd Academy around 1913. The last graduating class was in 1939, after which it was used for elementary grades. That same year, the high school moved to the present location of Floyd Elementary School. This building now houses School House Fabrics.

Teachers Vera (Sumpter) Shelburne and Annie Smith are seen at Check School in 1922. (MAS)

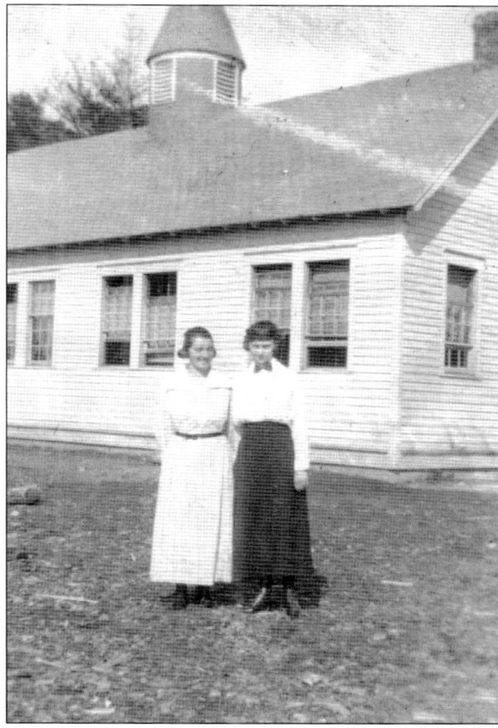

Toncray School, seen here in 1908, was on Old Furnace Road until it closed and was bought and moved to Black Ridge Road. Henrietta (Dillon) Shelor was a teacher there. It was the custom of the time for families to visit on special days, and this appears to be one of those days. (GS.)

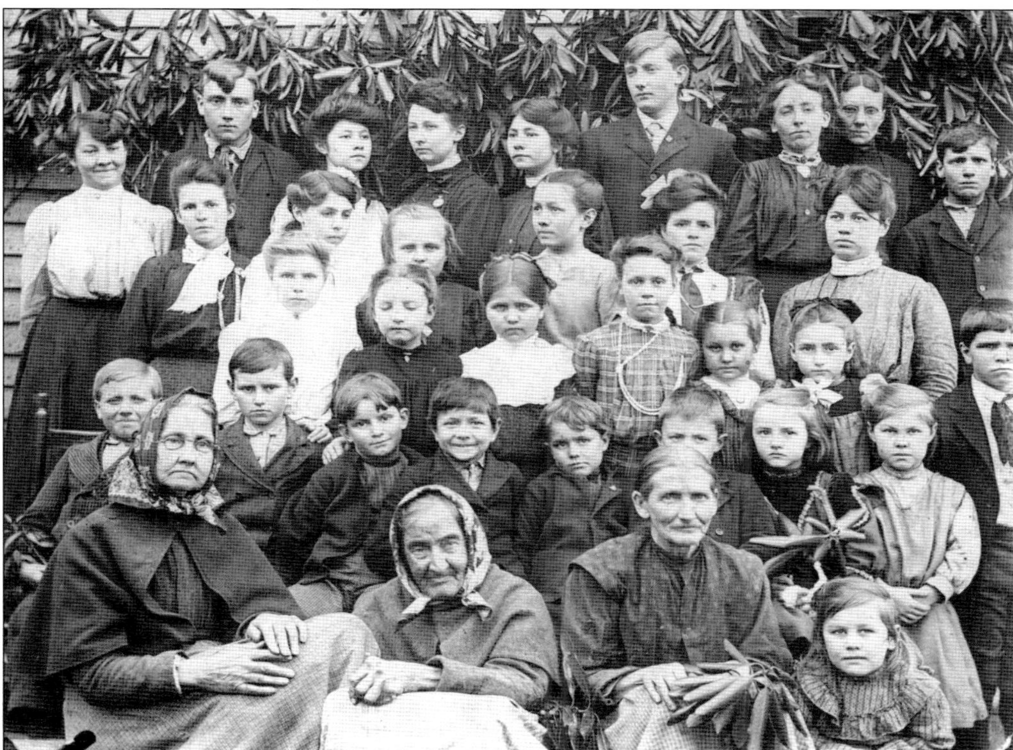

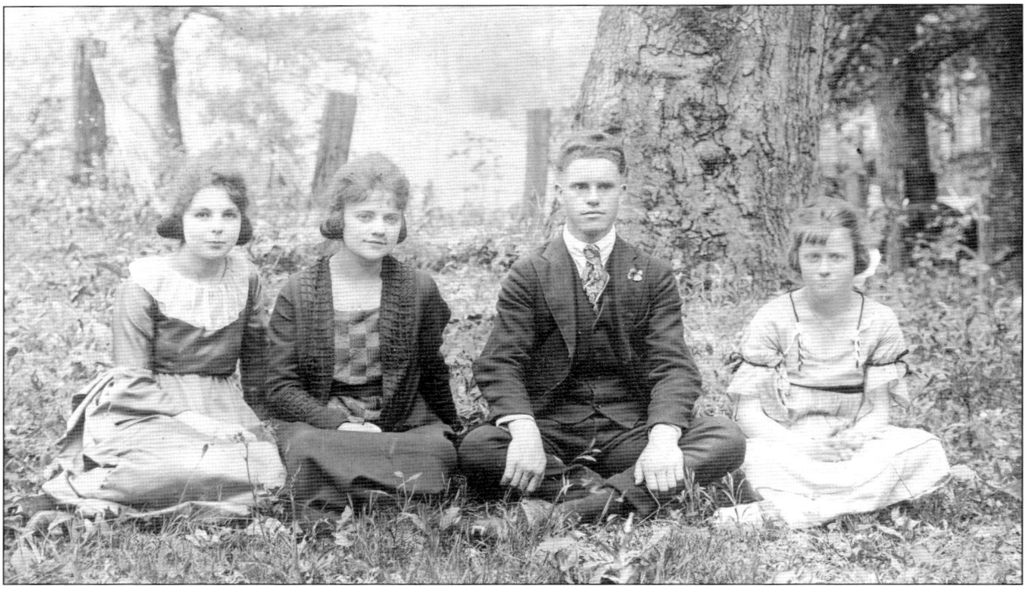

Students are seen here at Check School around 1921. They are, from left to right, Mary Cannaday, Iva Poff, Camden Reed, and Iris (Poff) Aldridge. (MAS)

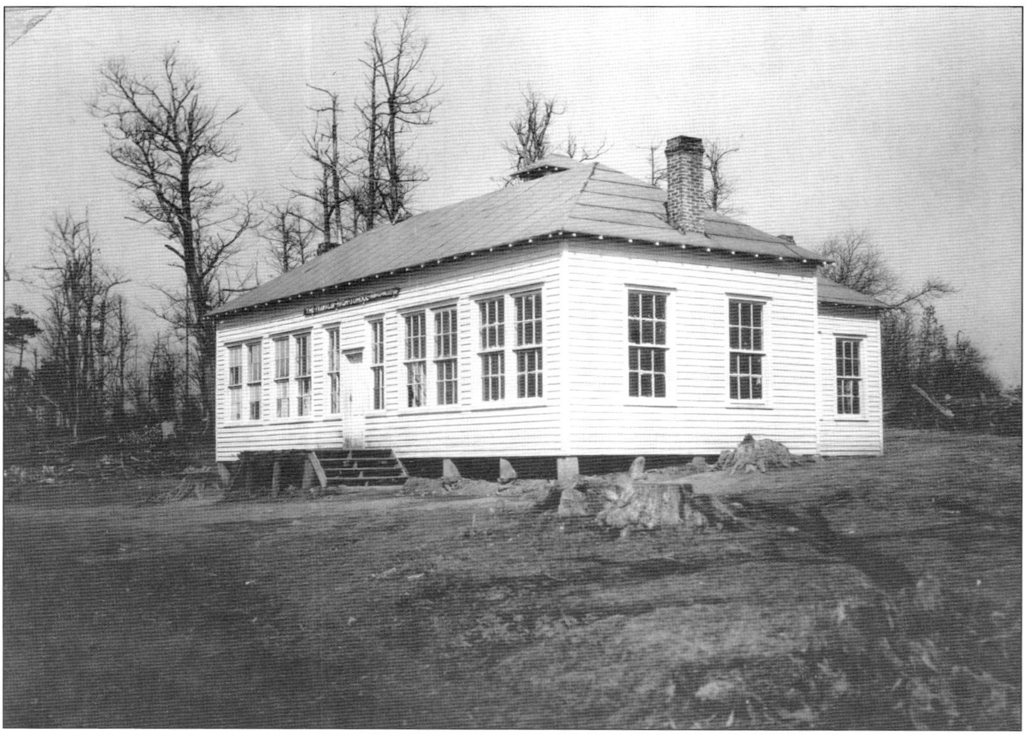

Franklin High School, a Harris Mountain school, was in Indian Valley. It served that part of the county from 1922 until 1930, after which Indian Valley students attended Willis High School. Granville and Cabell McGrady ran a store here for many years and lived in the back of the building. It is currently a private home on Macks Mountain Road. (DPM)

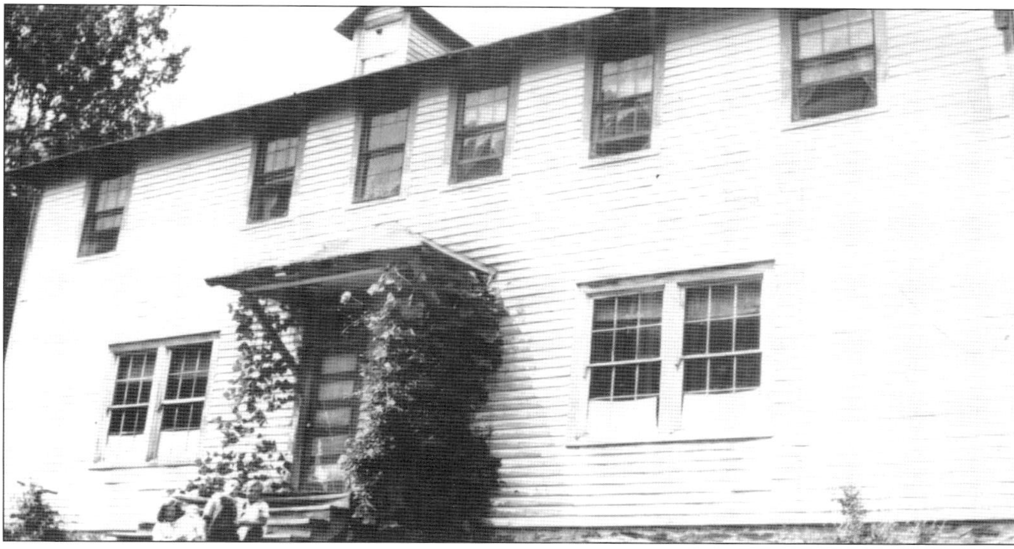

Reverend and Mrs. Y.P. Scruggs were principals of Shooting Creek School, one of the Harris Mountain Mission schools.

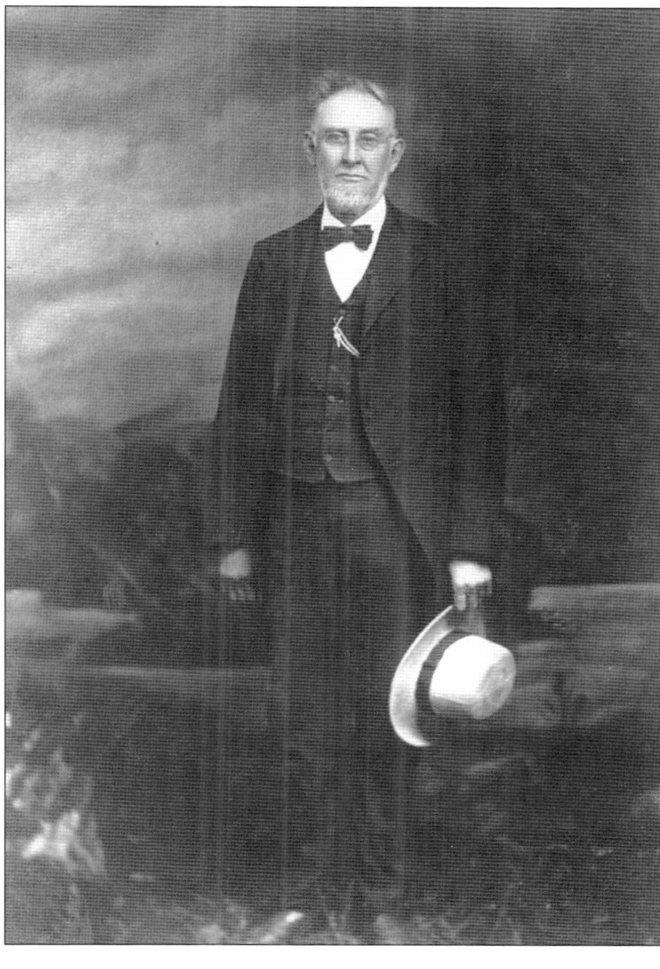

On May 15, 1872, Rev. John Kellogg Harris responded to the call of the Jacksonville Presbyterian Church. He and his wife, Chloe Minerva (Bigelow) Harris, also established the Oxford Academy, a college preparatory school, which was run by the Harris family from 1875 to 1904, except for a seven-year period when they were in Nebraska doing mission work. Chloe died in 1897 and John died in 1910.

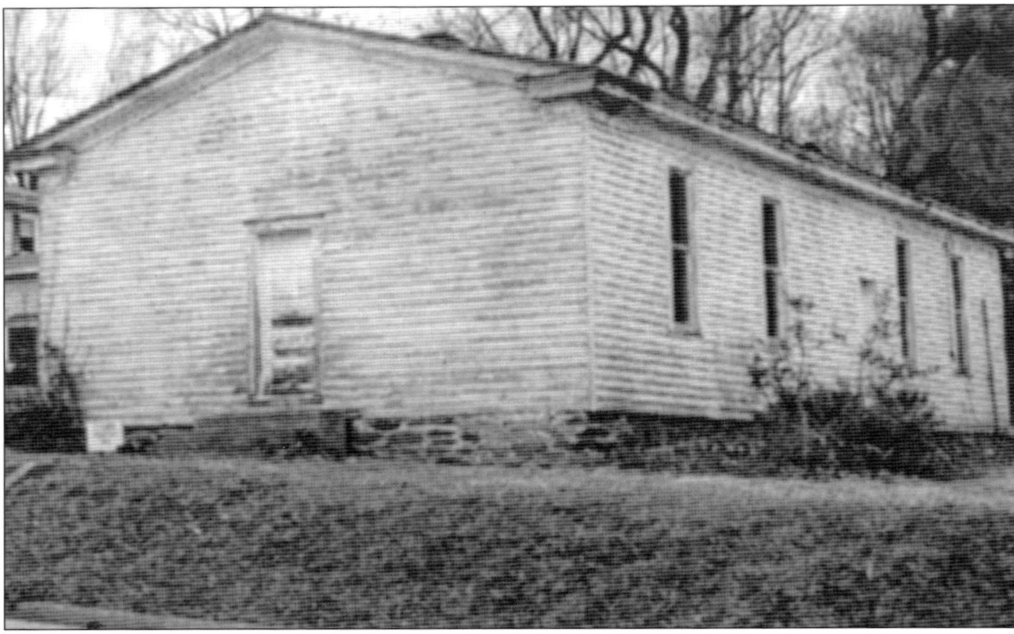

The original Oxford Academy was a log structure built in 1875. It burned down in the late 1890s and was replaced by this building, which still stands on Oxford Street. The Floyd County Historical Preservation Trust is currently renovating the building. (DRM)

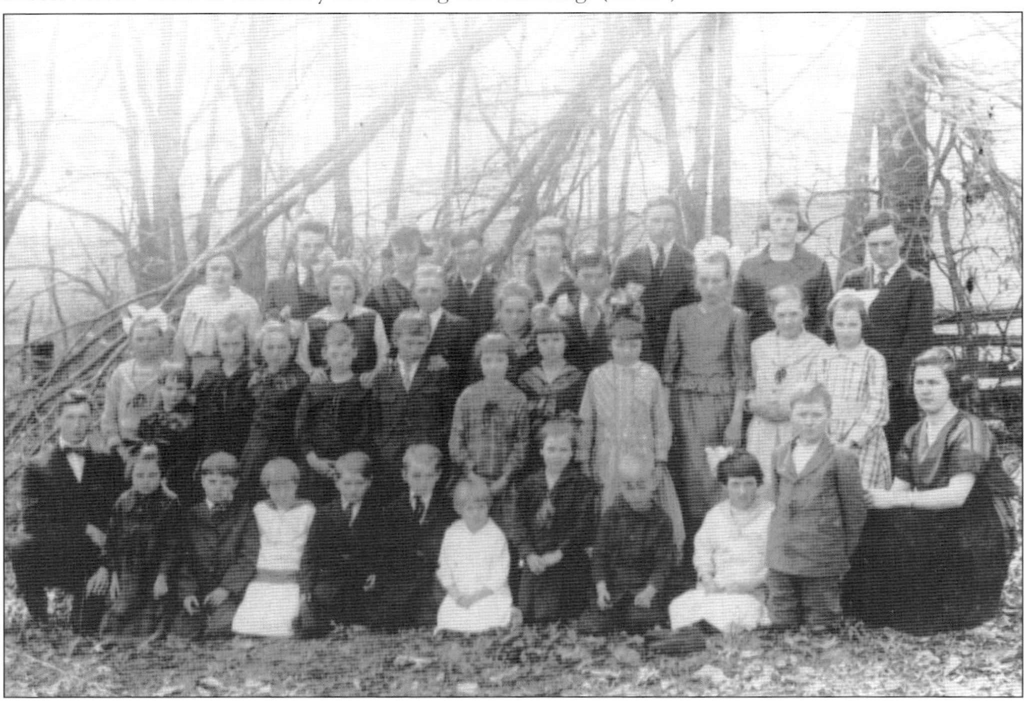

Principal Willie Hale (far left) and teacher Bess Sumner (far right) pose with students at the Red Oak Grove School around 1921. The students seen here are from the Hale, Sowers, Dobbins, Lampey, Bowman, Williams, Naff, McCann, Gray, and Smith families. (JGB)

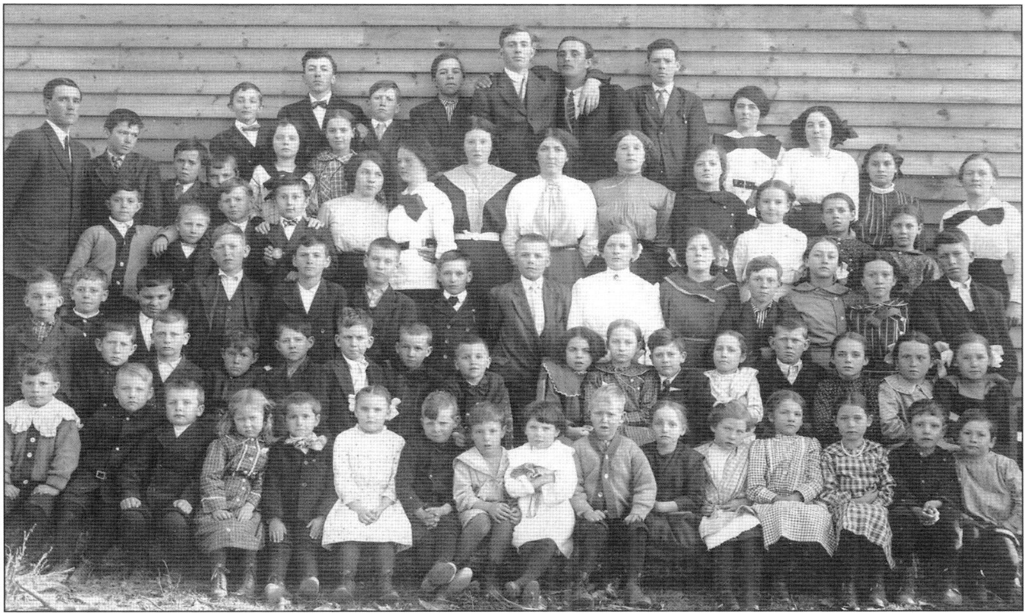

Alley School was on Indian Valley Road. Seen here are teachers Ida (Dulaney) Bishop (far right) and Doris Alley (far left). The students belonged to the Smith, Marshall, Wade, Cox, Bond, McPeak, Caldwell, Phillips, Akers, Duncan, Price, Mann, Lester, and Bishop families. (RC)

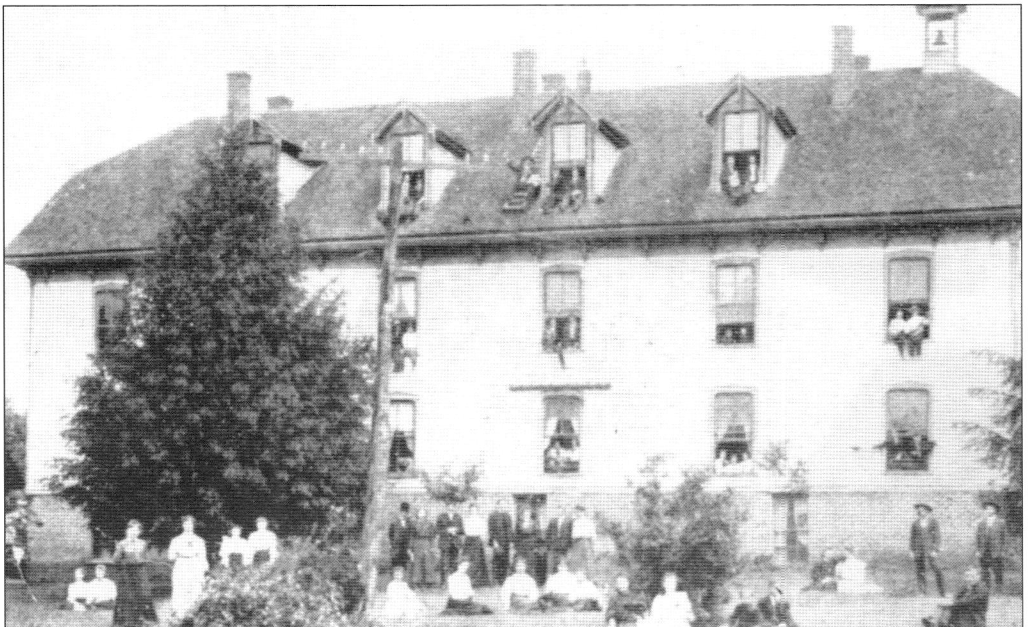

The Mountain Normal School in Willis opened in 1882 for a few seasons. Prof. John B. Wrightsman of Bridgewater College founded the private school that focused on teacher training. Later, Prof. J.H. Rutrough conducted a summer "normal" and often had 100 teachers and would-be teachers who he taught himself.

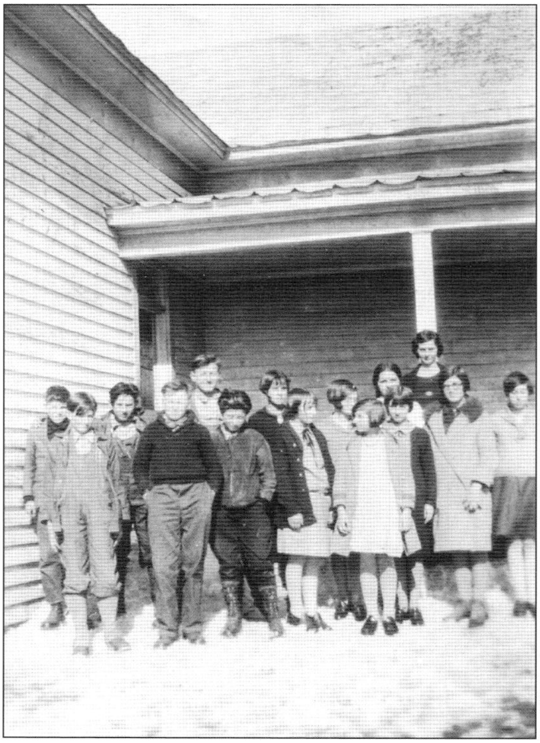

Teacher Annie (Williams) Smith poses with her class at Alum Ridge School in the late 1920s. (MAS)

This Alum Ridge School photograph shows unidentified students and teachers. Teachers known to have taught at this school include J.D. Wall, Marie Williams, Cathleen Wilson, Myrtle (Thompson) Mitchell, Violet Stafford, Pattie Gardner, Myrtle Shelor, Lorraine (Carr) Reed, Nan Howard, Alice Hylton, Ella Mae Reed, and Essie Lester. (RA)

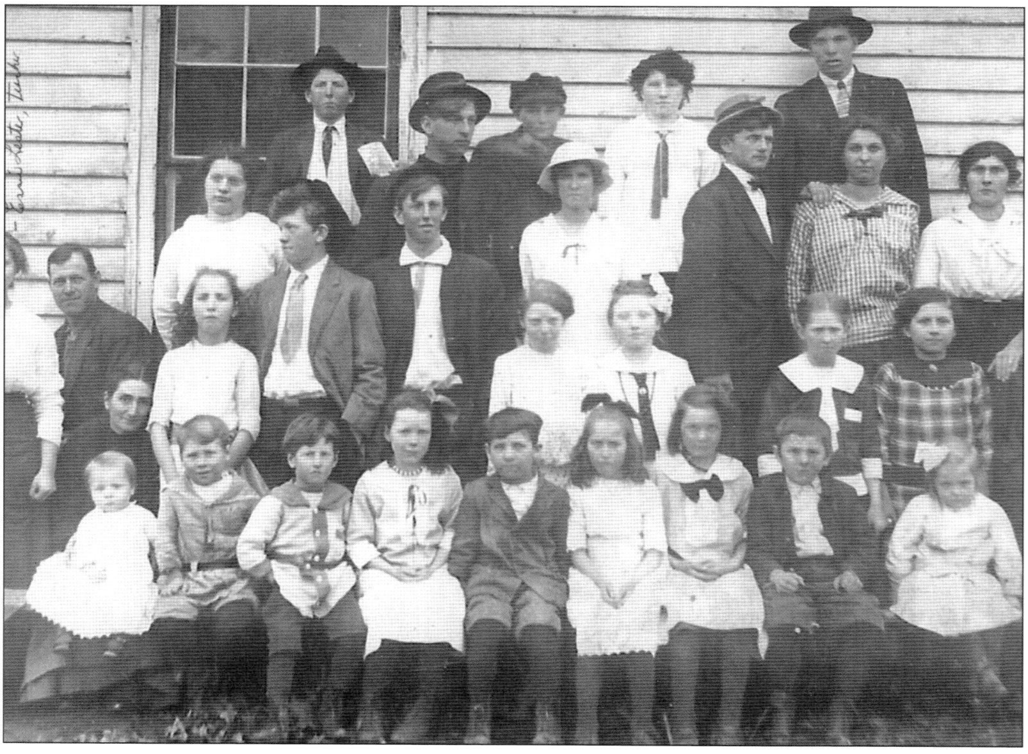

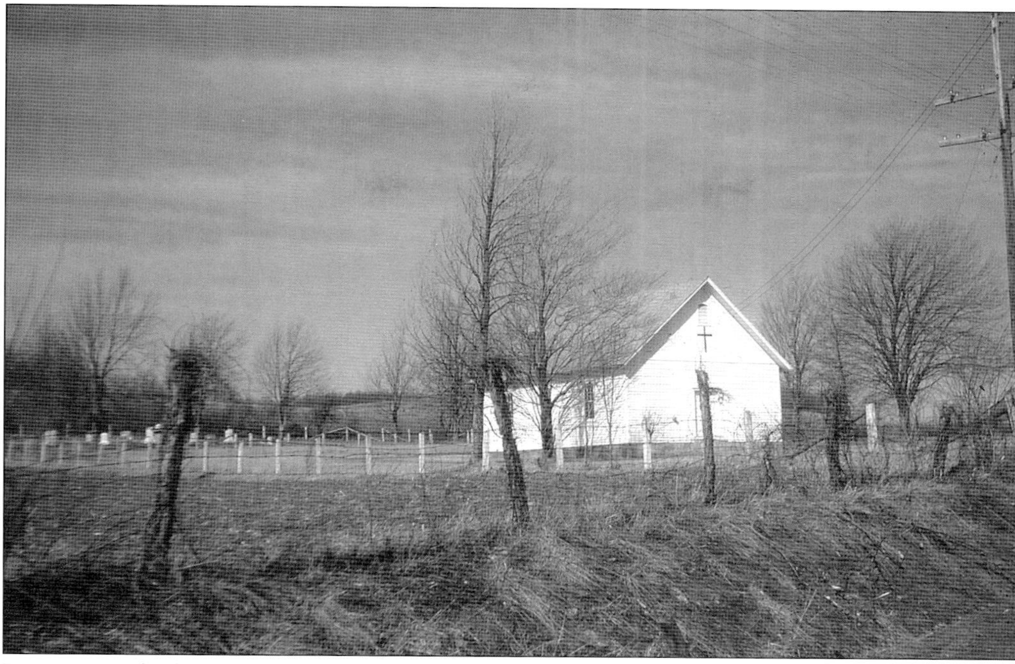

Harvestwood Church, built in the Pizarro community in 1916, was named for three men who helped found it: R.O. "Bob" Harvey, Lincoln Vest, and Greenville Wood. Dr. R. Gamble See helped start the church and keep it going. The old pump organ, played by Thelma (Turner) Houchins, is on display at the Old Church Gallery. Only the cemetery remains. (JTS)

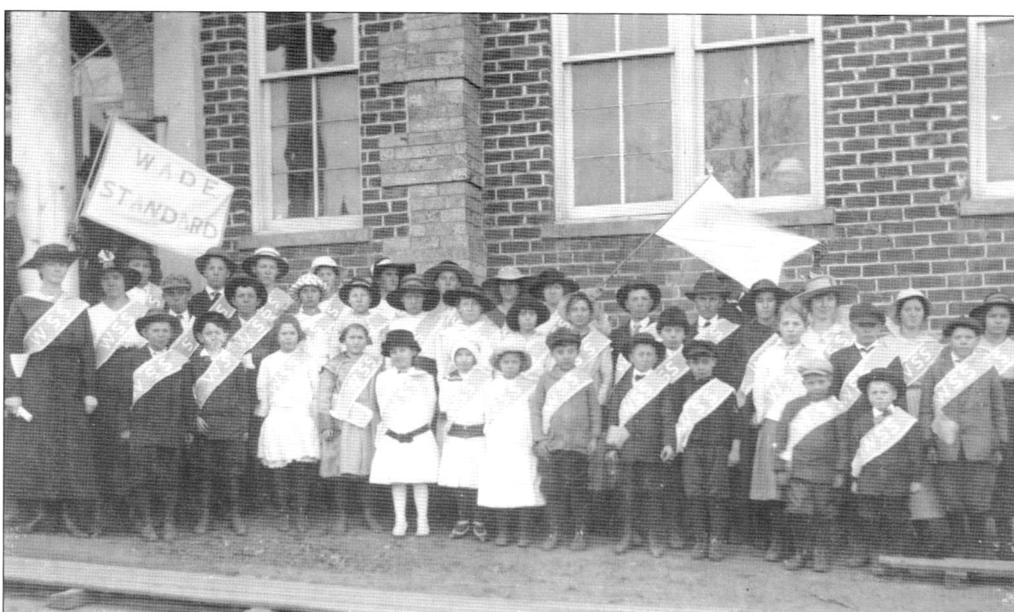

Annie (Williams) Smith (far left) was a teacher at the Wade School in Indian Valley. This class photograph was taken in the 1916–1917 school year during a visit to Floyd. (MAS)

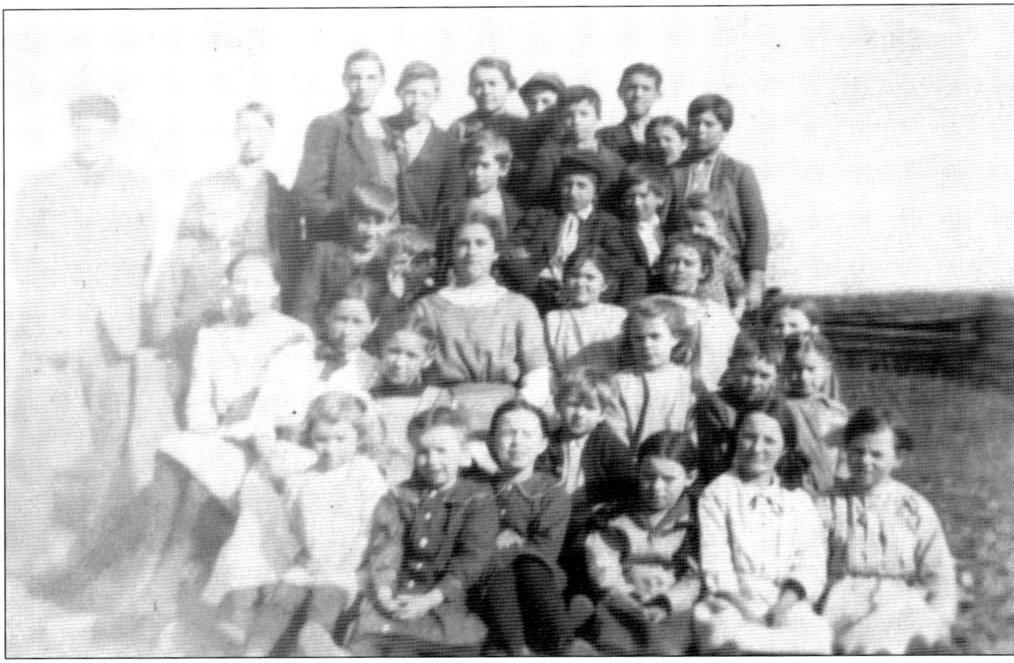

Mossy Dell School was near Pine Creek Church on Spangler's Mill Road. This is the class of 1922, which included children from the Hale, Smith, Sweeney, Bower, Boothe, Spangler, Hollins, Strickler, Lawrence, Aldrich, and Blackwell families.

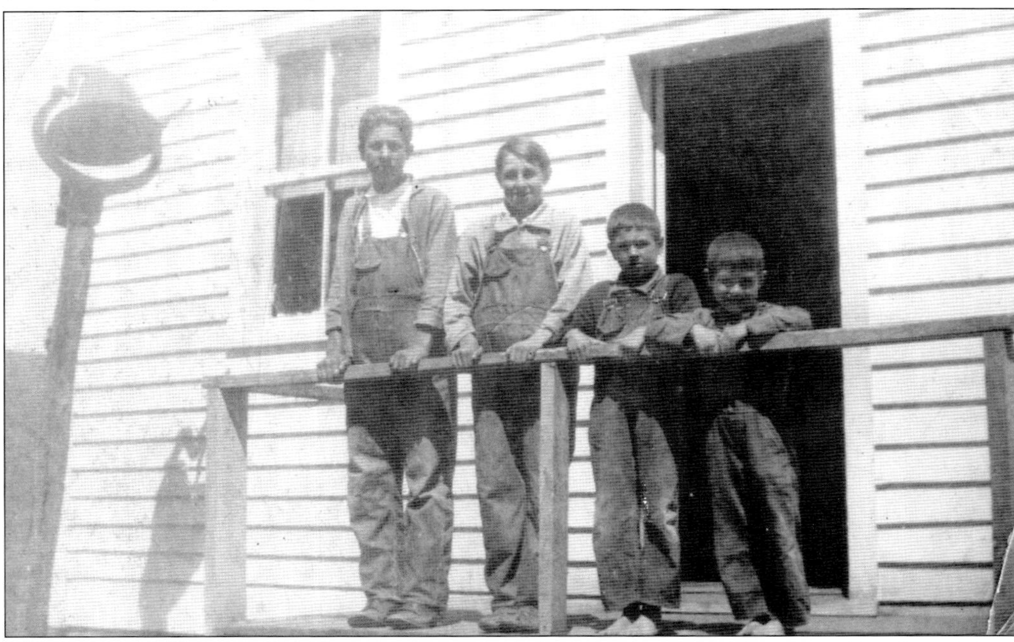

From left to right, Russell, Isaiah, Ernest, and Chester Quesenberry, the sons of Jonah and Cora Quesenberry, are seen here at Pine Grove School in Indian Valley. The school was later moved across the road and converted to a private home. It still stands on the Harold and Alta Turman farm on Indian Valley Road. (DDS)

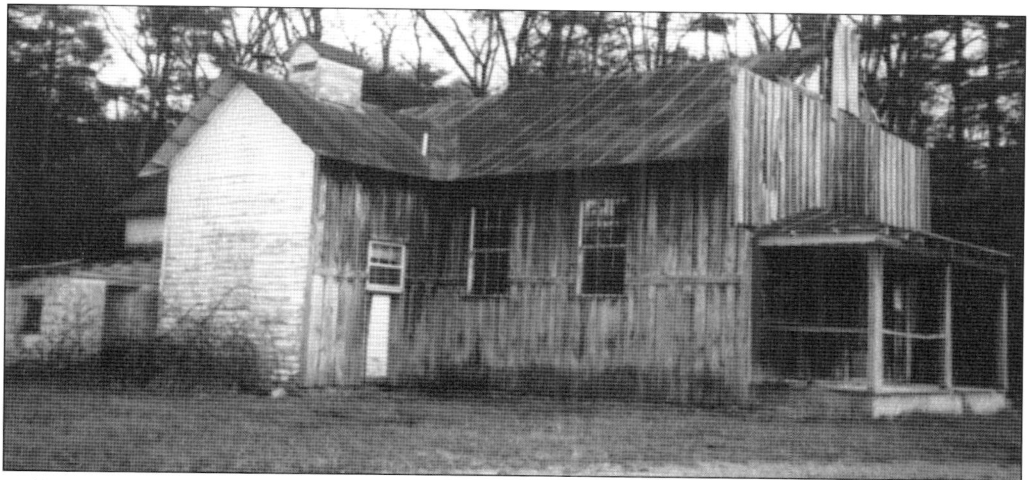

Kelley School, seen here in 1924, was located on Kelley School Road and closed in 1939. Moses Greer Kelley is believed to have been the first teacher. In 1915, the teacher was Annie Ellis. Other teachers through the years included Clara (Poff) Sink, Abagail King, Bill Hall, Daisy (Dewitt) Thomas, Annie (Kelley) Barnard, Irene (Peters) Poff, Lila (Vest) Thomas, and the three Kelley sisters, Gay, Emma, and Mamie. (AM)

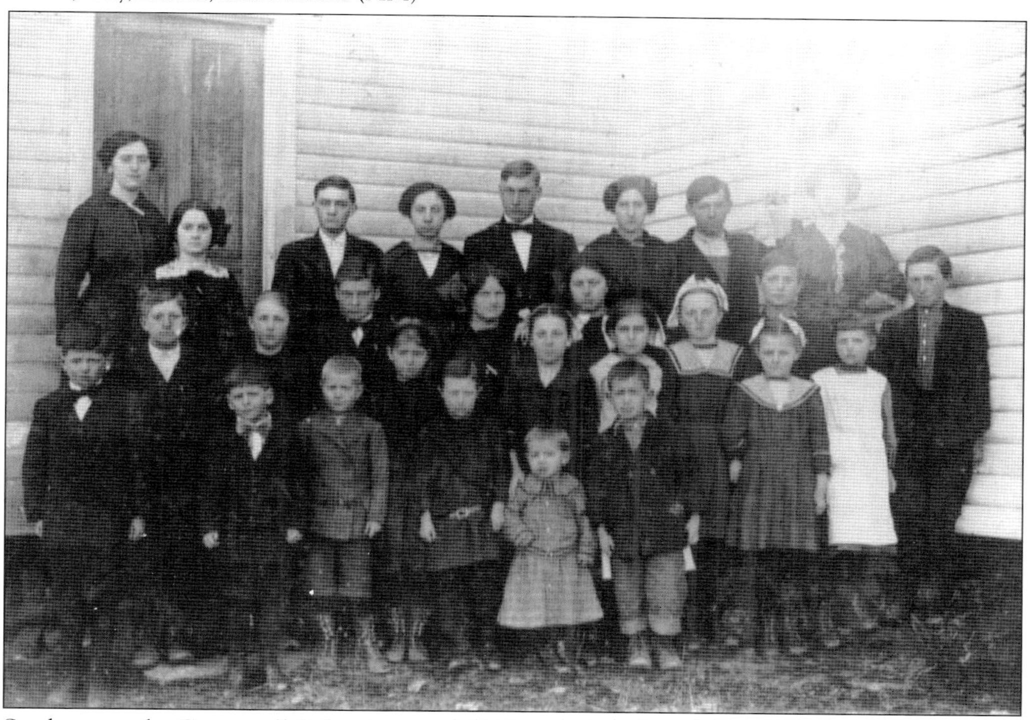

Students at the Stonewall School around 1915 included, from left to right, (first row) Elliott Whitlock, Edward "Boss" Whitlock, Clifford Hoback, three unidentified; and Carl Hoback; (second row) Wade Lawrence, unidentified, Frank Hoback, unidentified, Audrey Whitlock, Ether Hoback, Wilma Richard, Sally Hoback, Minnie Blackwell, Mary Blackwell, and three unidentified; (third row) teacher Kate (Williams) Whitlock, Effie Lawrence, Letcher Hoback, Lena Richard, Woodie Whitlock, Kate Hoback, unidentified, and Virgie Lawrence. (JGB.)

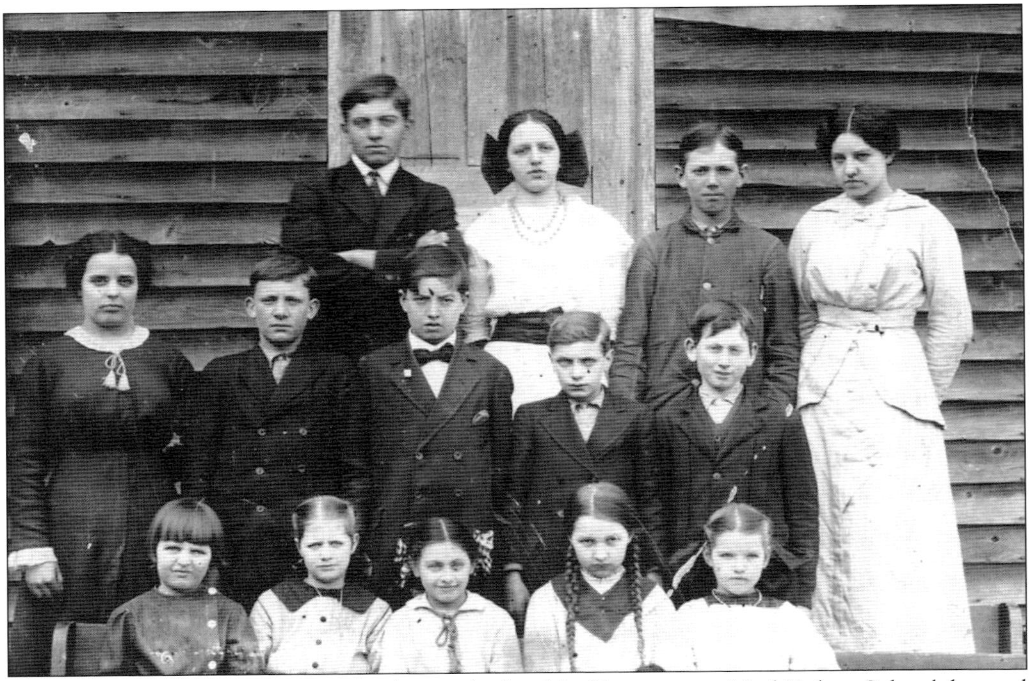

John Andrew Cannaday (1844–1933) gave the land for Howery—or Mud Hole—School, located in a potato patch on River Ridge Road, near Boothe Creek Road. Annie Kelley is the teacher and some of the children were from the Board, Cannaday, Fralin, Via, and Janney families. (GCS)

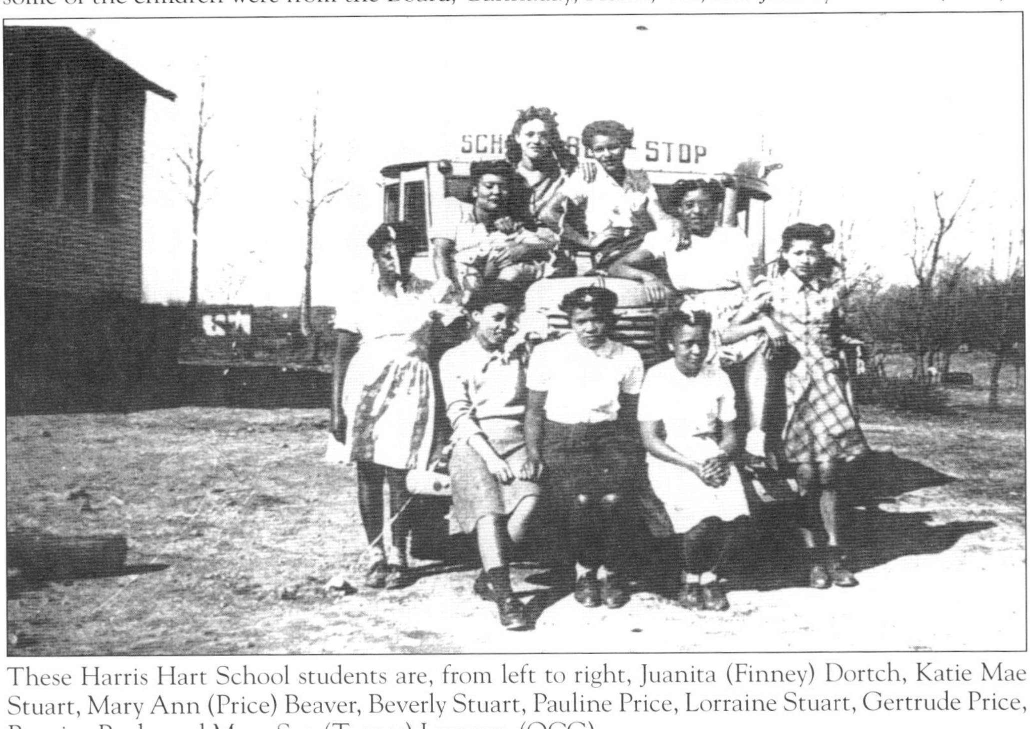

These Harris Hart School students are, from left to right, Juanita (Finney) Dortch, Katie Mae Stuart, Mary Ann (Price) Beaver, Beverly Stuart, Pauline Price, Lorraine Stuart, Gertrude Price, Bernice Pugh, and Mary Sue (Turner) Lemons. (OCG)

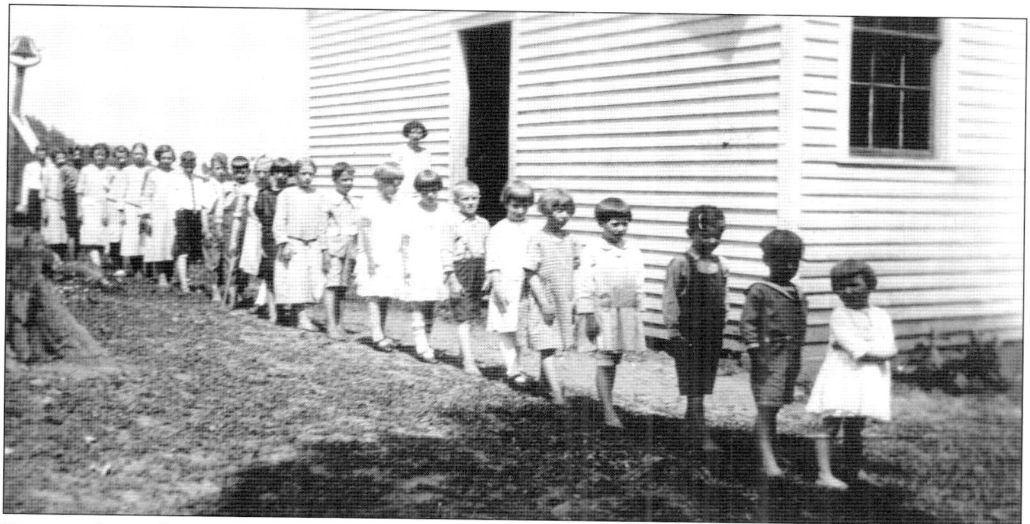

During the early years of schooling in Floyd County, one-room schools were common. In 1924–1925, Thompson School was taught by Velma Pratt, who is seen here with her classes. Lena Cannaday was a later teacher until about 1939, when the school closed and the students were taken to Willis to a school with separate rooms for each grade. It is now a private home. (GCS)

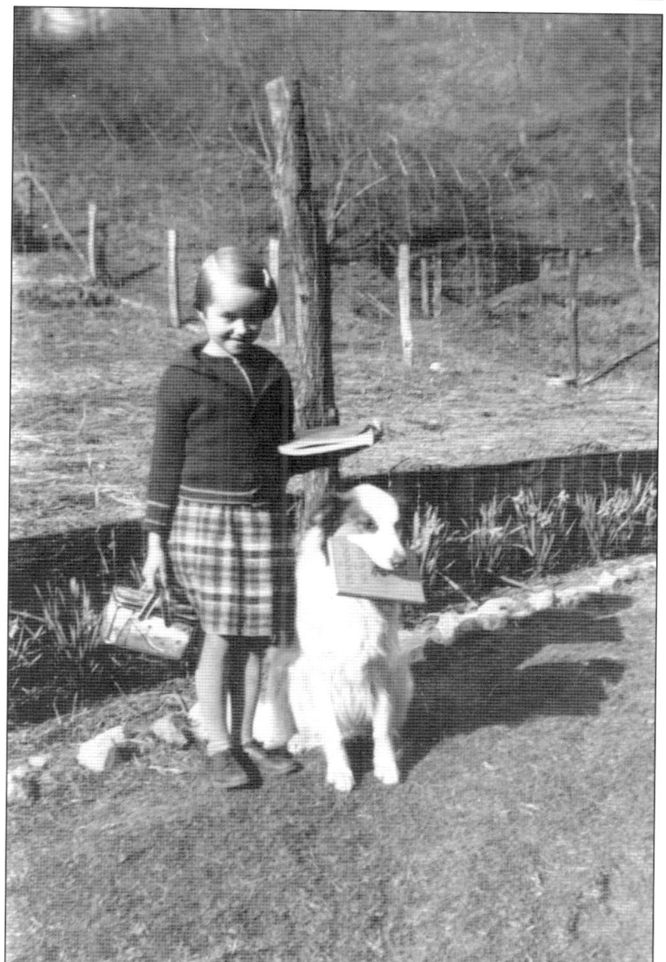

Genevieve Cochran is ready to go to the Thompson School as her dog waits patiently beside her. (GCS)

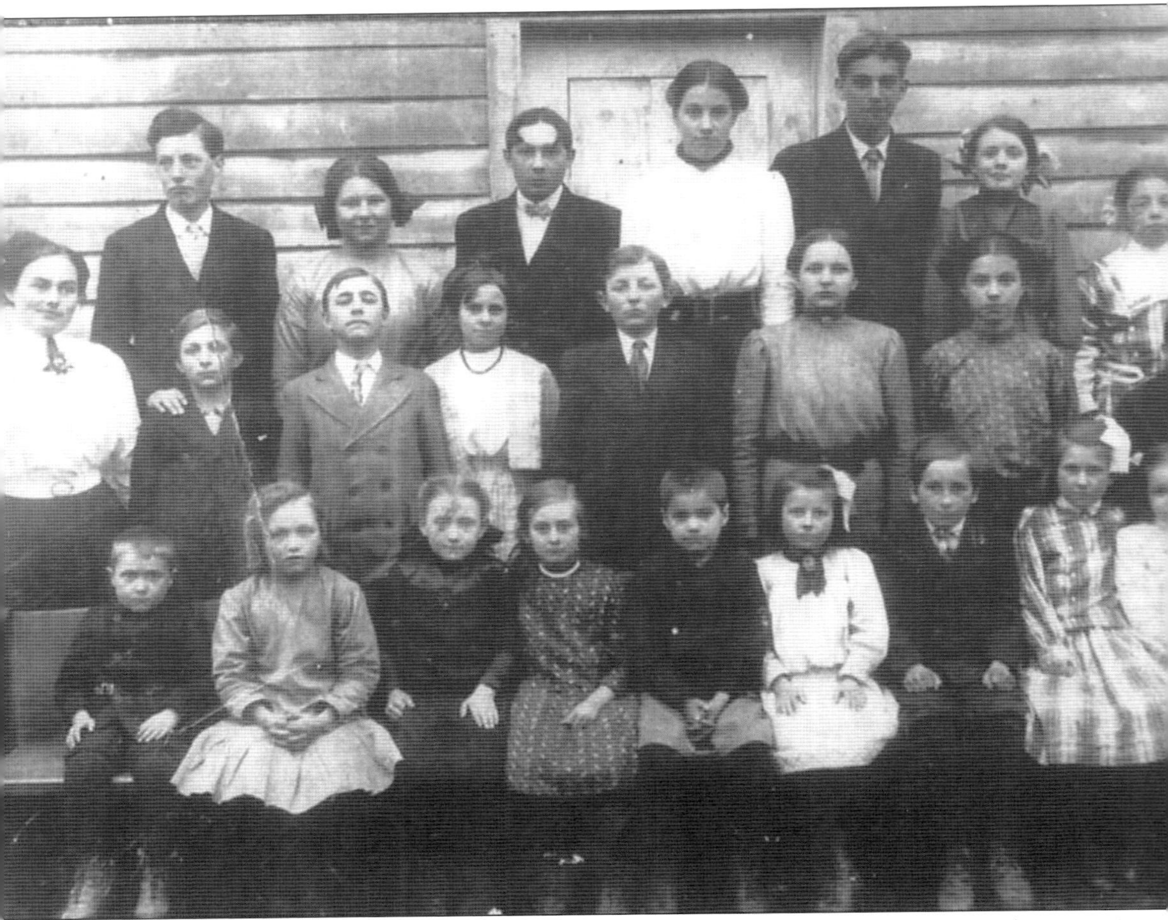

The Union School is still standing on Union School Road near the intersection with Conner's Grove Road. Seen here in 1914 are, from left to right, (first row) Otho Hylton, unidentified, Murlia Hylton, unidentified, Alvin Hylton, unidentified, Eli Hylton, unidentified, and Stella Pratt; (second row) teacher Pearl (Sutphin) Slusher, Tennyson Pratt, Harman Webb, unidentified, Frank Alderman, Velma Pratt, ? Hylton, and unidentified; (third row) Pierce Dickerson, unidentified, Ray Keith, ? Hylton, ? Hylton, and two unidentified. (APS)

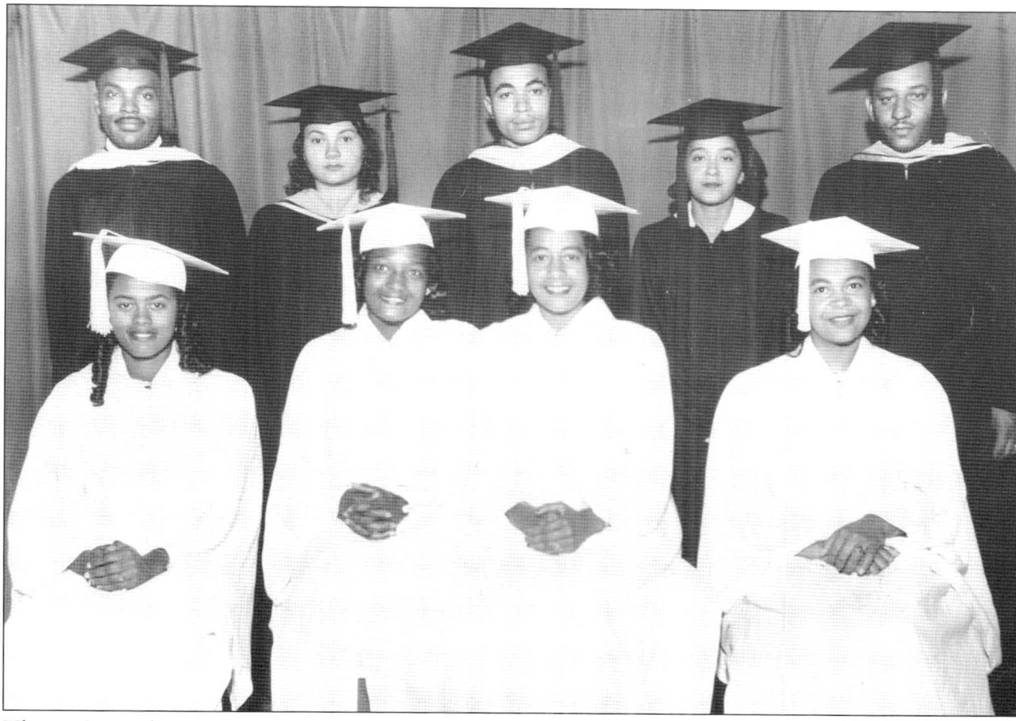

The 1950 graduating class of Harris Hart School are in the first row, from left to right, Jacqueline (Stuart) Majors, Alisha Floyd, Polly Ingram, and Catherine (Vaughn) Hubbard. Behind them are faculty members, from left to right, Mr. Brown, Mildred Milton, Charles Campbell, Grace (Claytor) Beale, and Walker Campbell. (WB)

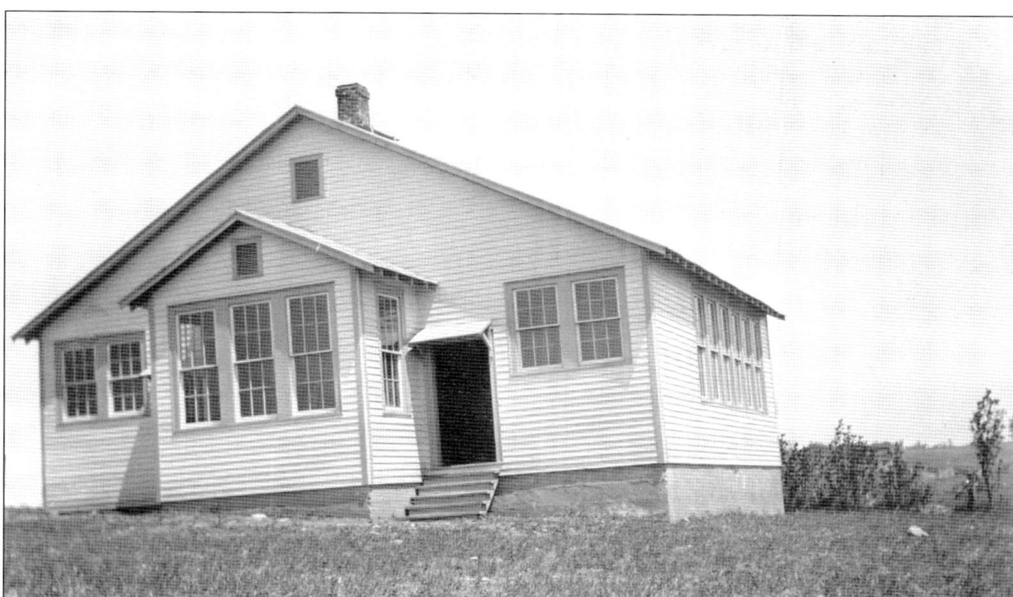

This photograph shows the original school building at Harris Hart School. (FU)

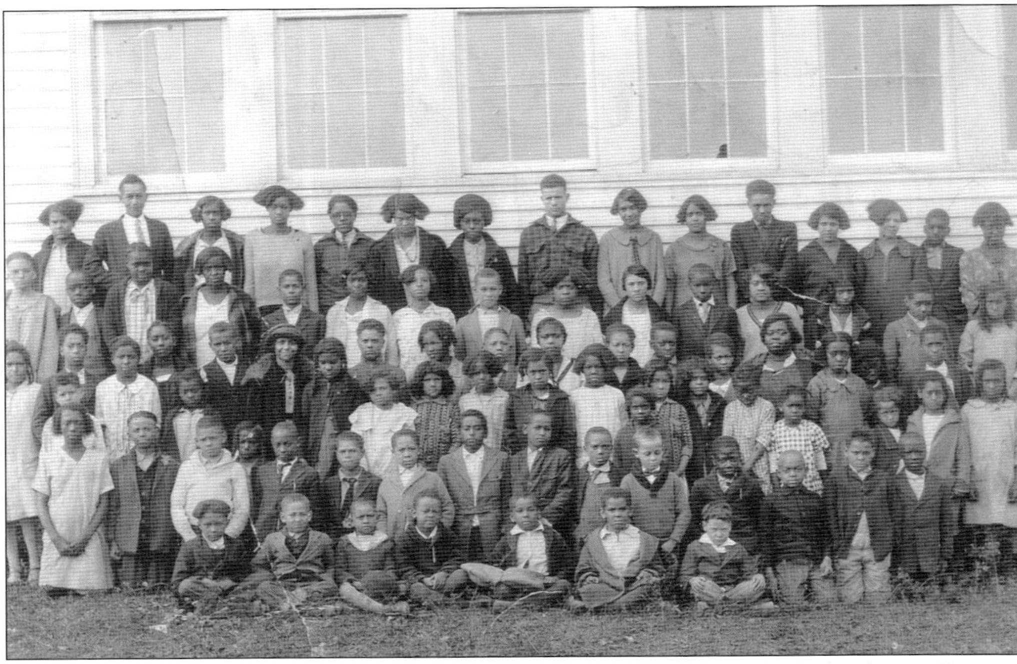

Students pose at Harris Hart School on Newtown Road in the 1922–1923 school year. Some of the students were from the Helm, Claytor, Parker, Beaver, Huff, and Stuart families. Virginia Hayden and a Ms. Stafford taught here. (WB)

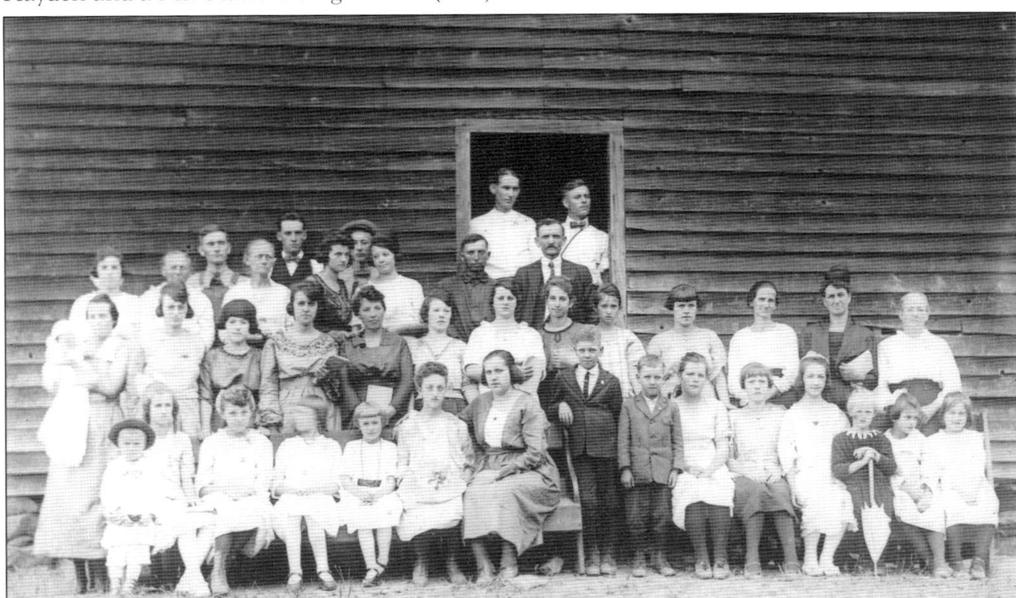

Singing schools were popular and were often held in churches, although this one was held at Greasy Creek School in 1921. A singing master would teach the attendees singing, especially shape-note singing, enabling students to learn to sight-read music. The singing master, Mr. Vass, is centered in the doorway. Burnett Marshall, seventh from the right in the first row, was 97 years old in 2012. (BM)

Four

Business, Industry, and Machines

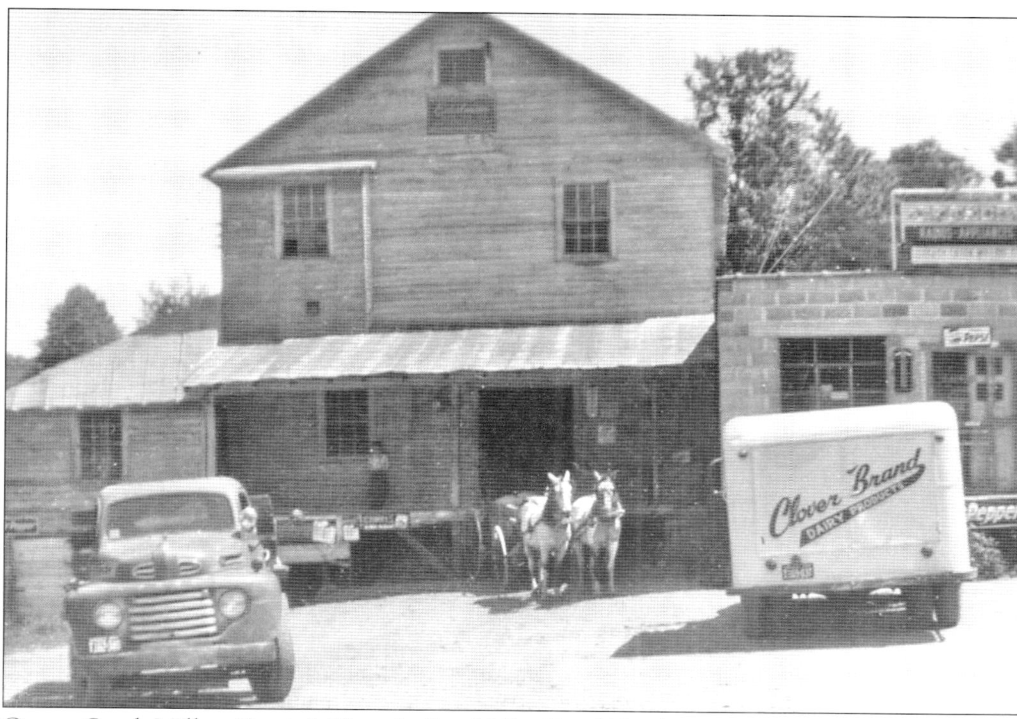

Greasy Creek Mill or Harris Mill on Indian Valley Road Northwest was the last roller mill built in Floyd County. When this photograph was taken in the mid-1950s, roughly 10 years before the mill closed, workhorse teams like Strawberry and Lady were being replaced on and off the farm by tractors and trucks. The store on the right carried general store items as well as televisions and home appliances. (RC)

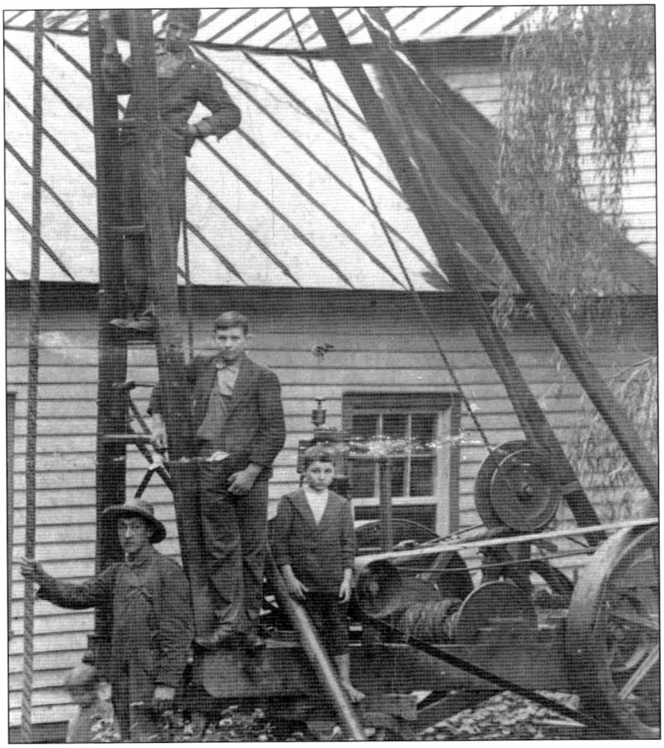

West Virginia native O.B. Pauley, with his hand on the rope, operated one of the first steam-driven well-drilling outfits in the county. The motion of a crankshaft acting on the rope alternately raised and dropped the heavy drill head. The force of the blow and downward progress were gauged by lightly grasping the heavy rope cable. Three generations of Pauleys drilled thousands of water wells in and around Floyd County. (CP)

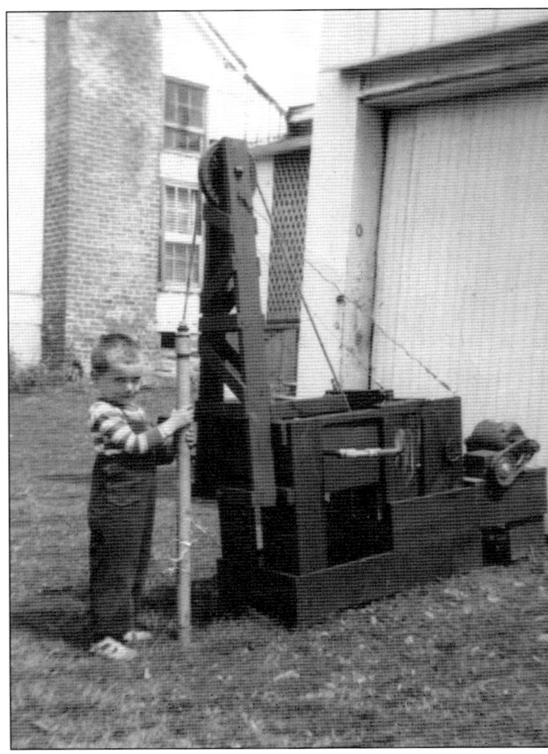

Third-generation well driller Kenneth Pauley began his career drilling holes in the family yard with a functional toy well-driller built by his father, Bud Pauley. In place of the steam engine that powered his grandfather's driller, a salvaged electric motor supplied the power to lift and drop the drill. (CP)

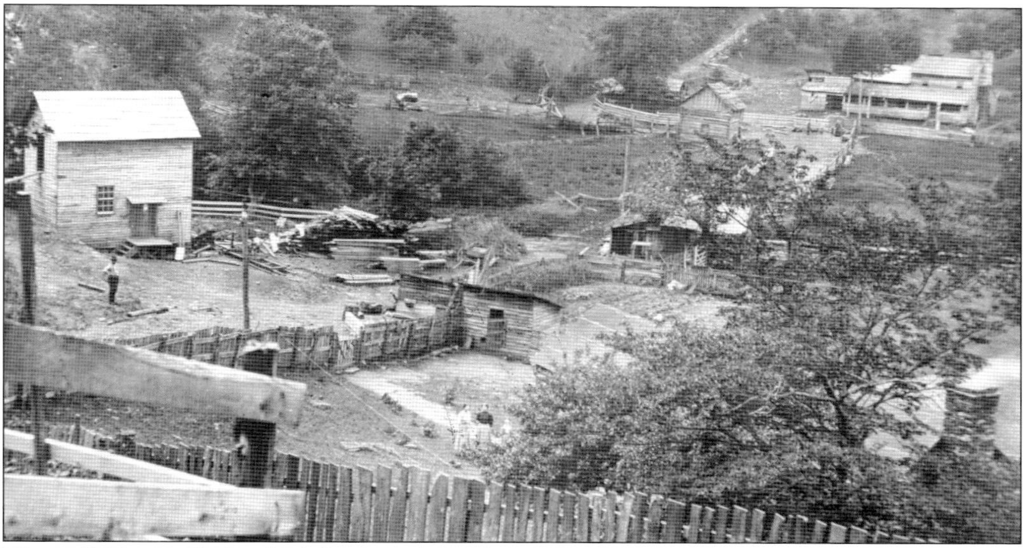

The mill Henry Slusher built here in the mid-1800s was replaced in 1907 by the Buffalo Roller Mill, which burned around 1910, making room for the Andy Alderman mill seen here. The water-powered sawmill below the nearly new gristmill was typical of the time. The earthen race that served all three mills remains on the east side of Burks Fork Creek north of Union School Road. (RC)

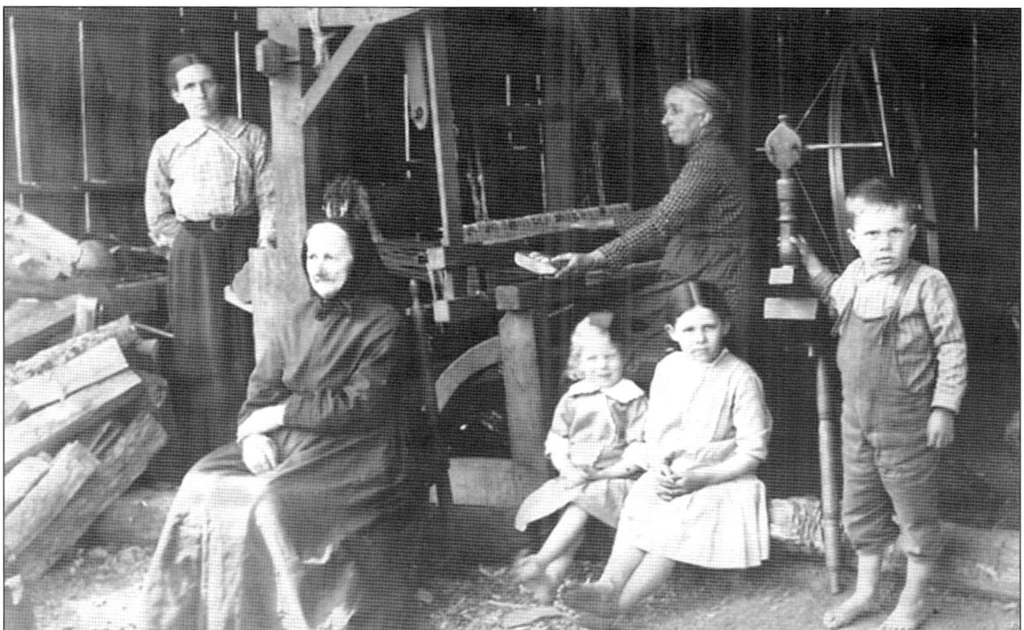

The clothing of the Hodge family, seen here, was probably a mixture of store-bought printed cotton and home-made wool, which was sheared, washed, carded, spun into thread using the hand-turned great wheel at right, dyed, and then woven into cloth or patterned coverlets on the loom in the center. Weavers continued to make rag rugs and carpet strips after home production of textiles disappeared around 1900. (OCG)

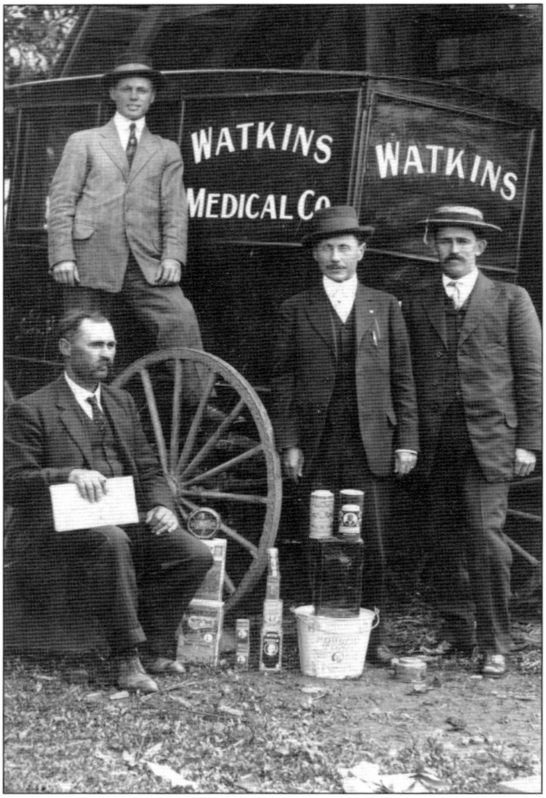

Visits from door-to-door salesmen representing companies like Watkins and J.R. Rawleigh supplied isolated farm families with patent medicines, spices, extracts, and flavorings as well as news and a welcome break from daily routines. Independent peddlers from as far away as New York sold everything from sewing supplies to eyeglasses. (JH)

Home to various retail businesses for more than a century, the Farmer's Store of Floyd County on South Locust Street, seen here around 1920, is now the Floyd Country Store, host of the Friday Night Jamboree.

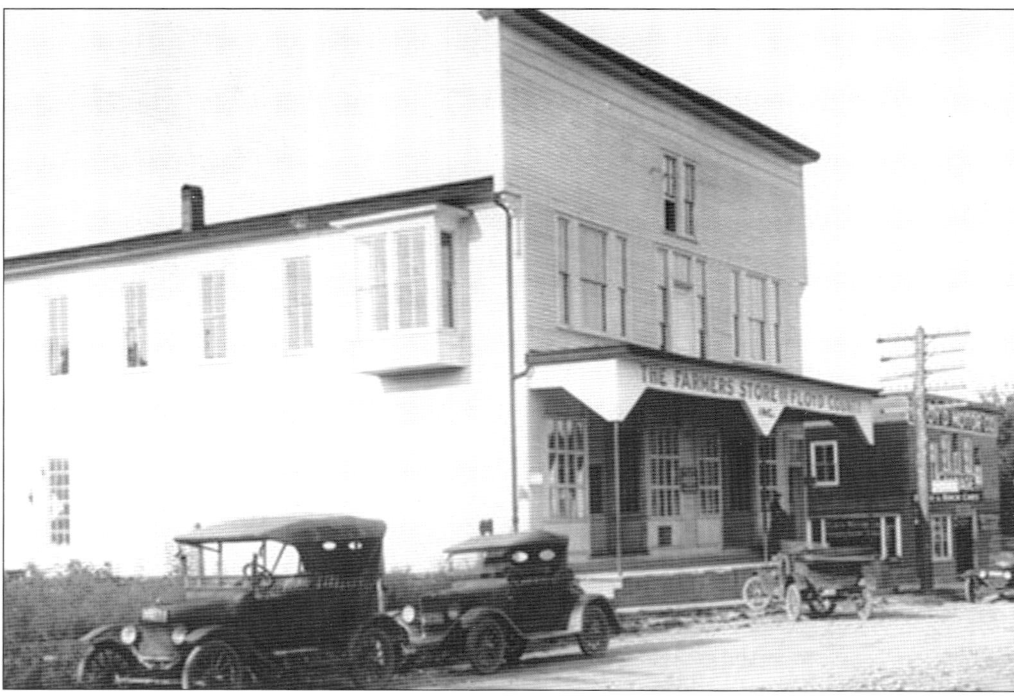

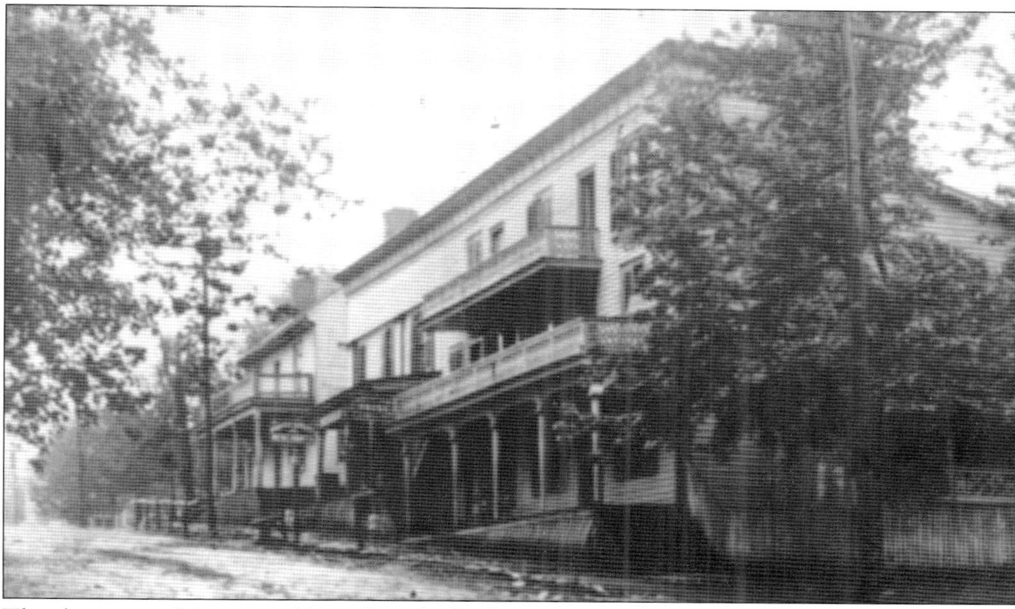

The three-story Mountain House Hotel, also known as Jett's Hotel, was one of several 1900-era lodging places available to traveling salesmen and visitors. Residents from outlying parts of the county, in town to conduct business or attend to legal matters, might also spend the night in one of Floyd's hotels. The Bank of Floyd occupies this site today.

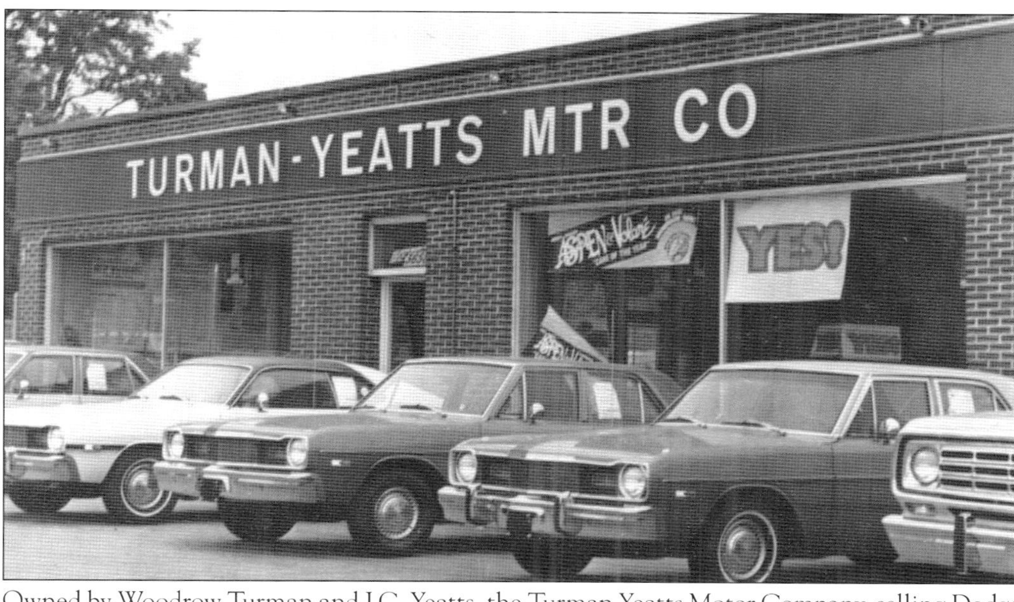

Owned by Woodrow Turman and J.C. Yeatts, the Turman-Yeatts Motor Company, selling Dodge and Plymouth cars and trucks, was one of three new-car dealerships in Floyd in the 1950s. Ironically, the four vehicles nearest the camera in this view include two Fords and a Chevrolet. New Dodge and Chrysler automobiles are still sold at this location on Route 8 just south of town.

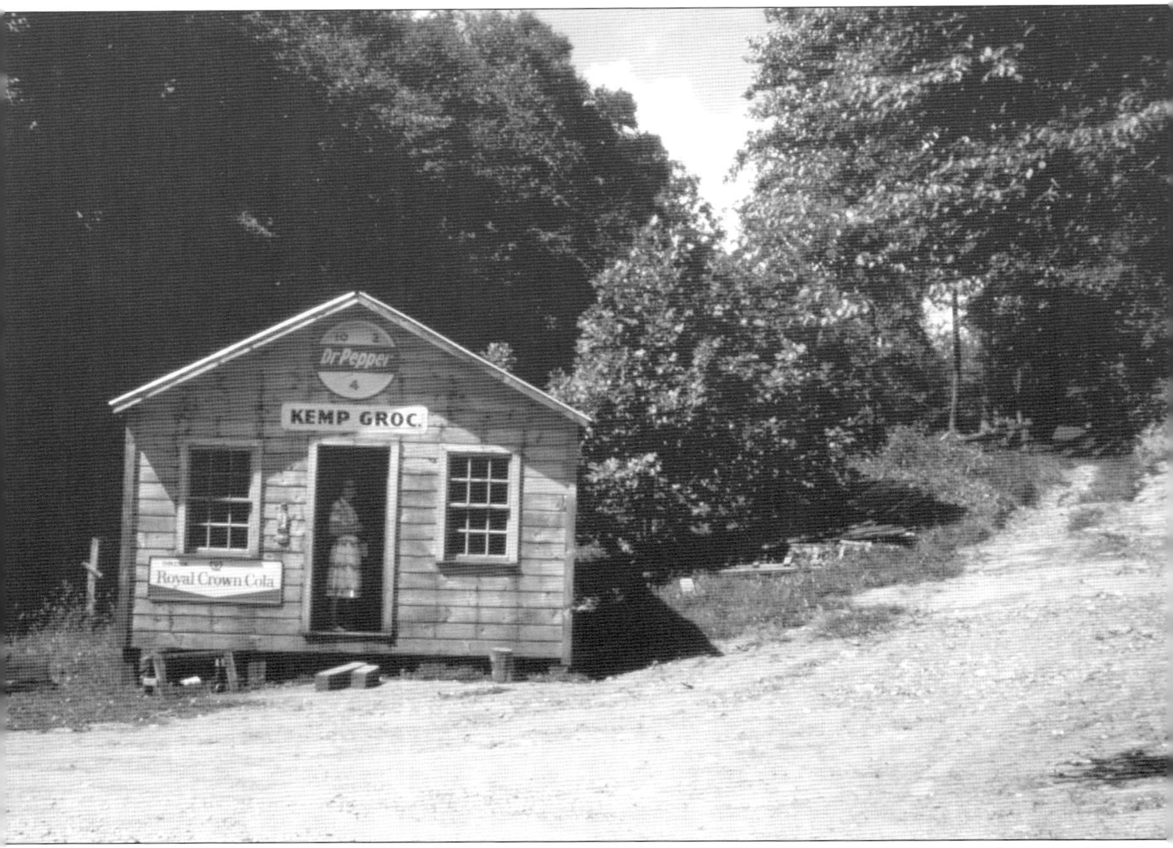

Thirsty patrons of stores like the Kemp Grocery near Buffalo Mountain were undeterred by the fact that the Dr. Pepper, Royal Crown Cola, and other brands of soda were not refrigerated until rural parts of the county got electric power in the late 1940s. Local stores were also social centers for residents in outlying sections of the county. The shaded figure in the doorway is Marguerite Tise.

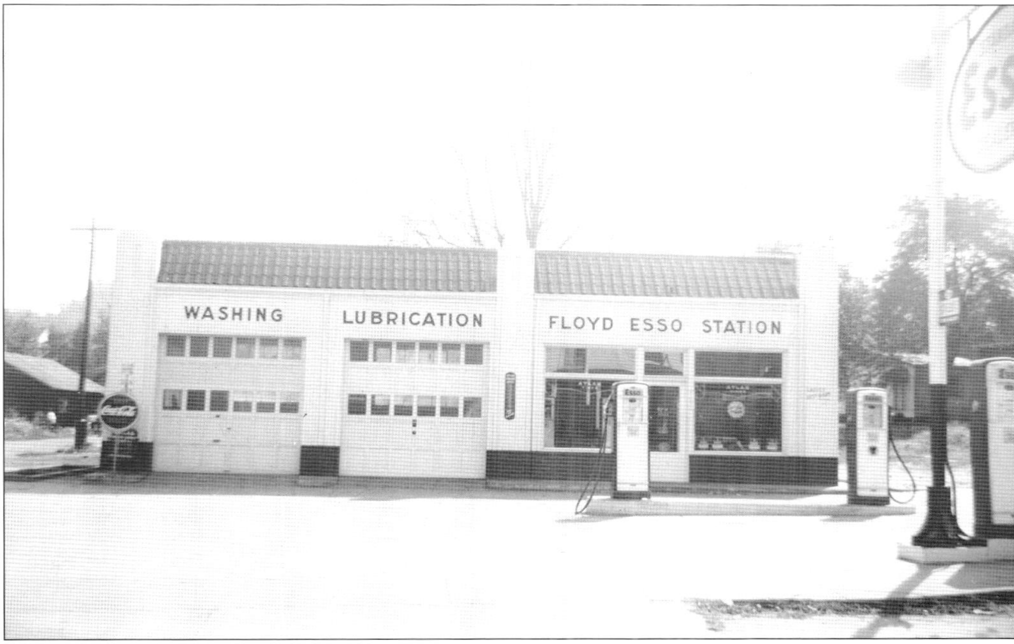

The Esso station on East Main Street was a typical full-service filling station. The distinctive tiled roof sections have been lowered and the doors and windows have been reconfigured, but the columns and double-bay garage are the same. The building now houses the antique store Finders Keepers.

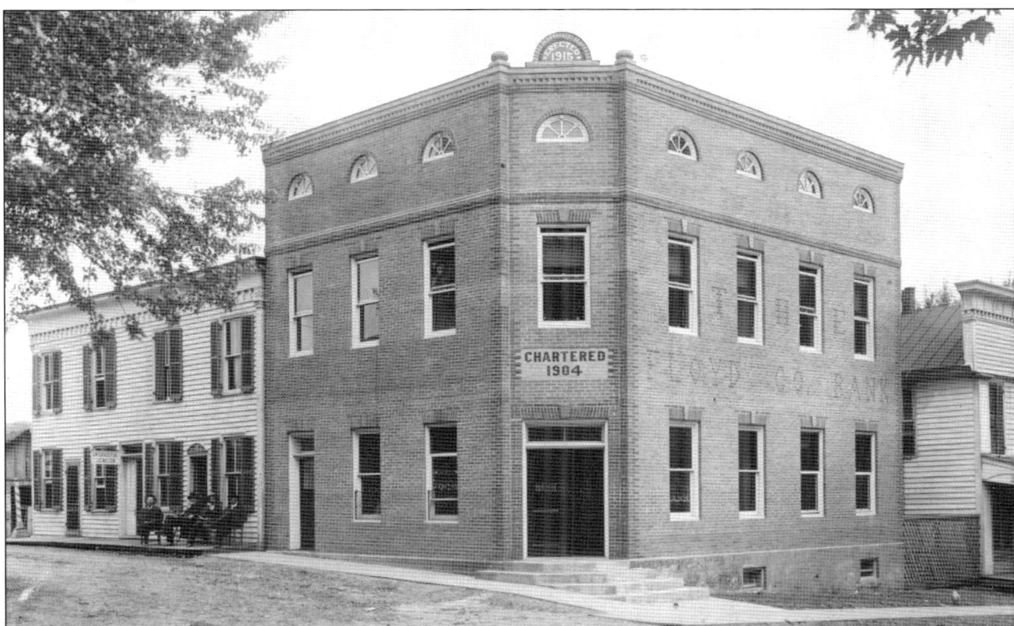

The Floyd County Bank building was later the Floyd Clothing Store. The striking brick building, with fan light windows illuminating the top floor, stood on the corner of what is now Main Street and Jacksonville Circle. (GW)

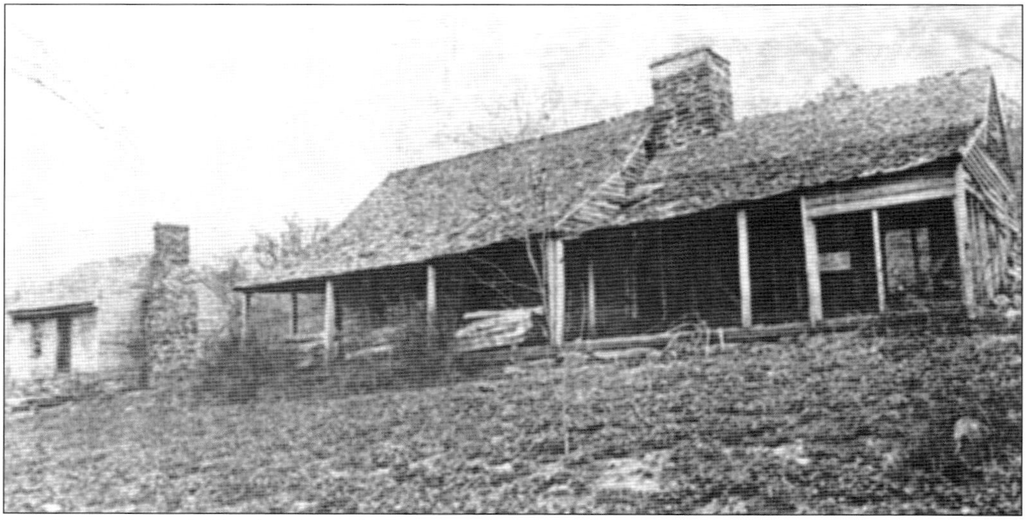

The law office of Charles Carter Lee, a brother of Robert E. Lee, was at Spring Camp in the southwest corner of the county on part of a 25,000-acre tract granted to their father, Henry "Light-Horse Harry" Lee III for his Revolutionary War service. Much of the land, which included parts of Floyd, Carroll, and Patrick Counties and Buffalo Mountain, was later owned by the Burwells, relatives of the Lees. (RFS)

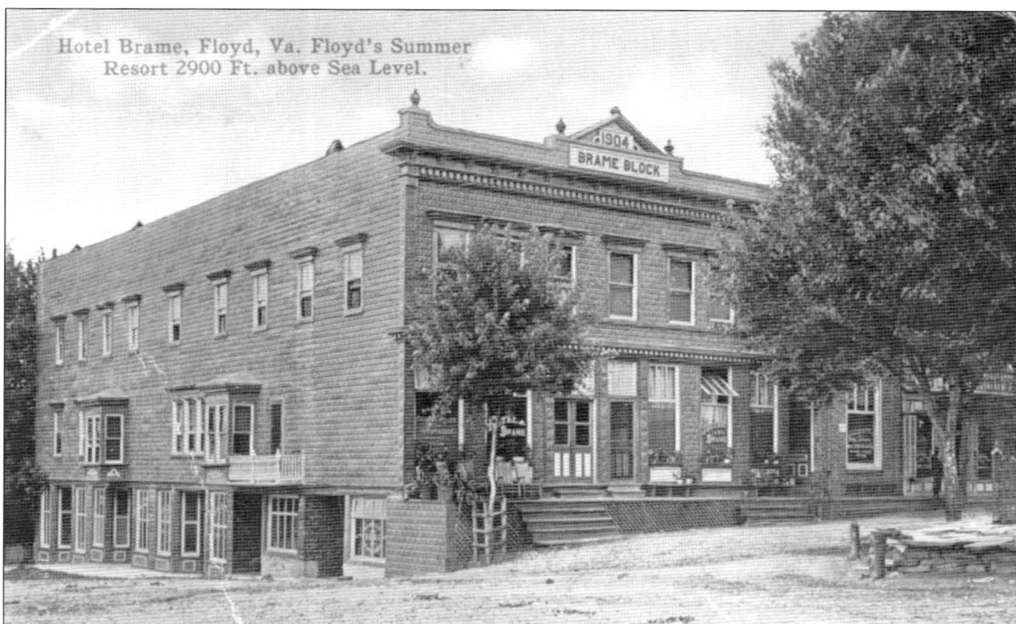

This 1910s postcard promotes the Hotel Brame as a summer resort. The wood-framed, metal-clad building housed at various times the town telephone switchboard, a butcher shop, business offices, People's Bank, Purcell's furniture store, and the original Slaughters' Supermarket. Built on the northwest corner of Main and Locust Streets in 1904, it was demolished in 1965 to make room for a smaller commercial building.

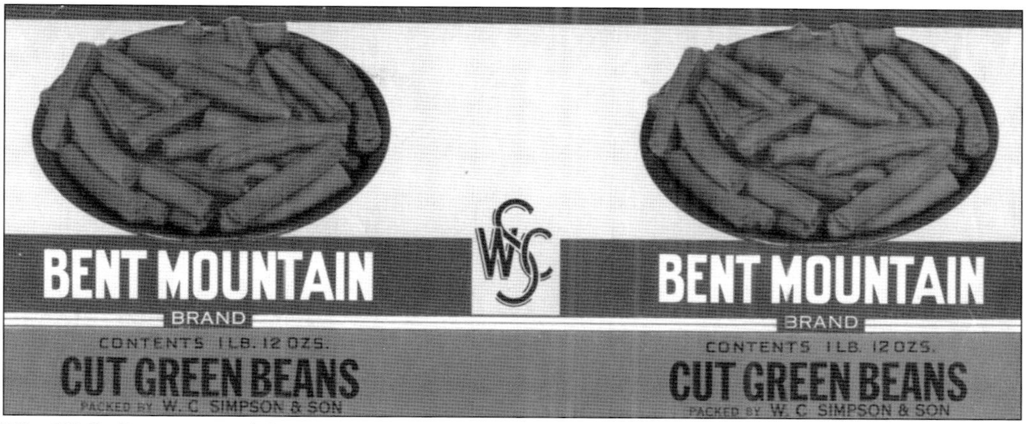

The W.C. Simpson and Son Cannery in Check was one of at least three commercial canneries buying local produce and providing seasonal work for men and women. Regional wholesalers also contracted with individuals to grow beans and tomatoes and can them in converted or purpose-built farm buildings. Wholesalers supplied seeds, metal cans, packing cases, and paper labels. Individual producers could be identified by a personal number stamped on each can.

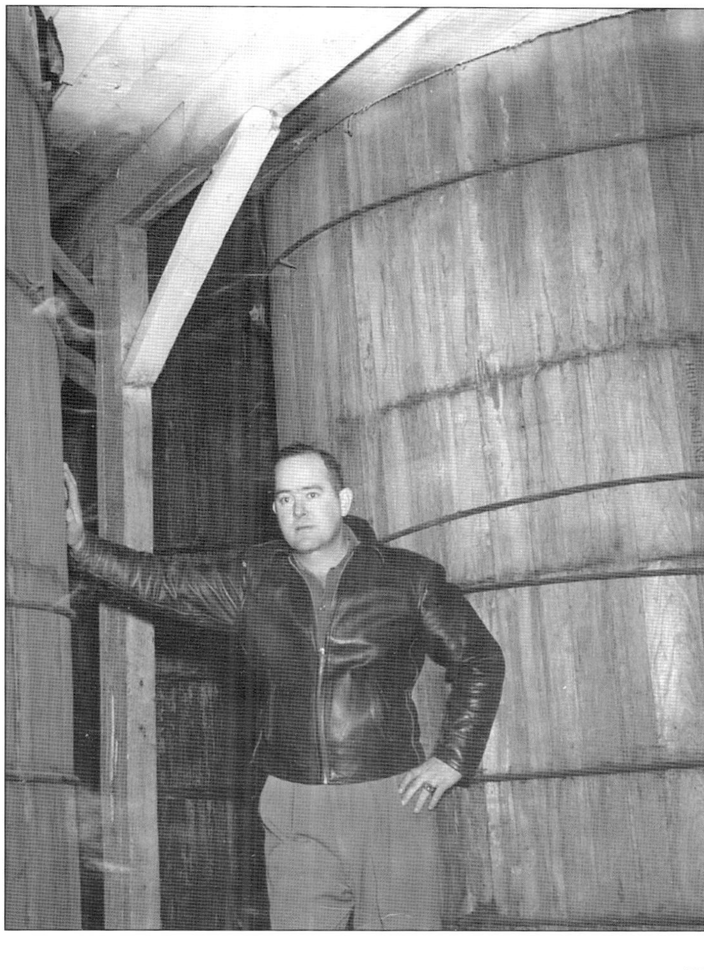

Basil Poff Simpson Sr. stands amid cypress tanks at the family canning factory in 1951. Born in 1918 in Check to Willard and Garnett Simpson, he graduated from Roanoke College and served in World War II. Simpson was elected at age 29 to represent Floyd and Carroll Counties in the House of Delegates. An educator and businessman, he worked to consolidate the high schools and integrate public education. (BPS)

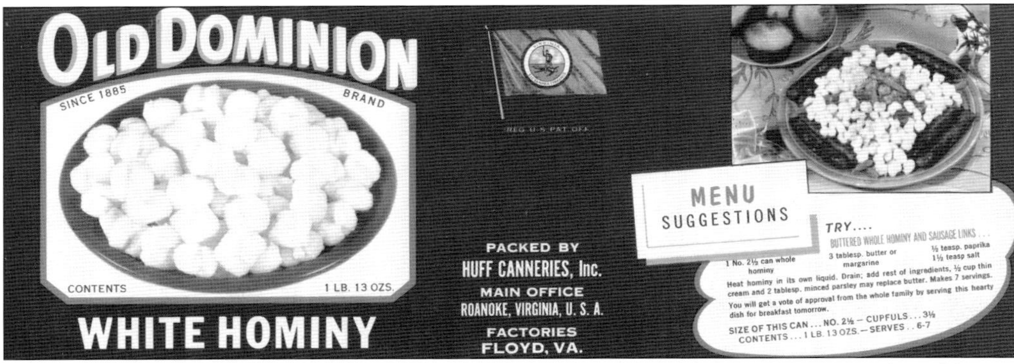

The Huff Cannery processed, canned, and shipped green beans, pinto beans, pork and beans, tomatoes, and sauerkraut under various trade names. Its rambling wooden structure still straddles Howell Creek at a spot once identified on maps as Shelor's Mill, at the intersection of Canning Factory Road and Route 221. (WS)

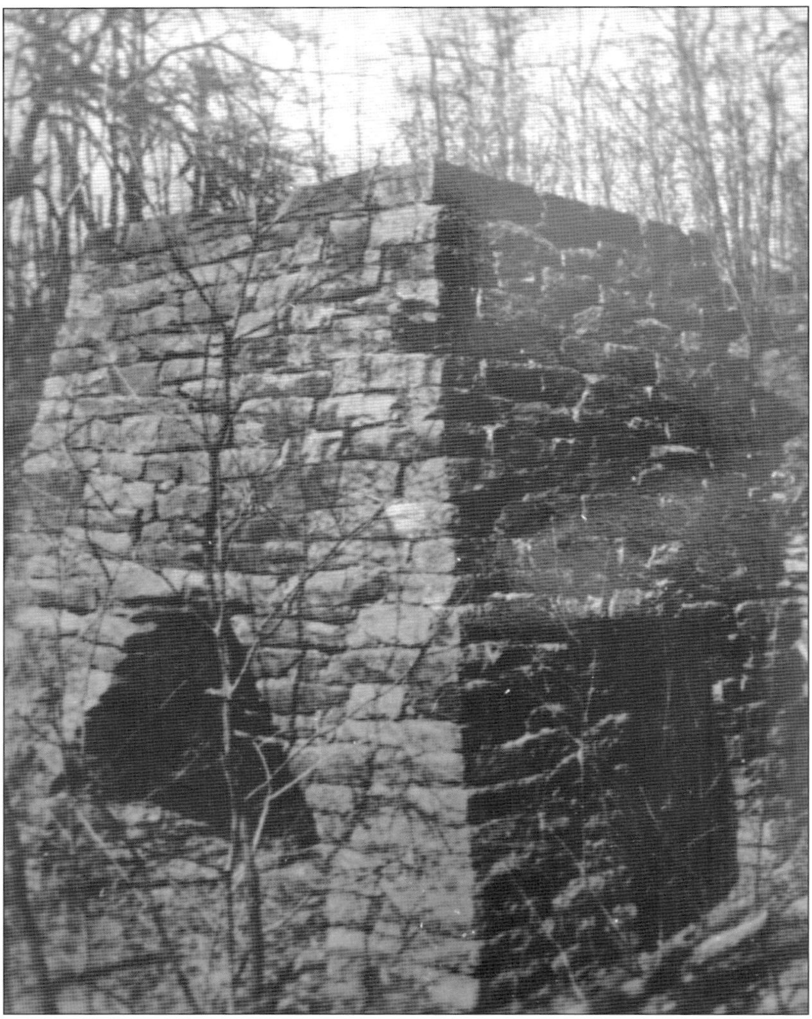

The last of at least two furnace stacks used in the long but sporadic history of iron and copper smelting still stands at Shelor Park on Old Furnace Road. Early owners included Revolutionary War veteran Capt. Daniel Shelor and Robert Toncray. Traces of copper in the iron ore yielded crack-resistant cast-iron cookware. Waterwheels drove bellows for the furnace and, at one point, a gristmill and sawmill. (NSA)

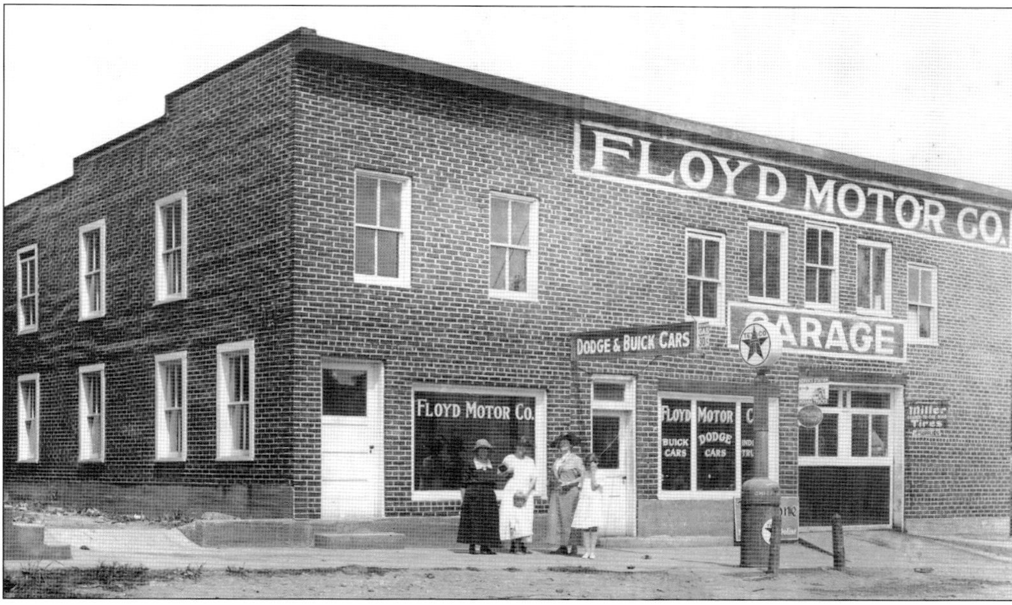

Walter Robertson owned a Dodge and Buick dealership and garage, seen here prior to a 1923 fire. From left to right, Mrs. Pettigrew, Mrs. Dobbins, Mrs. Slusher, and an unidentified girl stand out front. The Floyd Motor Company also retailed Texaco gasoline and lubricants. Tom Rakes bought the business and ran a Chevrolet dealership here for many years. A fast food restaurant stands at this East Main Street location today.

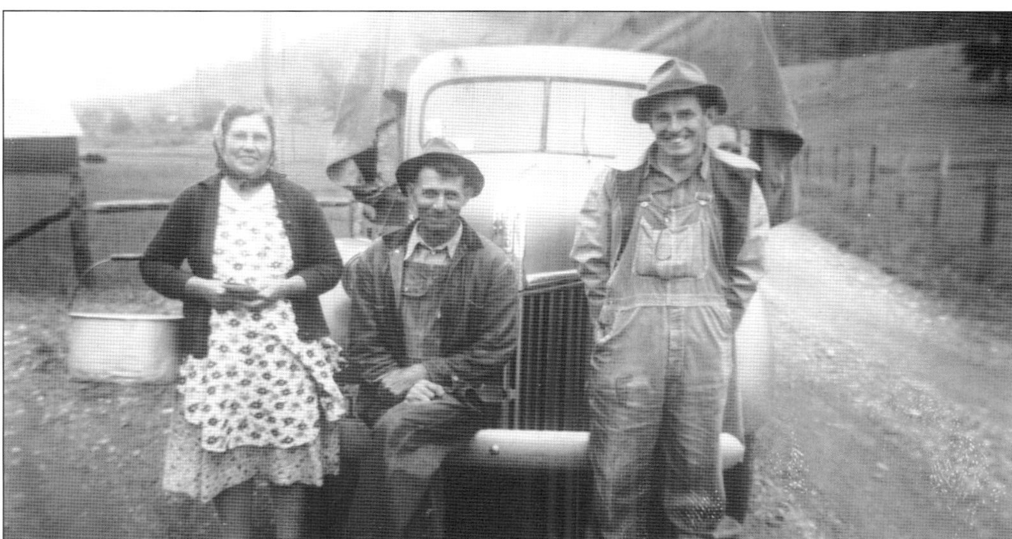

Hucksters like Claude Conner (right) covered regular routes buying eggs, butter, chickens, and other farm produce for resale in nearby trade centers and selling staple groceries, chicken feed, and items special-ordered from town. Many farmers were still without automobiles or decent roads despite increasing farm prices in the early 1940s. Romney and Ada (Harmon) Slusher enjoy this visit as well as the opportunity to trade. (APS)

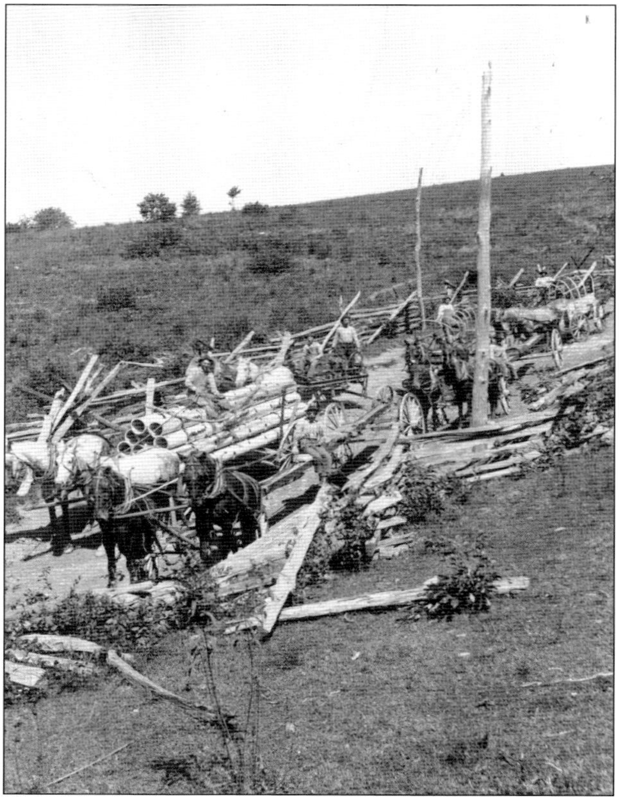

The presence of a horse-drawn grader close behind suggests that this load of pipes will replace wooden culverts or open "water lets" on this unpaved county road. Adequate drainage and roadbeds of packed stone were essential to making what had literally been dirt roads passable in wet seasons. (JH)

This crew crushes stone for graveling county roads around 1926 on what was then the county's Poor Farm on what is now Poor Farm Road Northeast. Henry Hatcher, seen here working with his sons, Donald, Roger, Herman, Harlow, Henry, and Hubert, rented the farm and his wife helped care for residents. Also in this image are Hatcher's nephew, Timond Hatcher, and his neighbors General Boyd and Moyer Wright. The truck is a 1924 or 1925 International. (RC)

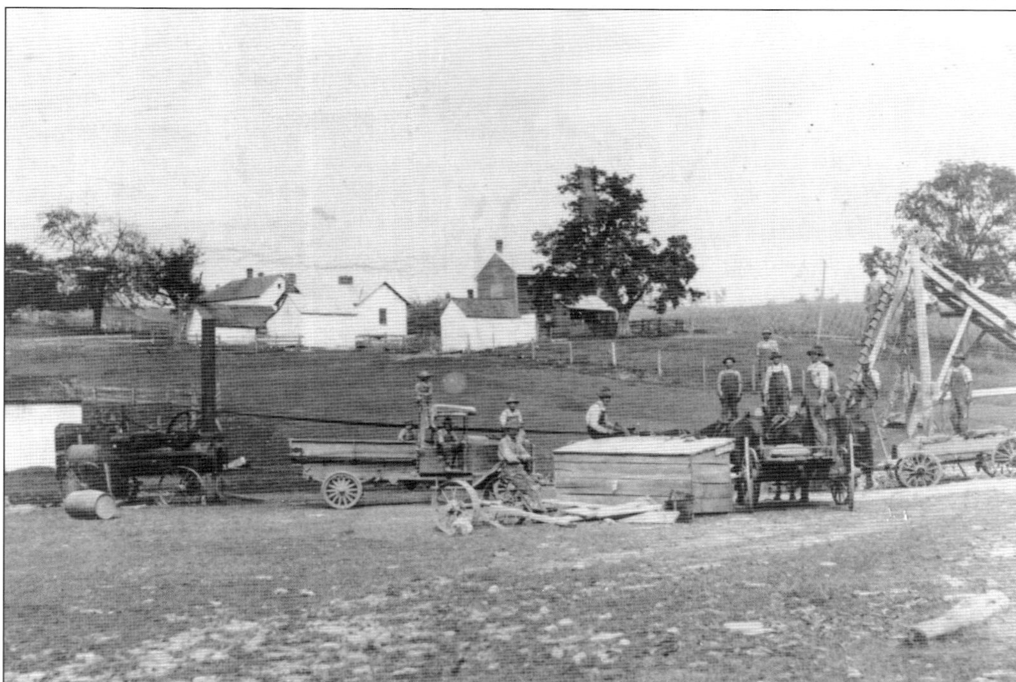

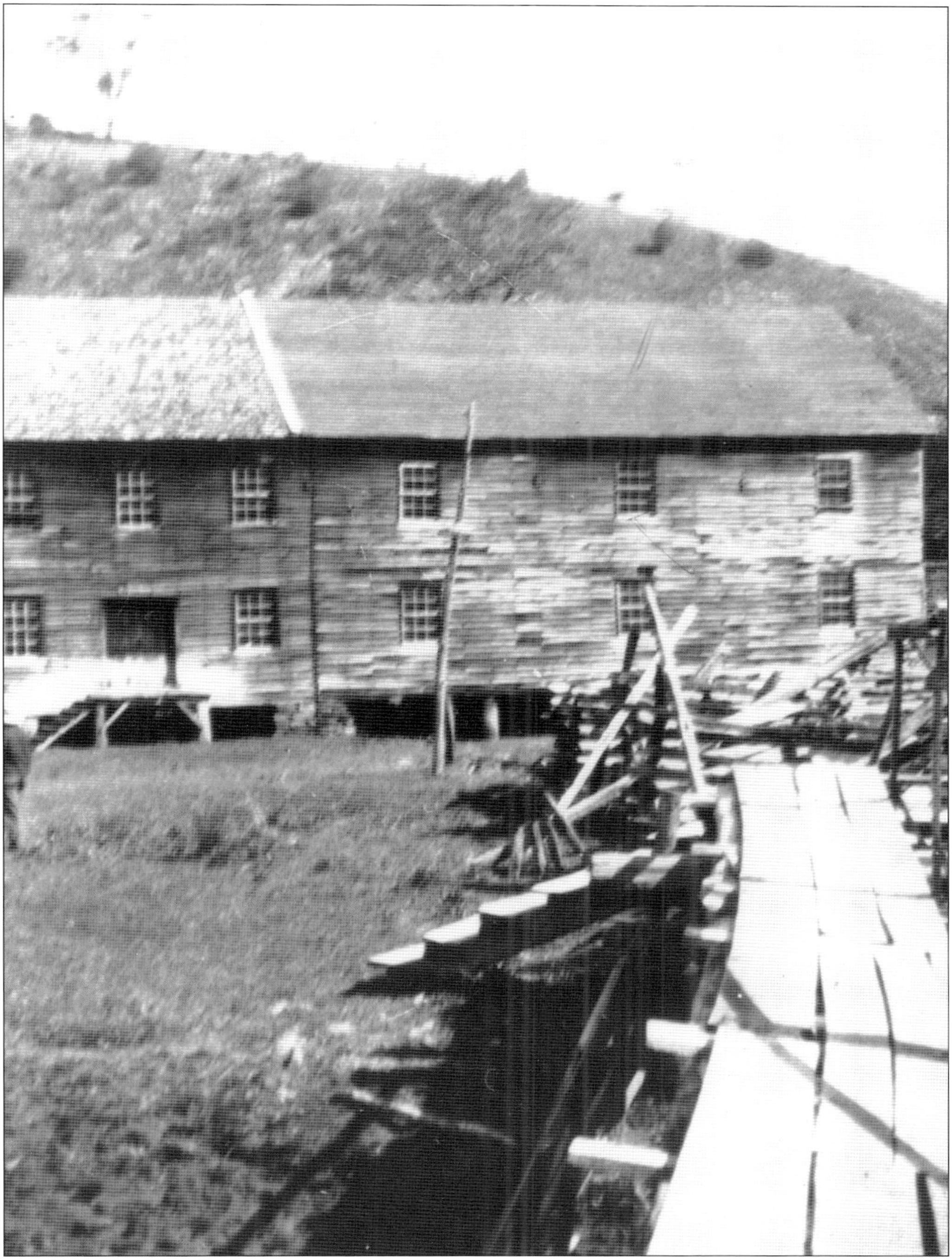

The Vaughn-Dunn Woolen Mill on Burks Fork Creek employed as many as 10 women and girls to wash, pick, card, spin, dye, and weave wool. In exchange for a portion of raw wool delivered to the mill, customers could have the remainder prepared for spinning and weaving at home. They could also exchange for or purchase finished fabric, blankets, and coverlets in a variety of colors and patterns.

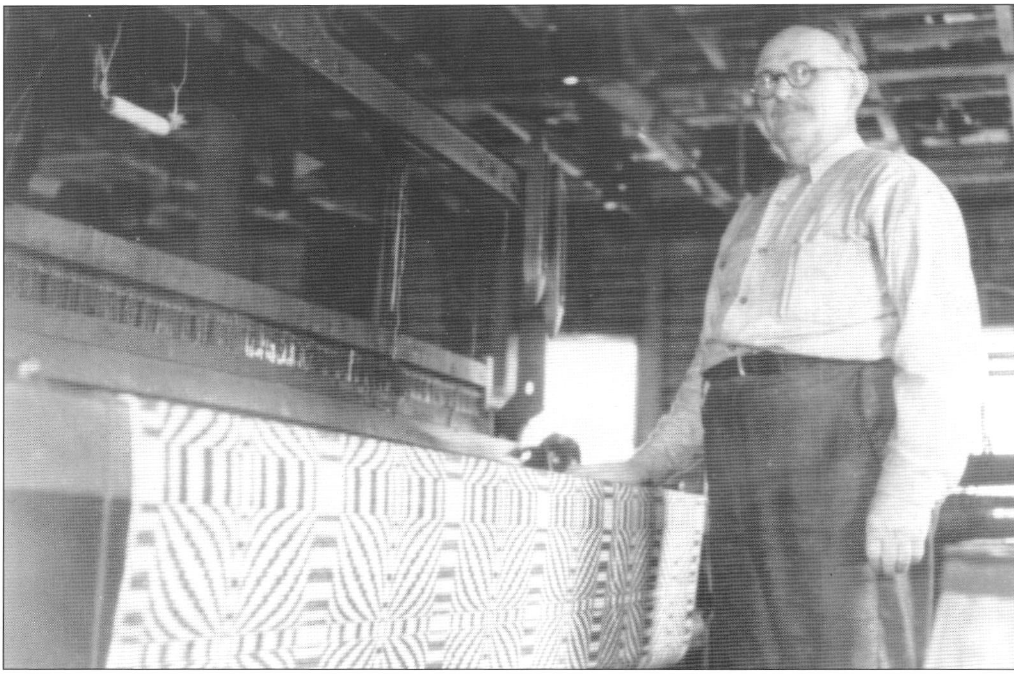

Hired around 1901 by the Vaughn brothers to install power looms in their Burks Fork weaving mill, J.T. Dunn married co-owner Columbus Vaughn's daughter and by 1920 had become sole owner of the company. The county's largest and most sophisticated wool processor operated until the mid-1940s. The machinery was sold or scrapped and the building was torn down after 1948.

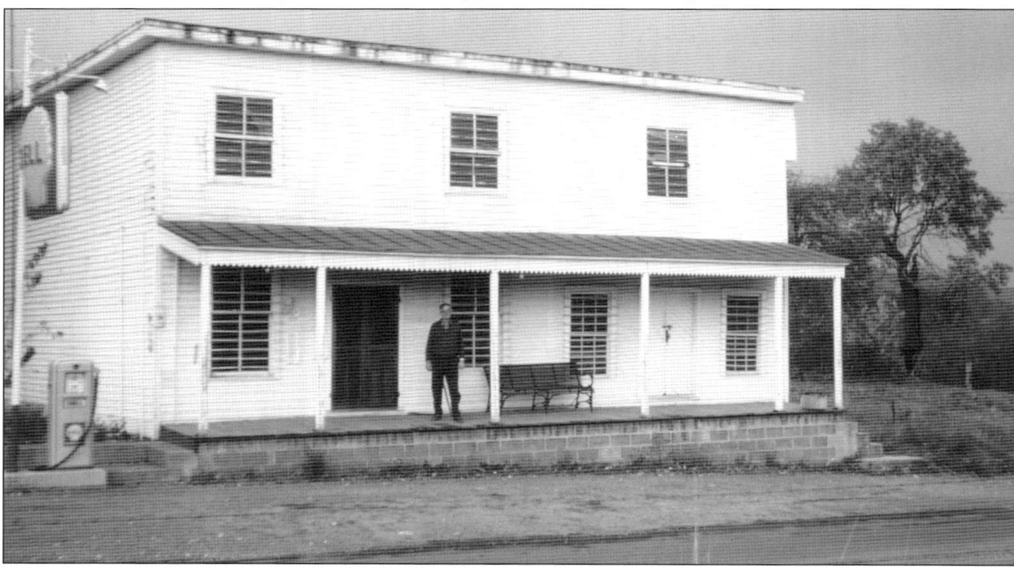

Greenville Wood built and operated this Franklin Pike store around 1900 and sold it to his niece, Dora (Wood) Turner, and her husband in the late 1940s. They sold grocery items, shoes, clothing, housewares, tools, and hardware, as well as animal feeds and gasoline to Floyd and Franklin County customers. Mrs. Turner taught school before her marriage to Cameron Lee "Cam" Turner, who was also a farmer and a county supervisor.

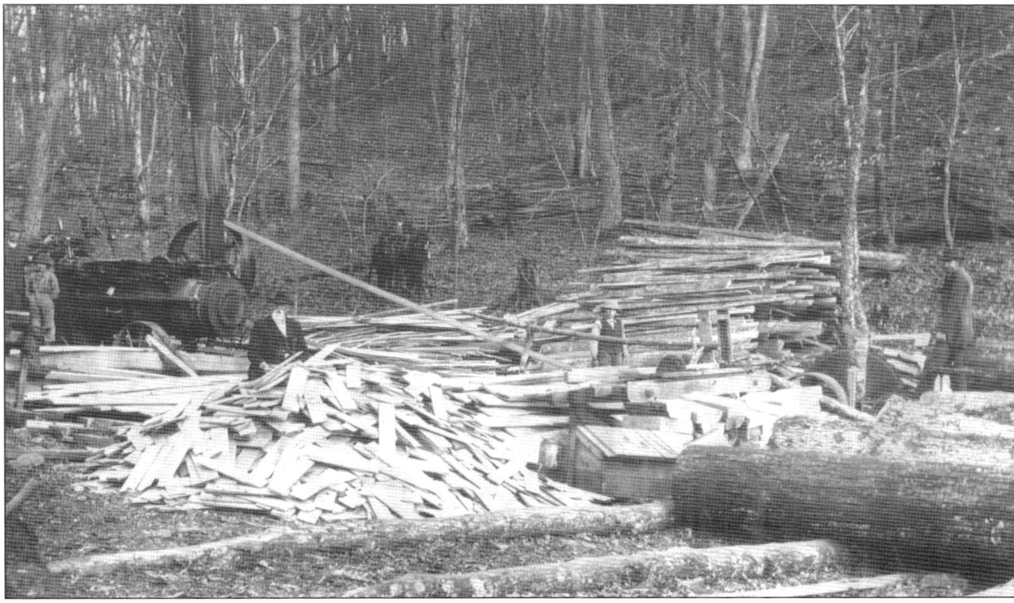

Matthew Weeks (with beard) and John Poff (far right) oversee the process of making sawn shingles. After squaring and removing sapwood with the large circular saw, the logs were crosscut to shingle length and split into shingle bolts. These were fed through a second steam-driven, rip-cut saw. A ratcheting mechanism gave a slight, lengthwise taper to each of the shingles piled in the foreground. (JH)

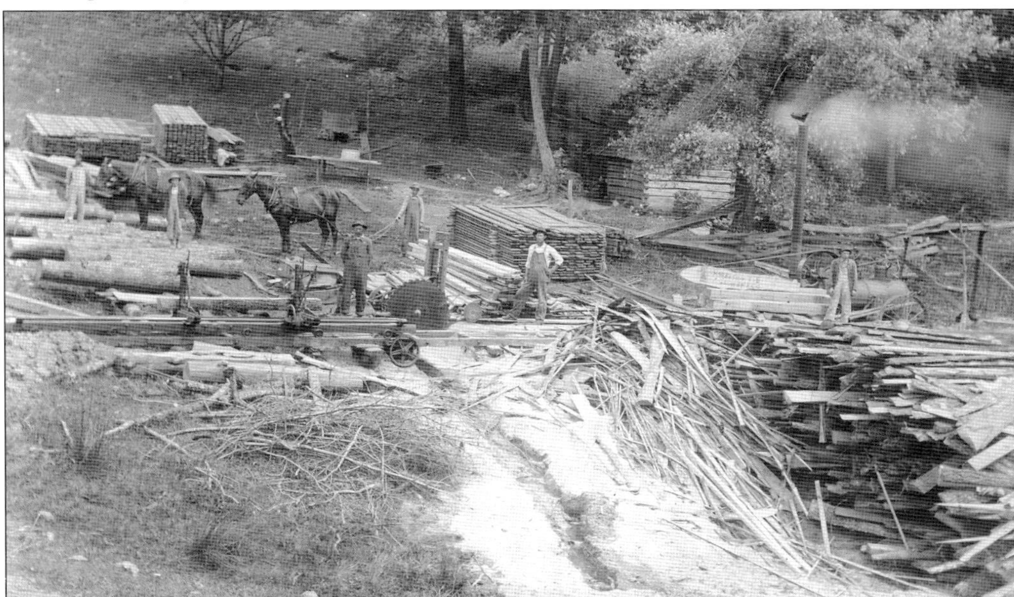

Working under contract for the Harrison Tie and Lumber Company, sawyer Arthur Bond and his crew produced crossties, lumber, and a big slab pile. A convenient stream carried sawdust to nearby Mira Fork Creek. Henry Martin and his sons, Sterling, Herman, and Raymond, handled logs and lumber. Early Quesenberry piled the slabs. Board edges and slabs fueled the steam boiler. Quesenberry Road Northwest passes this spot today.

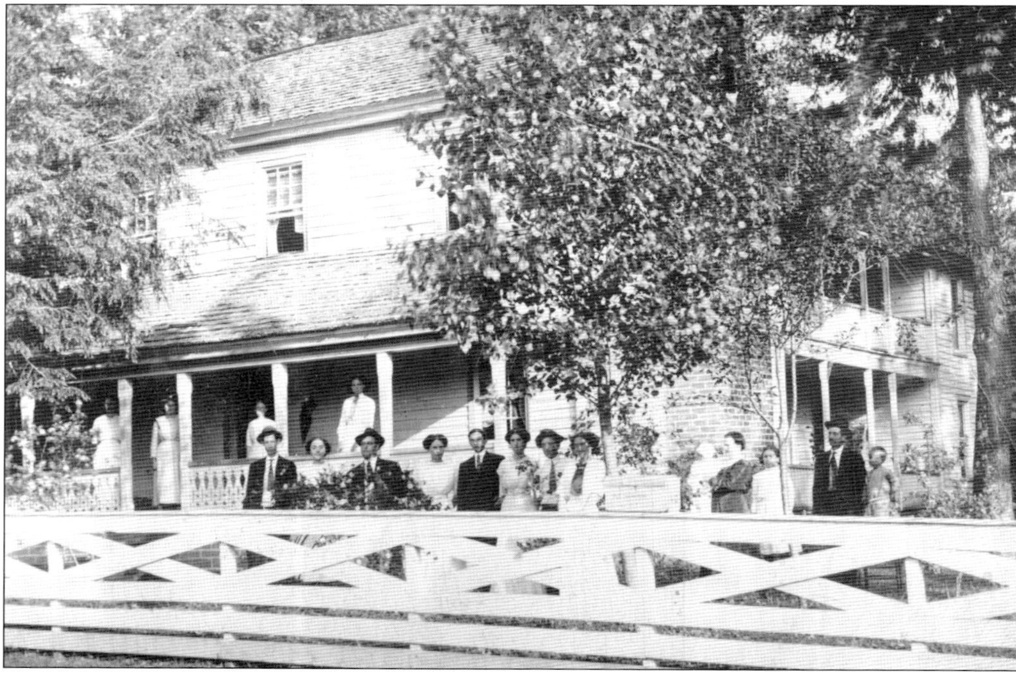

The Albert Gardner family ran a boardinghouse for and stabled the horses of as many as a dozen young men and women, all of whom were attending Willis High School or preparing for teaching careers at Mountain Normal. Gardner bought the Hardin Hylton house in 1905 and added the back section. The house still stands by Route 221, across from the intersection with Indian Valley Road (Route 787). (JSK)

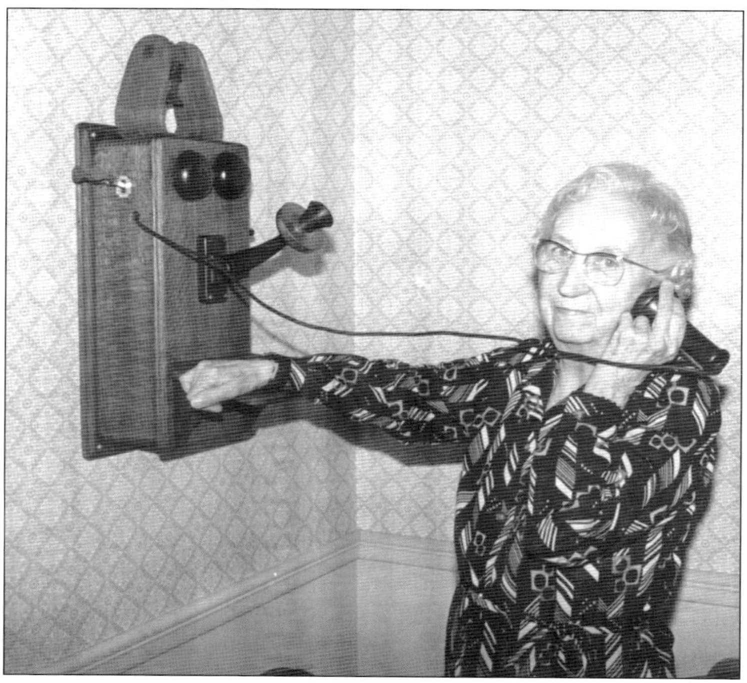

Telephone operator Lena Whitlock, "the voice of Floyd," maintained the town switchboard in her West Main Street home, bought for this purpose by the Floyd Telephone Company in 1926. The house still stands two doors up from the Jessie Peterman library. The switchboard was previously located up and across the street in the Hotel Brame. (RFS)

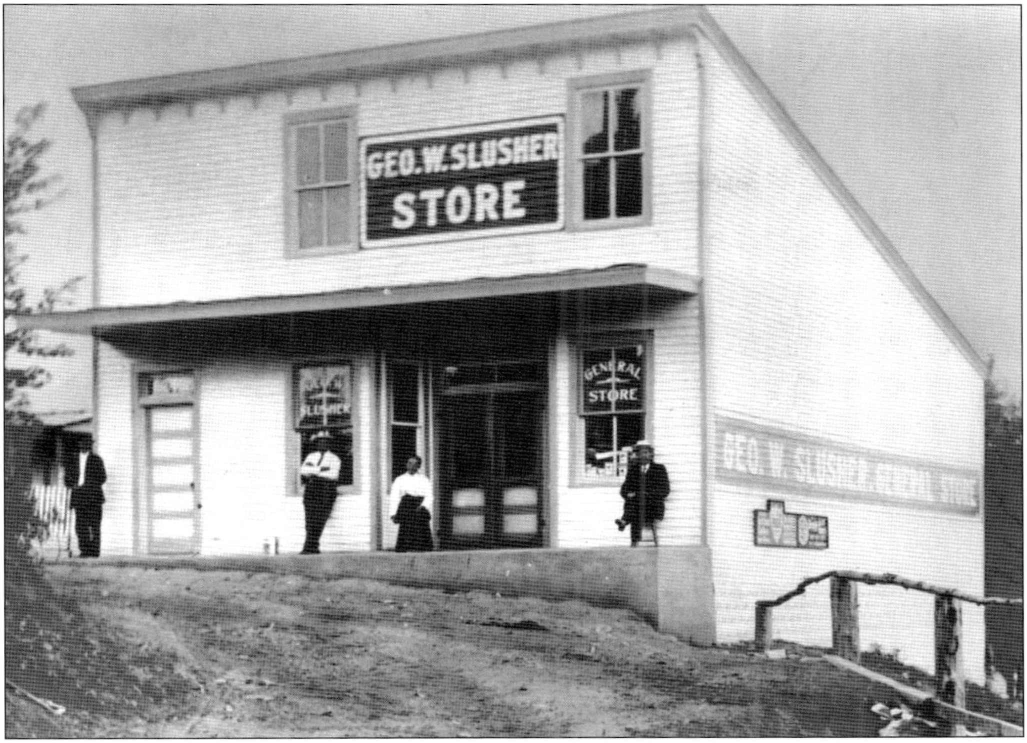

George W. Slusher's sons regularly made the two-day wagon trip to the railroad station in Cambria (Christiansburg), hauling butter, chestnuts, and other goods and returning with dry goods for their Penn Avenue store. Slusher's daughters clerked in this store, where the Nazarene Church stands today. A former mayor of the town, Slusher (seated, right) is seen on the porch of the store with his wife, Clementine Corn Slusher (seated, left). (JSK)

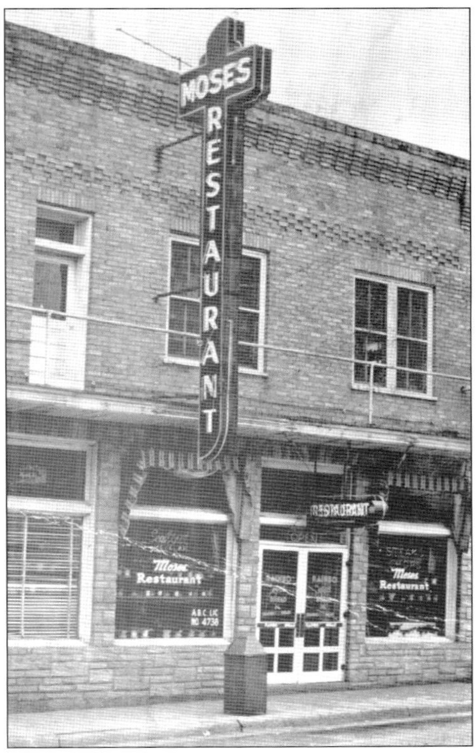

Roy and Willie Moses's restaurant on North Locust Street was a longtime fixture in the town of Floyd and a landmark for townspeople and visitors alike. This postcard mailed by Mrs. Moses in 1965 shows the distinctive brick front sawn from locally quarried soapstone. Oddfella's Cantina occupies the space today.

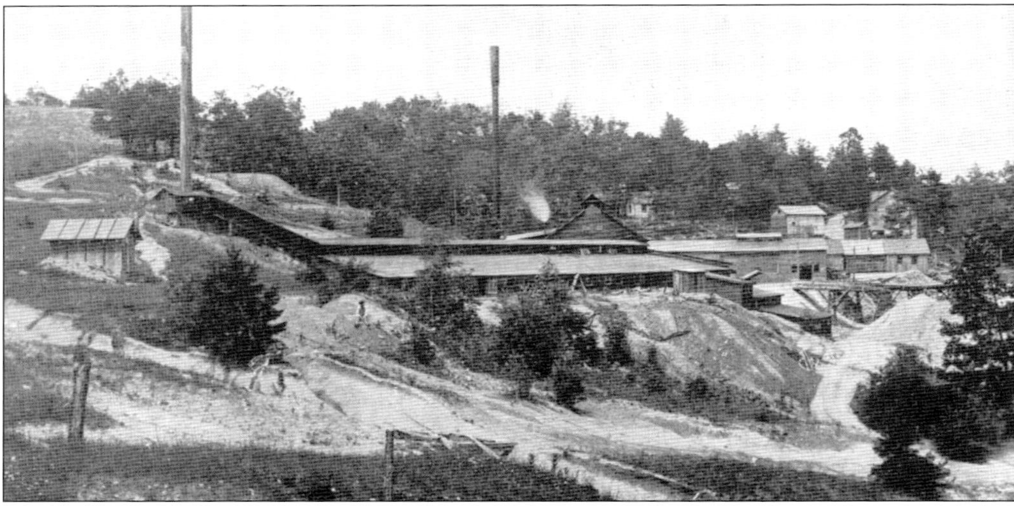

Said to have been one of only two such facilities east of the Mississippi, Floyd County's arsenic mine lay about 1.5 miles southeast of Huffville near the Eastern Continental Divide. First worked by the United States Arsenic Mine Company in 1903, the facility closed at the end of World War I but was still considered a valuable mineral resource in an industrial survey published in 1930. (DRM)

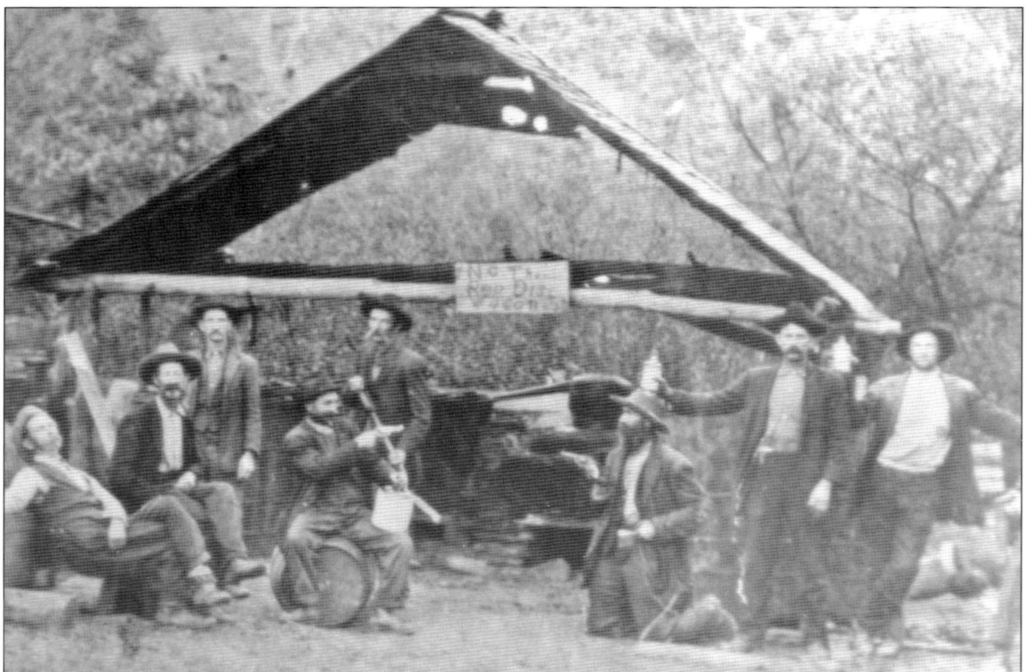

Licensed distilleries like Nathaniel C. Thomas's in the Paynes Creek area were common before Prohibition, with at least 40 reported in Floyd County in 1890. Government agents collected taxes and certified the proof of whiskey and brandy retailed both on and off premises or shipped out of the county in barrels. The low value and difficulty of transporting bulky grain and fruit made distilling an attractive alternative or supplement to farming. (RC)

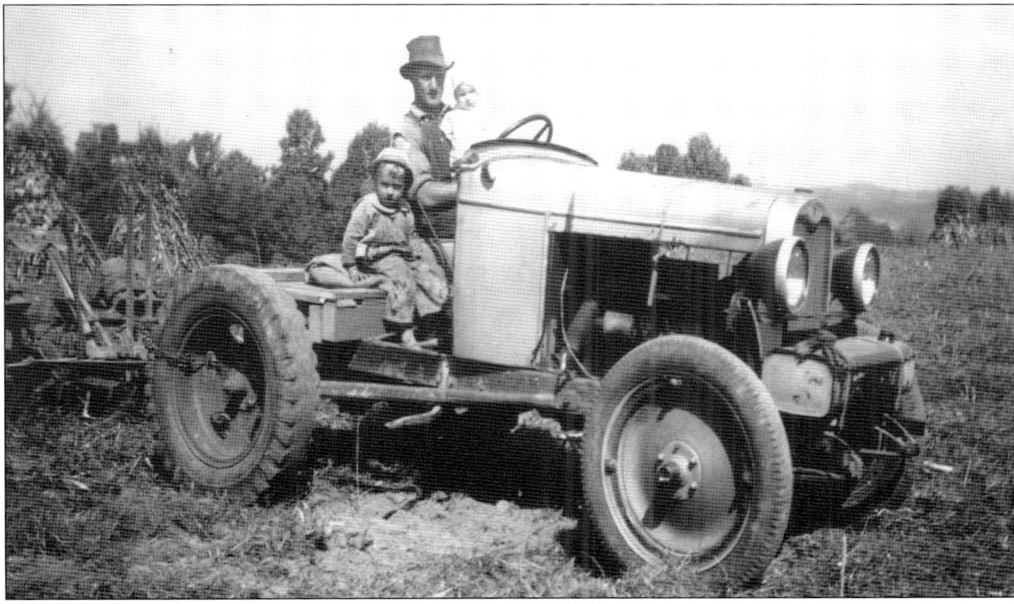

Leonard Boothe of Wills Ridge made his own "Doodlebug" tractor by installing a heavy truck rear end, minus the suspension, in a car or pickup frame. Homemade tractor plans appeared in do-it-yourself magazines like *Popular Mechanics* during the Depression and World War II, but many, like Boothe, worked without them. His daughter Marie Daniels and son Arnold are along for the ride around 1940. (SAB)

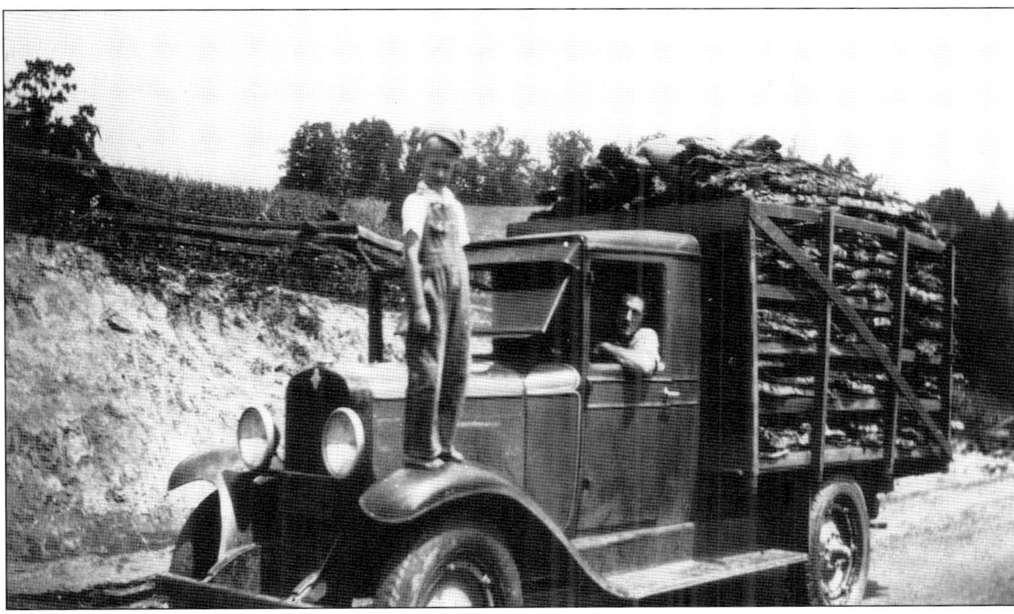

Leonard Boothe and son Lowell head to Christiansburg with a load of tanbark. Peeled in rings of uniform length from tannin-rich trees, tanbark was easier to handle and transport than the logs from which it was taken. Income from tanbark, used for tanning leather, was a bonus for timber men and farmers since bark left on sawlogs and cleared trees ended up in the slab pile or steam engine firebox. (SAB)

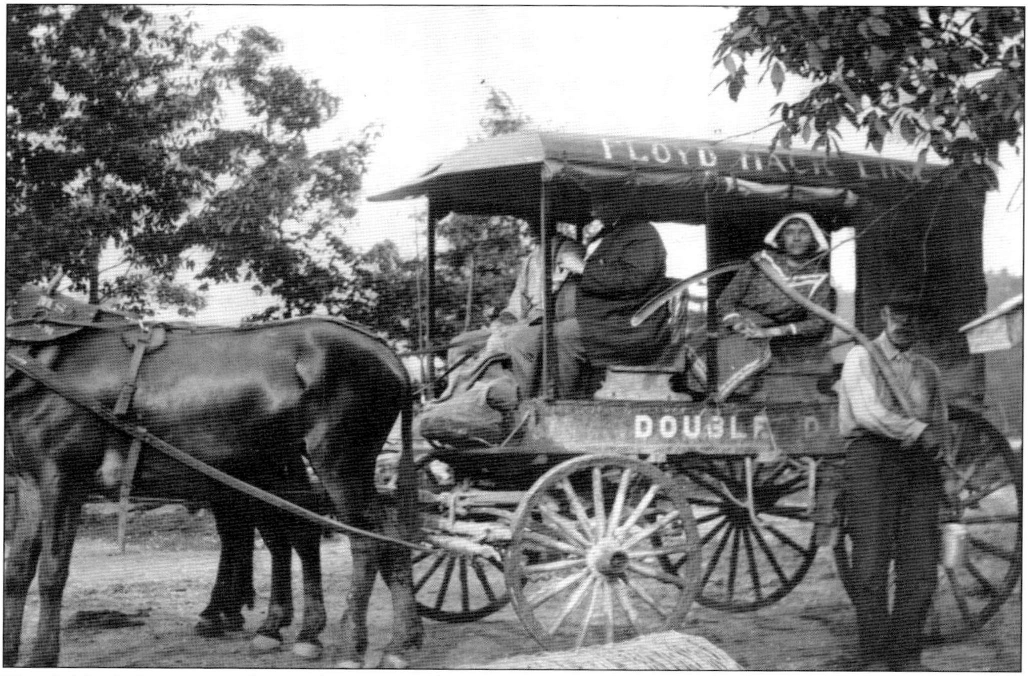

Floyd Hack Line was the early taxi in the area. Howard Stump ran the "Double Daily" hack line from the depot and stables near Hensley Road at the current Winter Sun location via the Christiansburg Turnpike (Route 615) to Cambria train station. Charles Henry Agnew is holding the scythe.

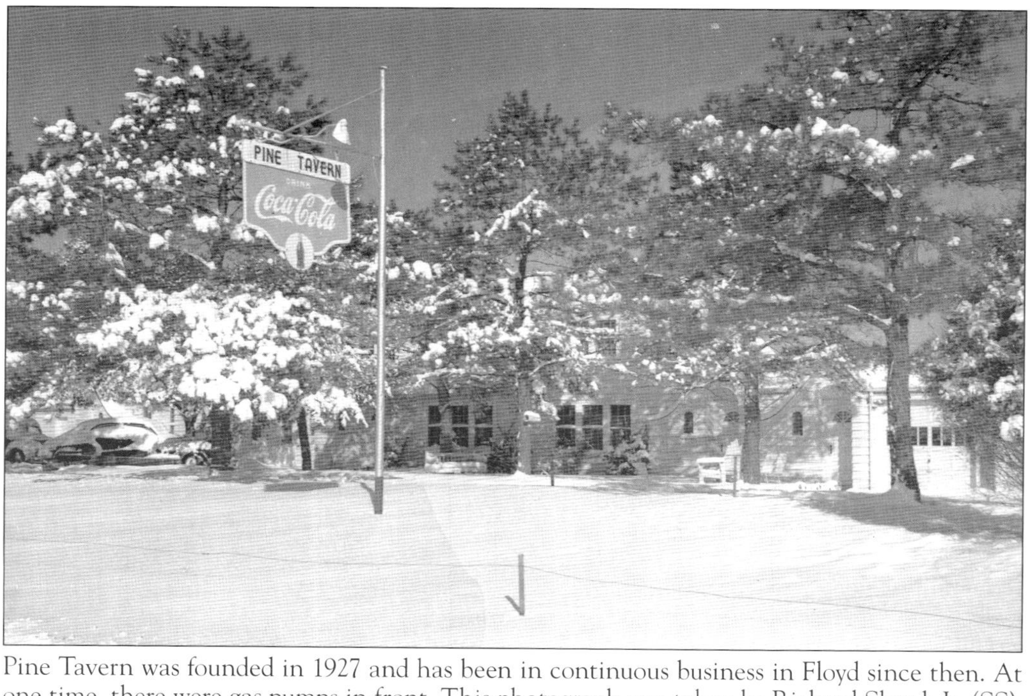

Pine Tavern was founded in 1927 and has been in continuous business in Floyd since then. At one time, there were gas pumps in front. This photograph was taken by Richard Shank Jr. (SS)

Five

Sports, Recreation, and Leisure

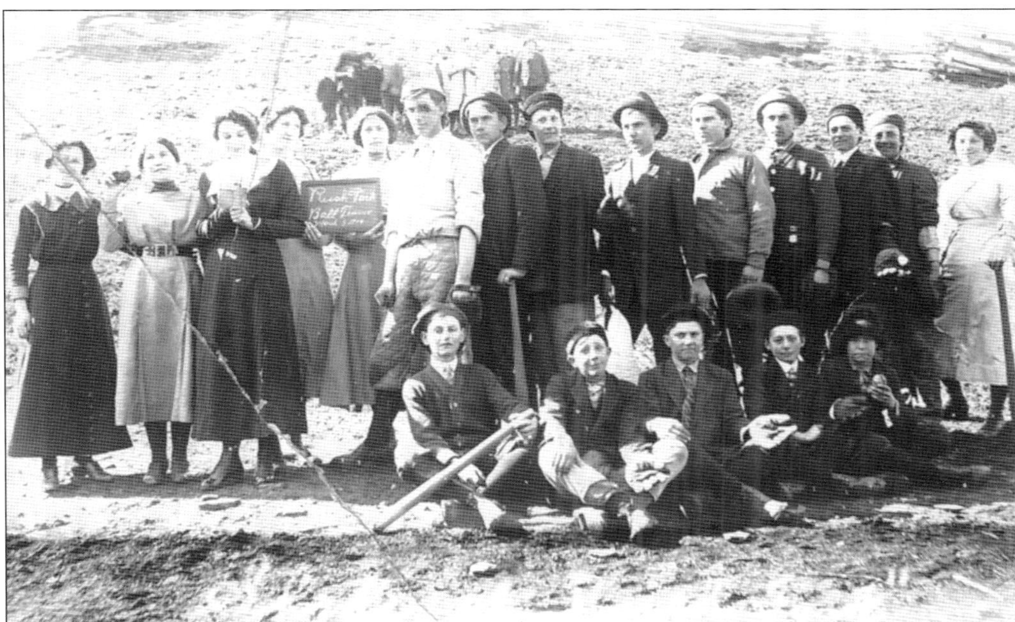

The Rush Fork baseball team joins some of their fans in 1914. Roger Oliver Slusher Sr., standing to the right of the slate, was the catcher. Dewey Cannaday, George Slusher, and Roy Weddle are among the seated players. Bess, Effie, and Martha Slusher are also in the image. (APS)

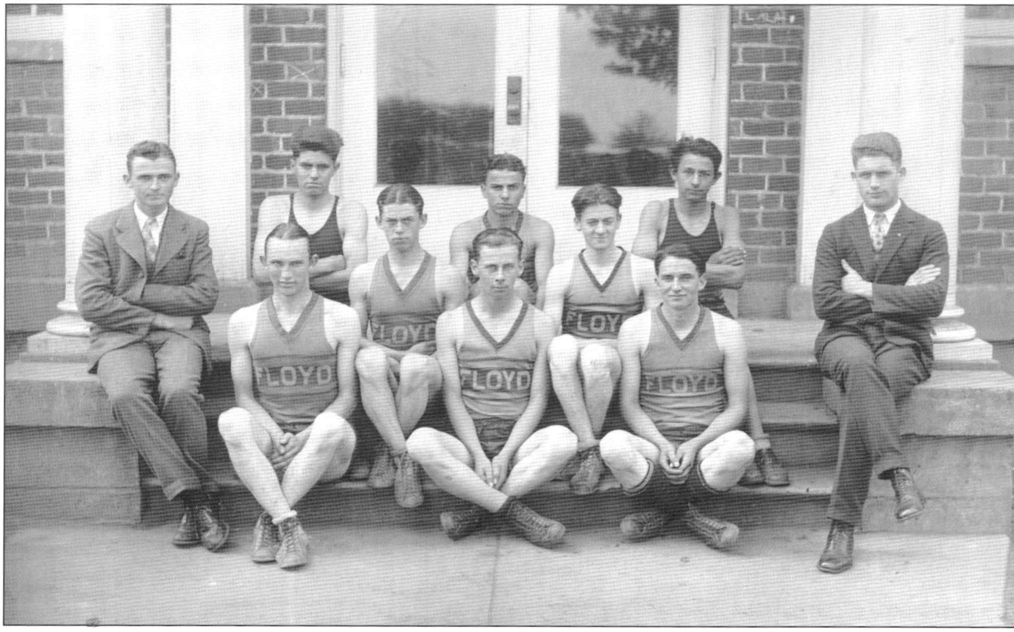

Floyd High School's boys' basketball team from the 1926–1927 season poses in front of old Floyd High School. The team included, from left to right, (first row) unidentified, Guy Williams, and Trent Weeks; (second row) Principal Joe Poff, Bernard Lee, Ed Lee, and unidentified; (third row) three unidentified.

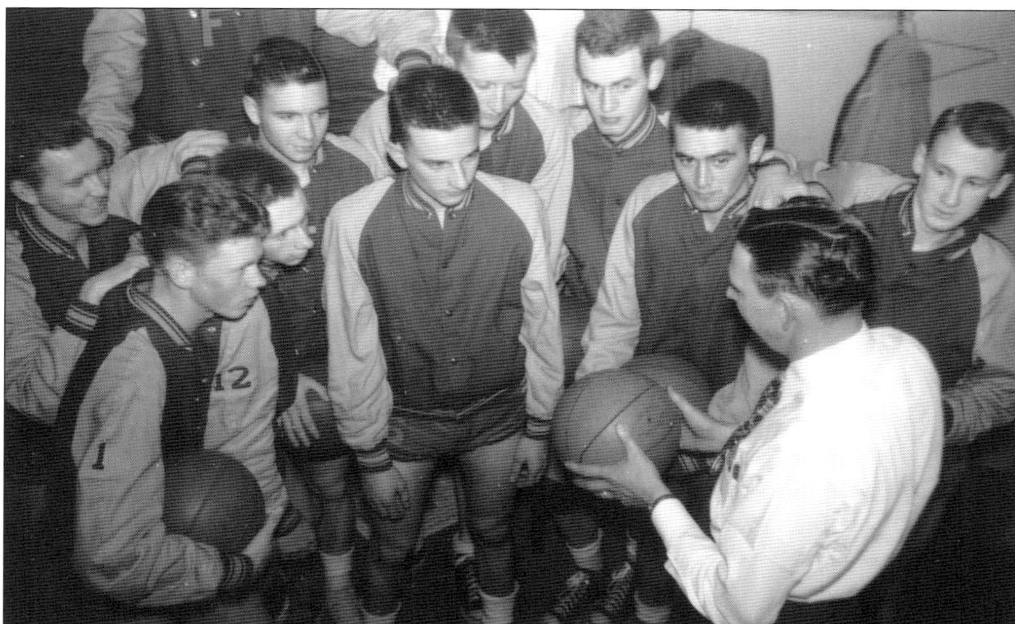

Coach John R. Graham poses with some of the 1951 Floyd High School Golden Eagles. The team was the District S, Group III champion. The team included, from left to right, Bill Casteel, Milton Ogle (No. 1, holding ball), Claude Royal (No. 12), Dock Sweeney, Billy Weddle, Pete Williams, George Vaughan, Ralph Cannaday, Coach Graham, and Dean Beckleheimer. (JG)

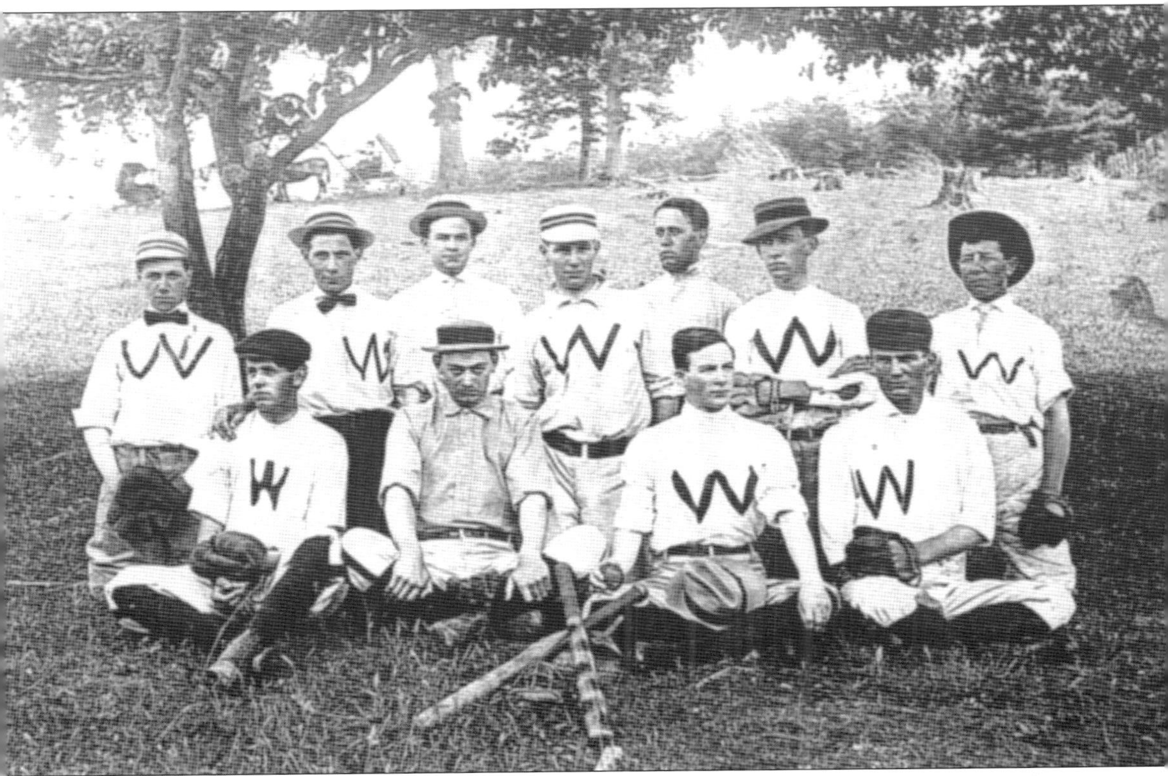

The 1906–1907 Willis baseball team poses in the foreground with some of their fans behind them.

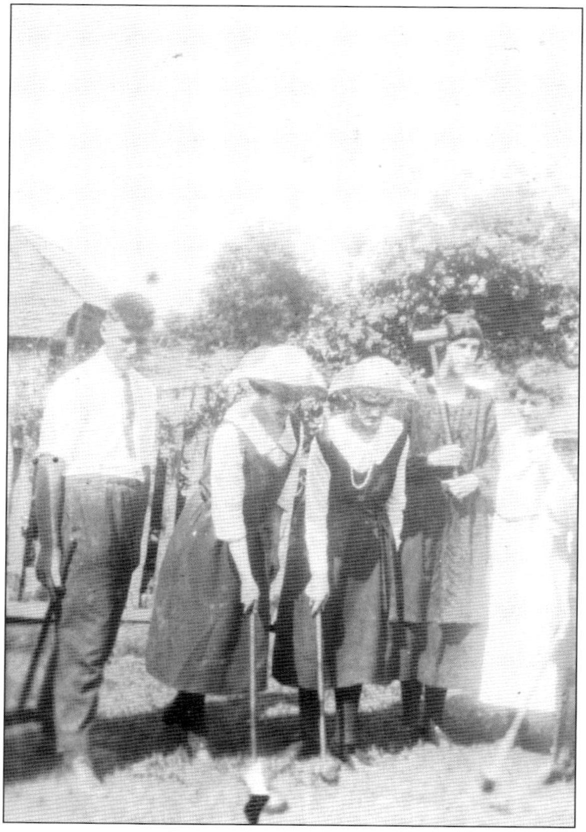

The croquet players in the picture are, from left to right, William Spangler, Elsie Epperly, Mattie Epperly, Myrtle Epperly, and Ressiemaine Epperly Spangler.

This baseball team was from the Sears community near Willis and was one of the most successful in the county from 1912 to 1915. The team included, from left to right, (first row) pitcher Cephas Hylton, outfielder Dayton Harman, shortstop Ted Alley, catcher Roger O. Slusher Sr., and outfielder Lonnie Quesenberry; (second row) first baseman Earl Sutphin, third baseman Chris Hylton, scorekeeper Dr. Will Hylton (standing), second baseman John Harman, utility player Clarence Hylton, and outfielder Ray Harman. (APS)

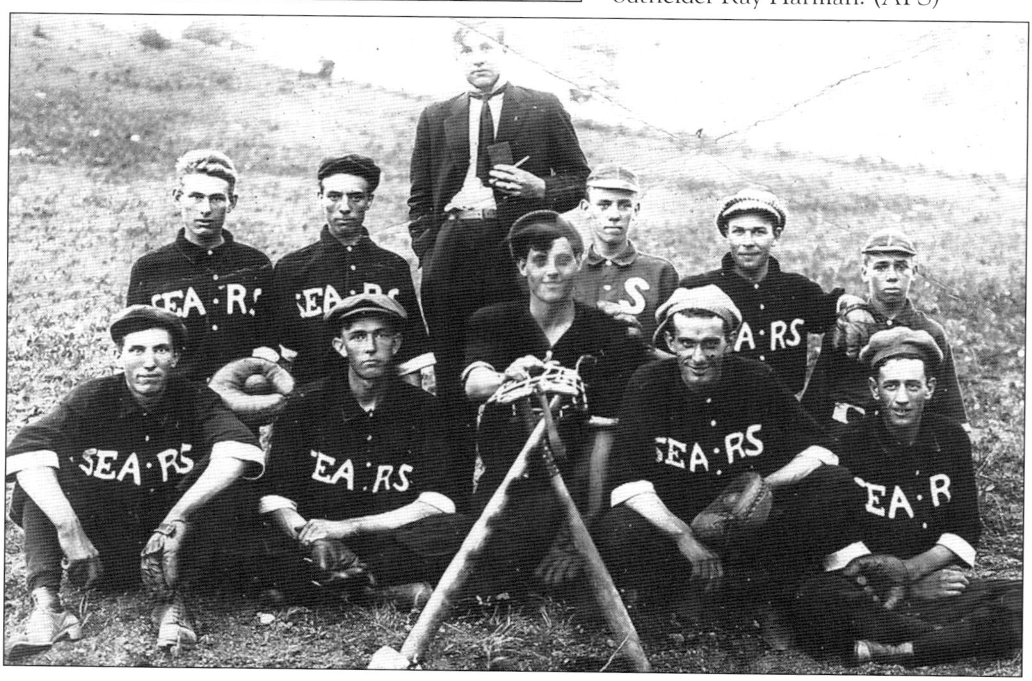

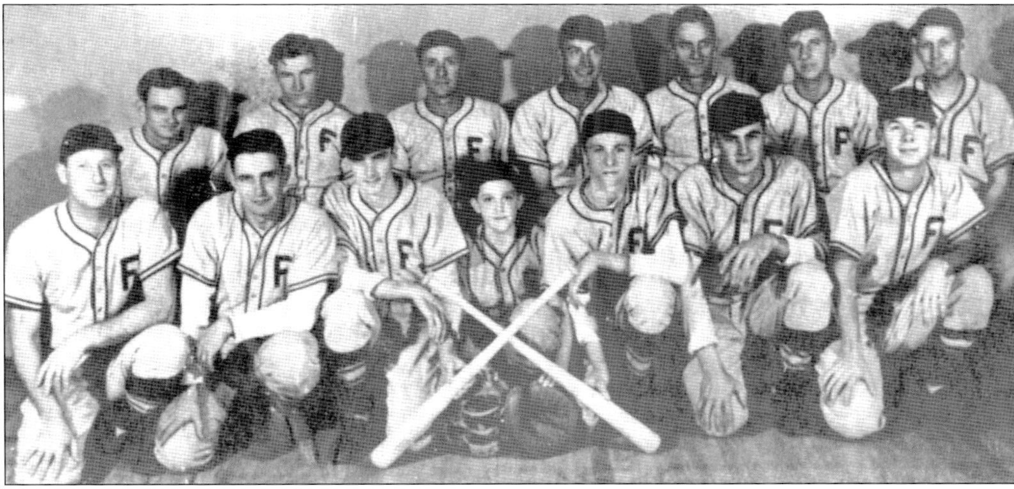

The Floyd Blue Sox amateur baseball team was organized in 1947 and played until the mid-1950s, winning four championship trophies and one pennant. The team included, from left to right, (first row) Vernon Harris, Bryce Yopp, Ross Williams, bat boy Charles Kingrea, Deward Williams, Gene Williams, and Maurice Slusher; (second row) Ralph Yopp, Morris Agee, coach Ray Williams, R.O. Slusher Jr., Henry Casteel, John Graham, and Walter Moore. (CHM)

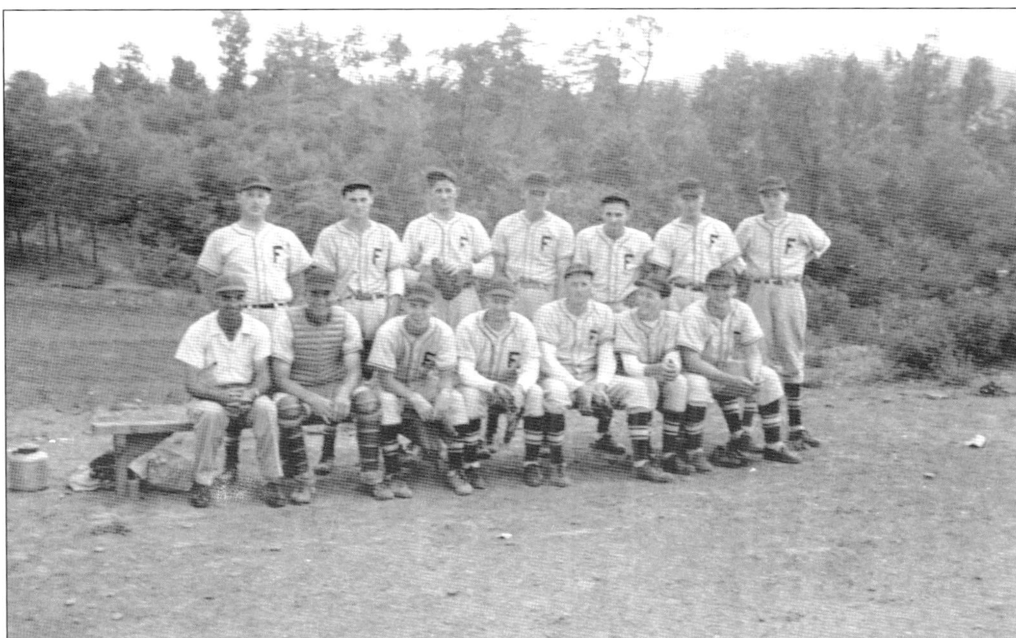

Several members of the Blue Sox were offered professional contracts; both Deward and Don Williams signed with the Pittsburgh Pirates. The team played on Saturdays and Sundays, drawing big crowds to what is now the Floyd Elementary School field. Included in this image are, from left to right, (first row) scorekeeper Henry Whitlow, R.O. Slusher, Maurice Slusher, Walter Moore, Ray Williams, Don Williams, and Marvin Agee; (second row) manager Vernon Harris, Gene Williams, Henry Casteel, Glen Tolbert, Ralph Yopp, Morris Agee, and Deward Williams. (MS)

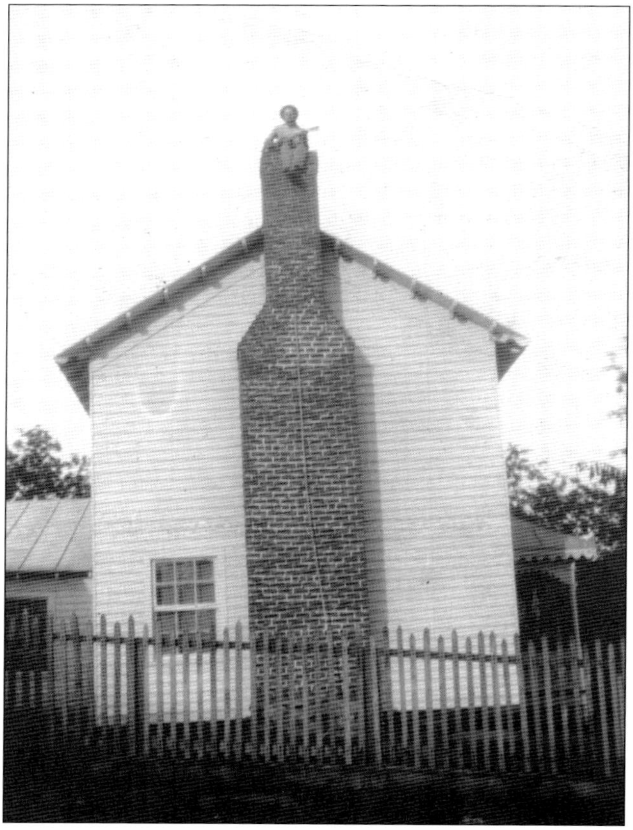

Dewey Joel Keith, the son of John William and Naomah Weddle Keith, plays guitar atop the chimney of his parent's house in Union, in the Willis area, in the 1920s. (JSK)

The 1925 Floyd High School girls' basketball team poses on the front steps of Floyd High School. From left to right are (first row) Wilma Cox, India DeHart, Mildred Roberson, and Catherine Morgan; (second row) Elizabeth Williams, Mary Custis Burwell, and Lillian DeHart; (third row) teacher Miss Wartman, assistant coach Ruth See, Dot Slusher, and Mary Watkins; (fourth row) Coach Joe Poff and Edna Roberson.

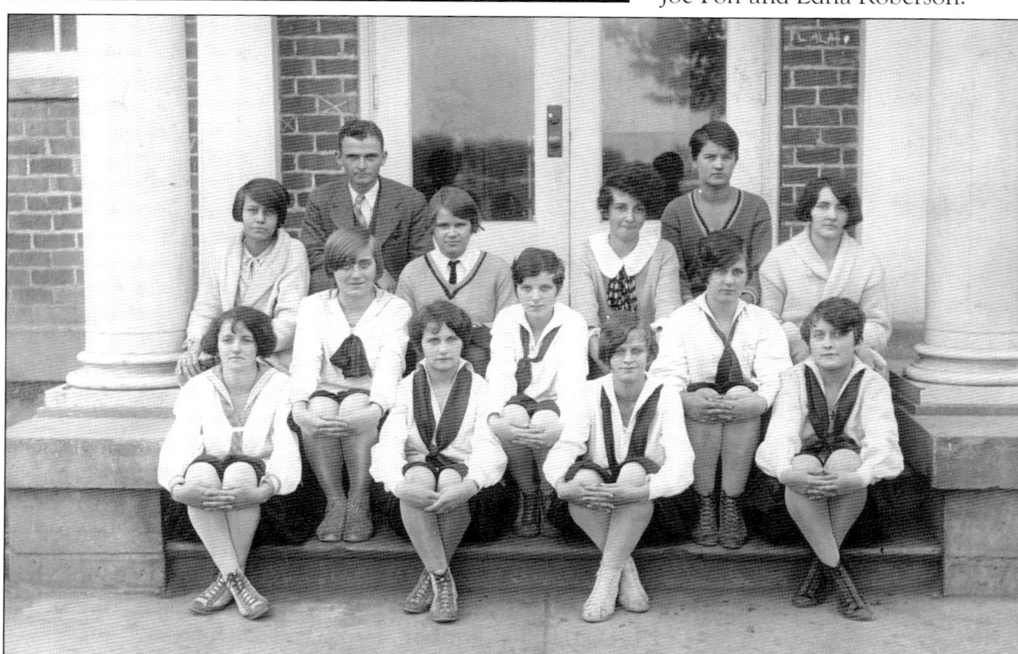

Tom Rakes, the president of Floyd Motor Company, hands Coach John R. Graham the controls of the new electric scoreboard the company donated to the high school as principal Kenneth Fulp looks on. (JG)

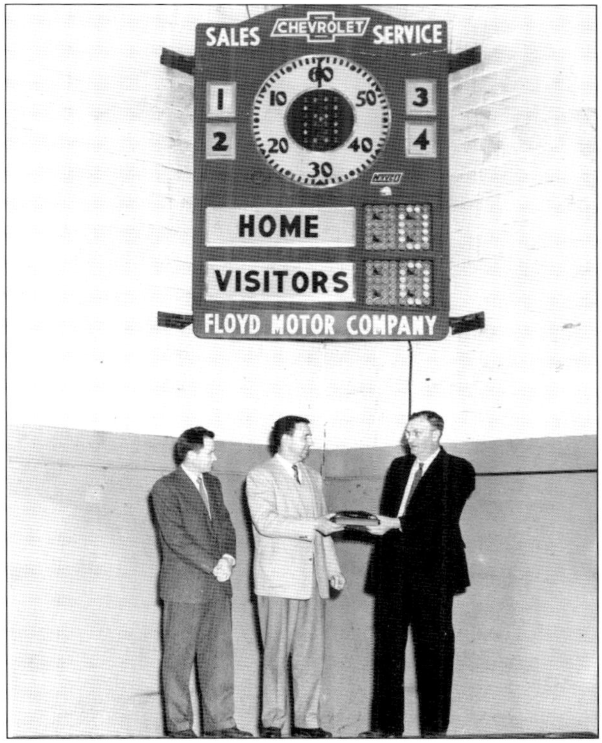

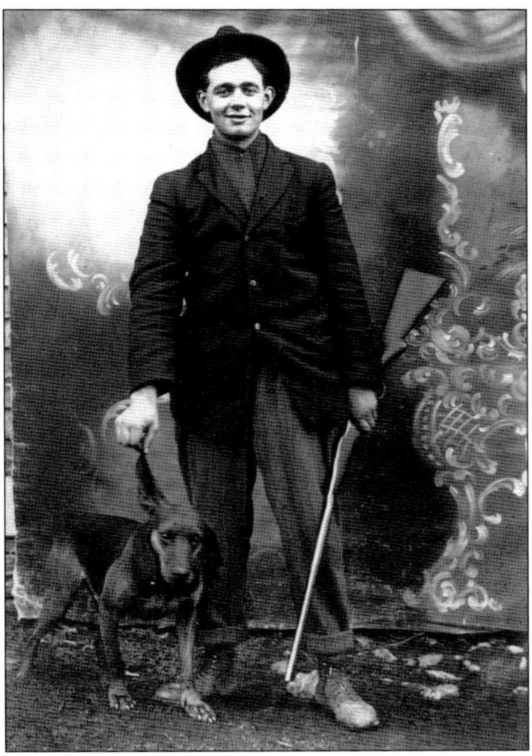

Luther Helms poses proudly with his coon dog and shotgun. (JH)

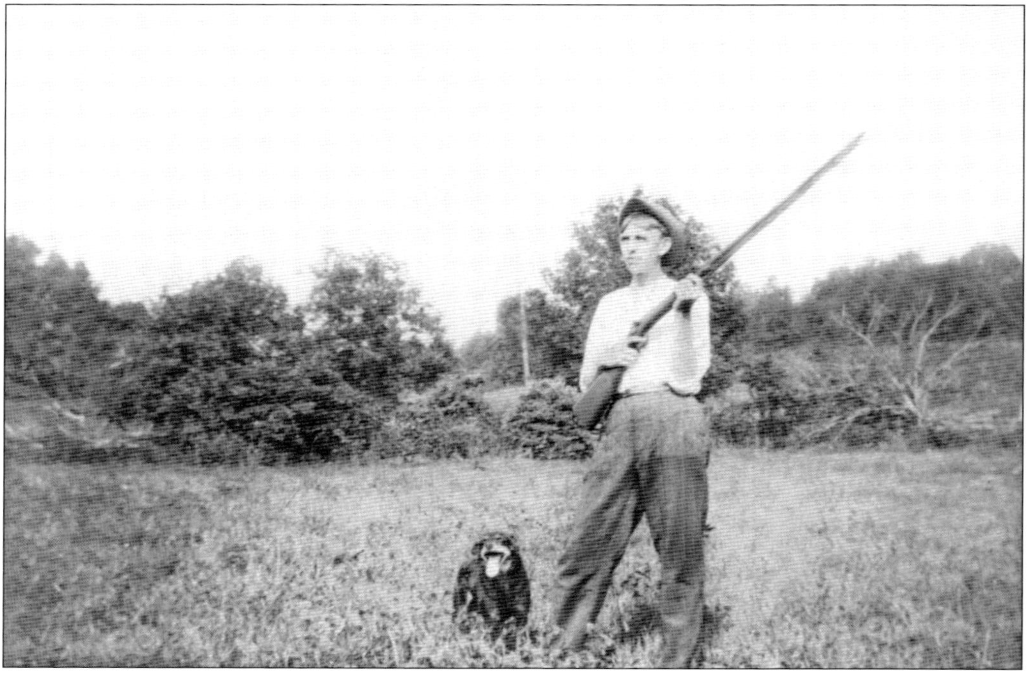

Vauban Lancaster poses dramatically with his hunting dog and rifle.

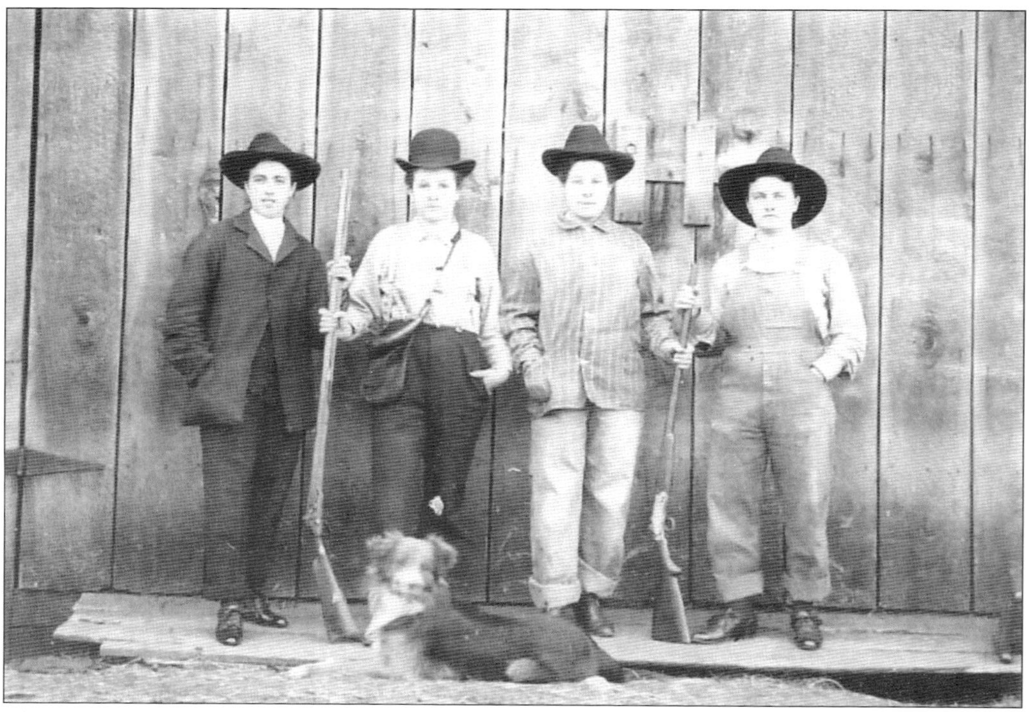

These ladies, dressed as men perhaps for a hunting trip, are, from left to right, Minnie (Wood) Webb, Dora (Vaughn) Harman, Ella (Harris) Harman, and Mattie (Hurd) Webb. (JH)

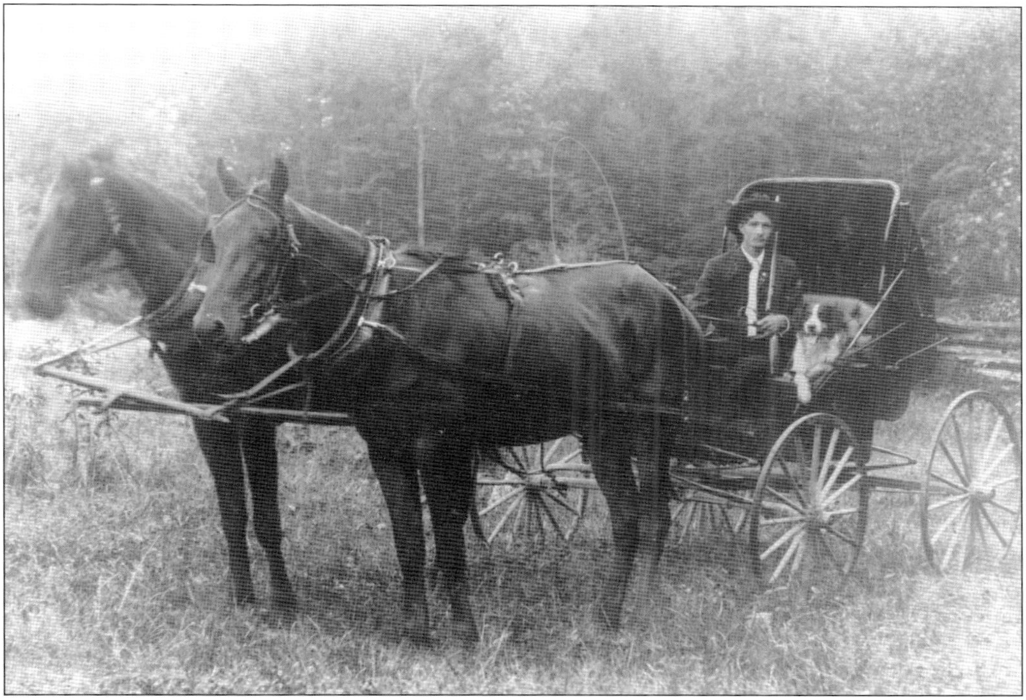

Rural mail carrier Will Reed, who worked out of the Willis post office, is seen here on his route with his dog and his gun around 1920. (JH)

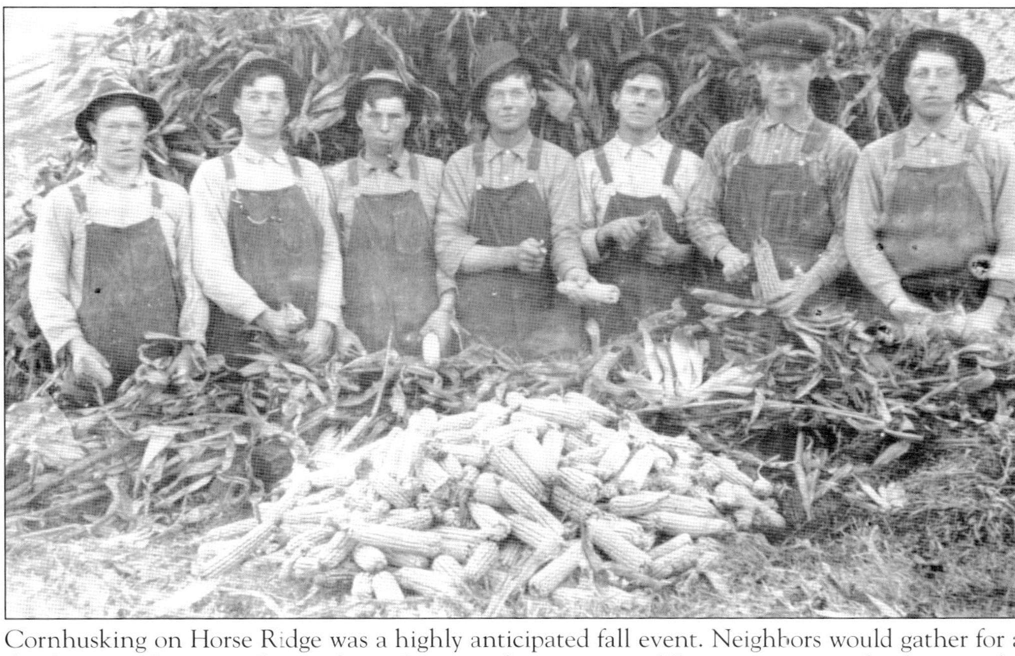

Cornhusking on Horse Ridge was a highly anticipated fall event. Neighbors would gather for a shucking, working together and socializing at the same time. These young men shucking in the 1920s are, from left to right, Oakley Dalton, Paul Cox, Roy Phillips, Perry Cox, Draper Young, John Cox, and Jett Dalton. (DDS)

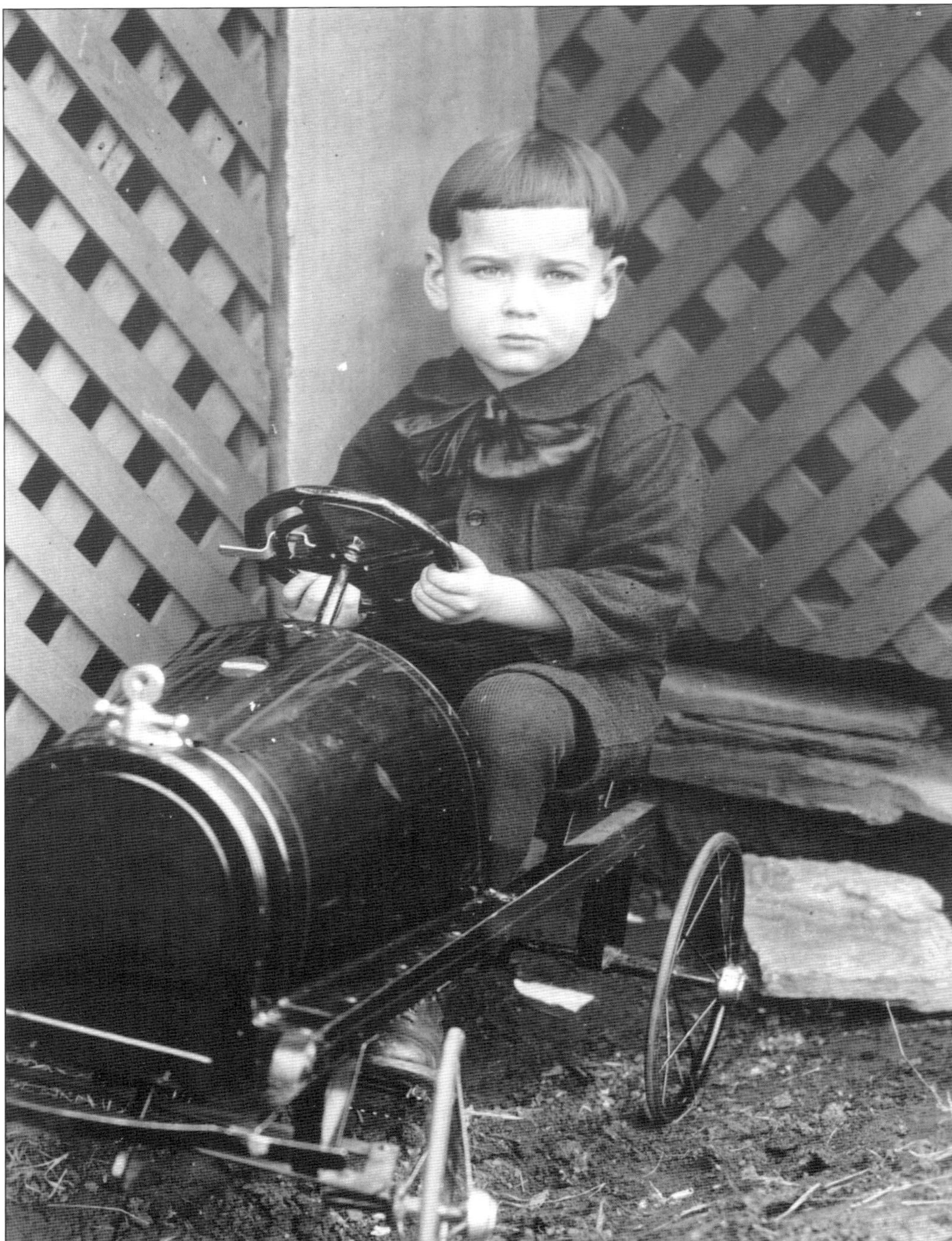

A well-dressed young J.P. Walton Weeks, sporting the "bowl" haircut of the early 1920s, poses in his pedal-propelled car. Like many Floyd citizens, Weeks later worked at the Radford Arsenal. He was elected to four terms on the board of supervisors. Weeks's daughter, Rebecca Weeks, is the current president of the Floyd County Historical Society. (RAW)

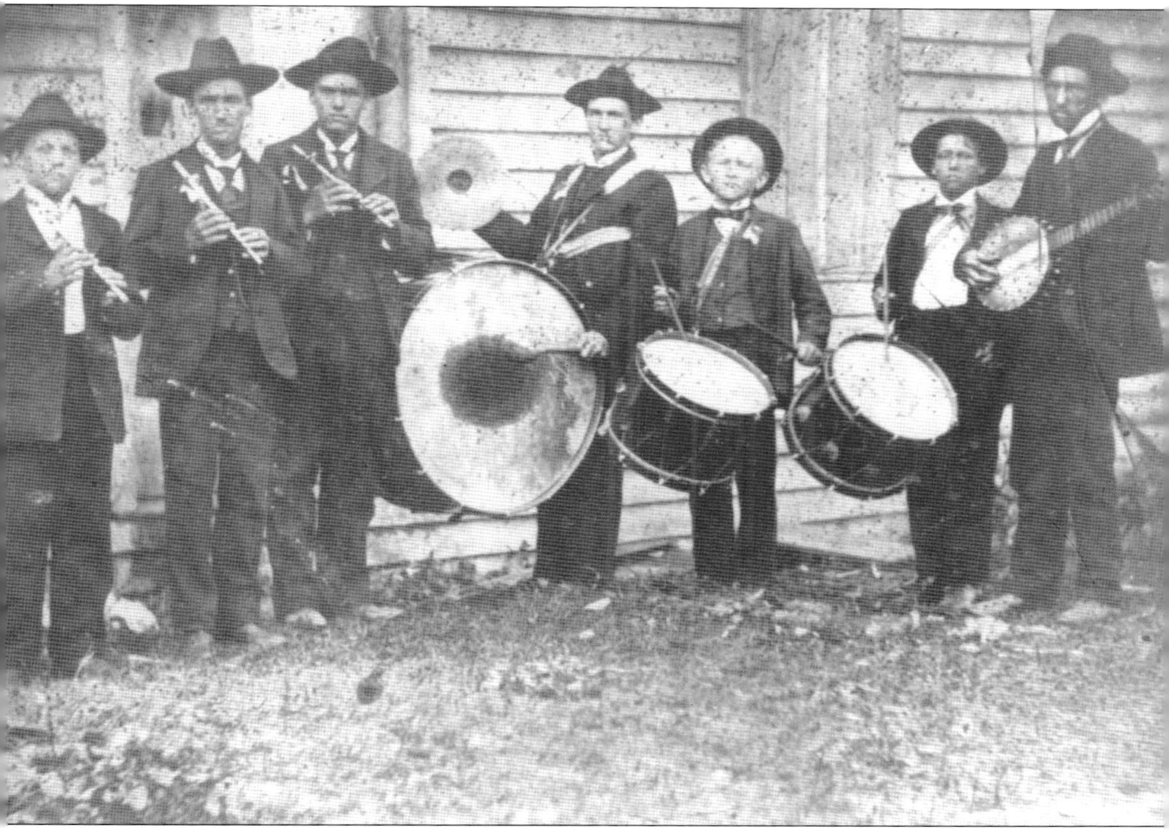

The Hylton Band, posing around 1900, featured, from left to right, Charlie Vaughn, Weldon Hylton, Sherman Hylton, Manuel Hylton, George Hylton, Watt Vaughn, and Arnon Hylton. (JH)

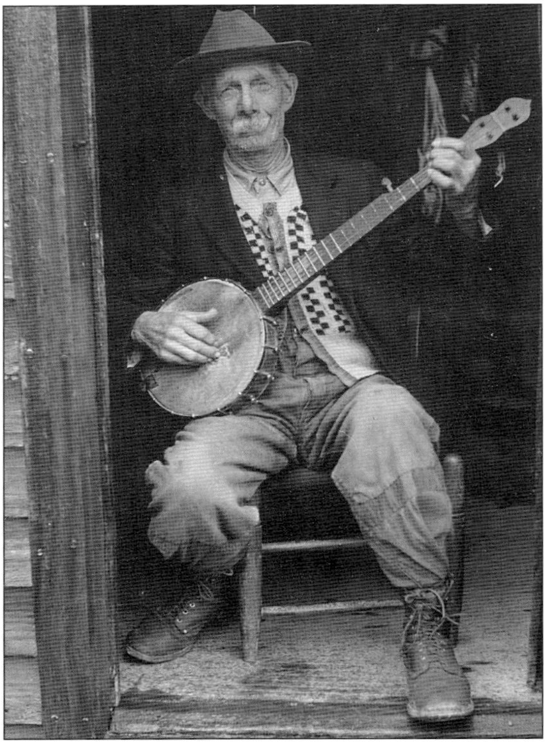

Alonzo "Newton" Hylton (1872–1957) seen here picking on his banjo, was a farmer, musician, blacksmith, miller, and millwright. He built many of the wooden waterwheels used in southwestern Floyd County, including two for Mabry Mill.

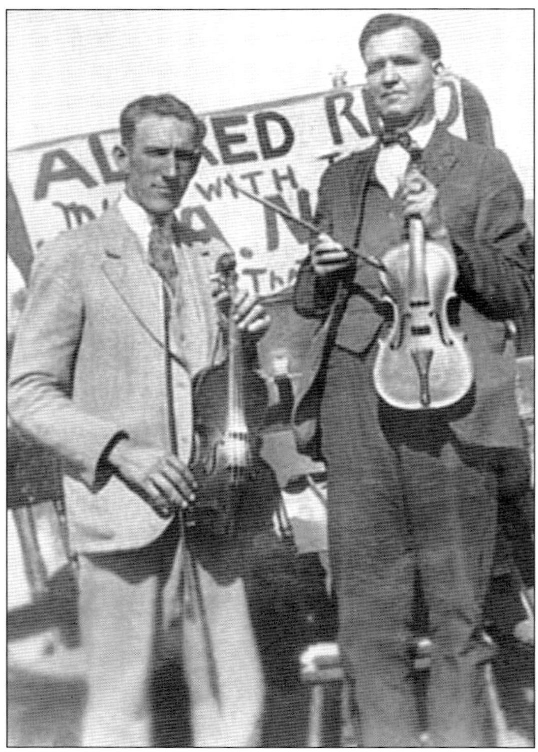

"Blind" Alfred Reed, on the right with Fred Pendleton, was born blind in Floyd in 1880. He supported his wife and six children by playing his fiddle at events and on the street, giving music lessons, and selling his songs. He is remembered for playing at the famous Bristol Sessions in 1927. He later moved to West Virginia, and after his death in 1956, he was inducted into the West Virginia Music Hall of Fame. (DRM)

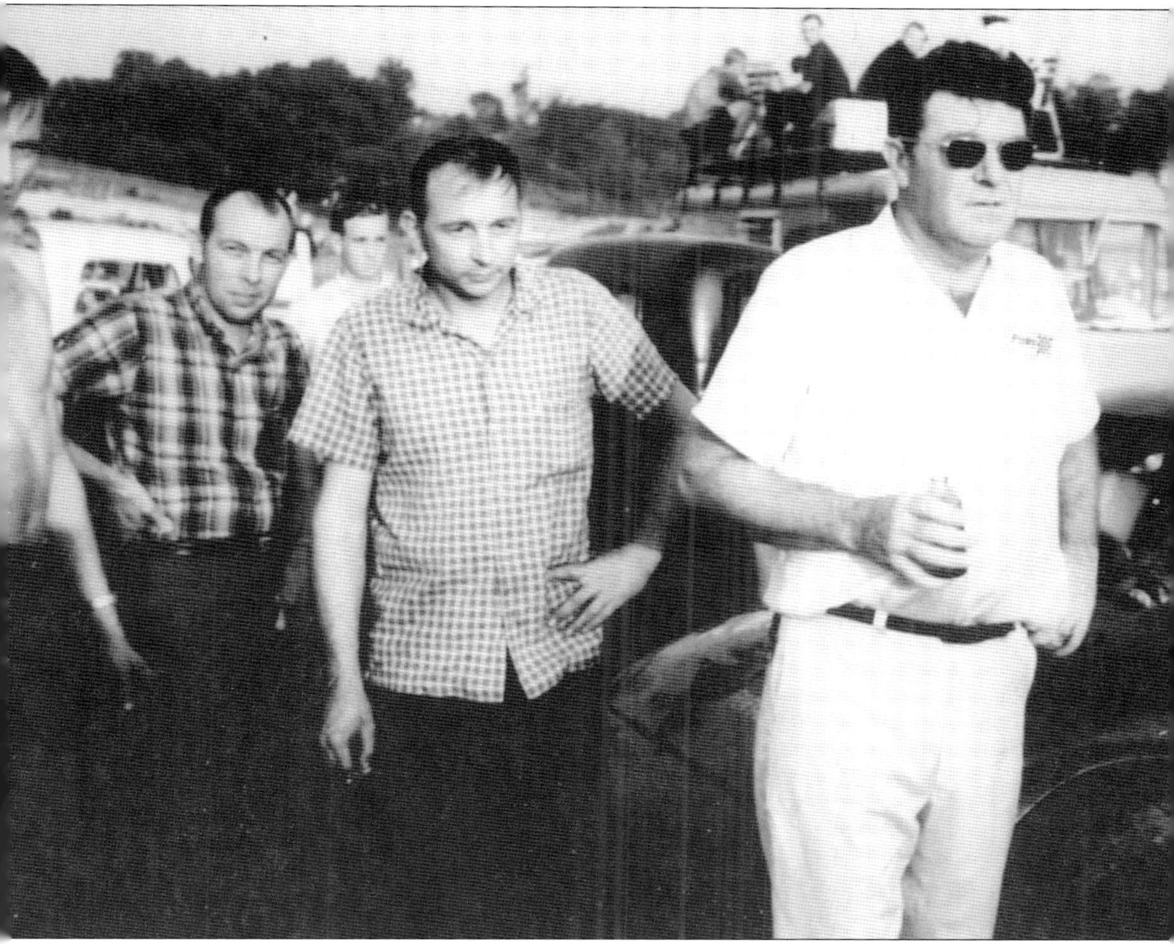

NASCAR legend Curtis Turner (far right), who built the Charlotte Motor Speedway, was a Floyd native who got his start outrunning "revenuers" while delivering moonshine. He is seen here before his last race in 1968 at the dirt track that is now the Motor Mile Speedway in Pulaski County. His career was cut short when he died in a plane crash in 1970. With him are, from left to right, Doug, Bruce, and Barry Sweeney. (BS)

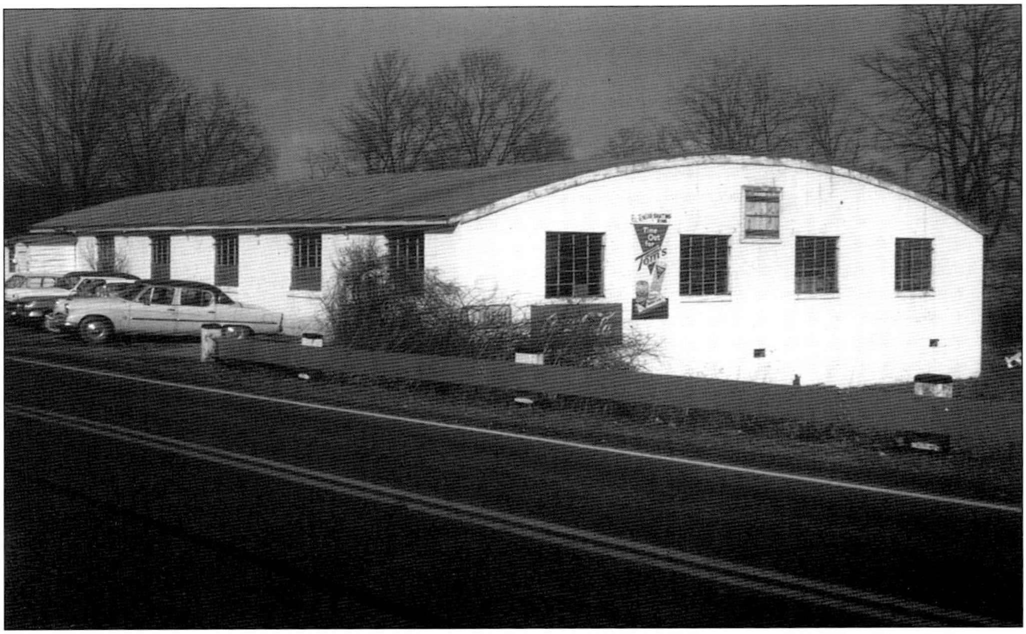

El Tenedor skating rink, built in the 1940s, was a popular gathering place for Floyd County youths. In the early 1950s, a week's activities included a dance, a night for African Americans to skate, and a couple of nights for church groups to skate. This building still stands on Route 221 northeast of Floyd and has been used as a polling place and a shop for lighting manufacturing. It is currently a woodworking business. (BH)

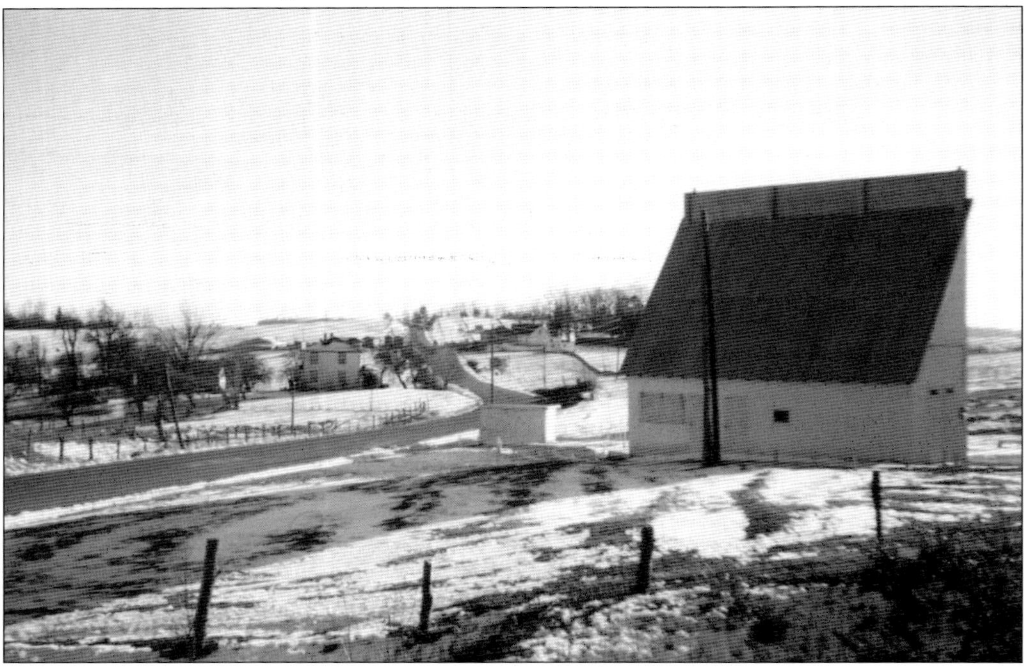

Vest Drive-in Theater, north of Check on Route 221, was the last active drive-in theater in Floyd County. This photograph shows the back of the screen. (SAB)

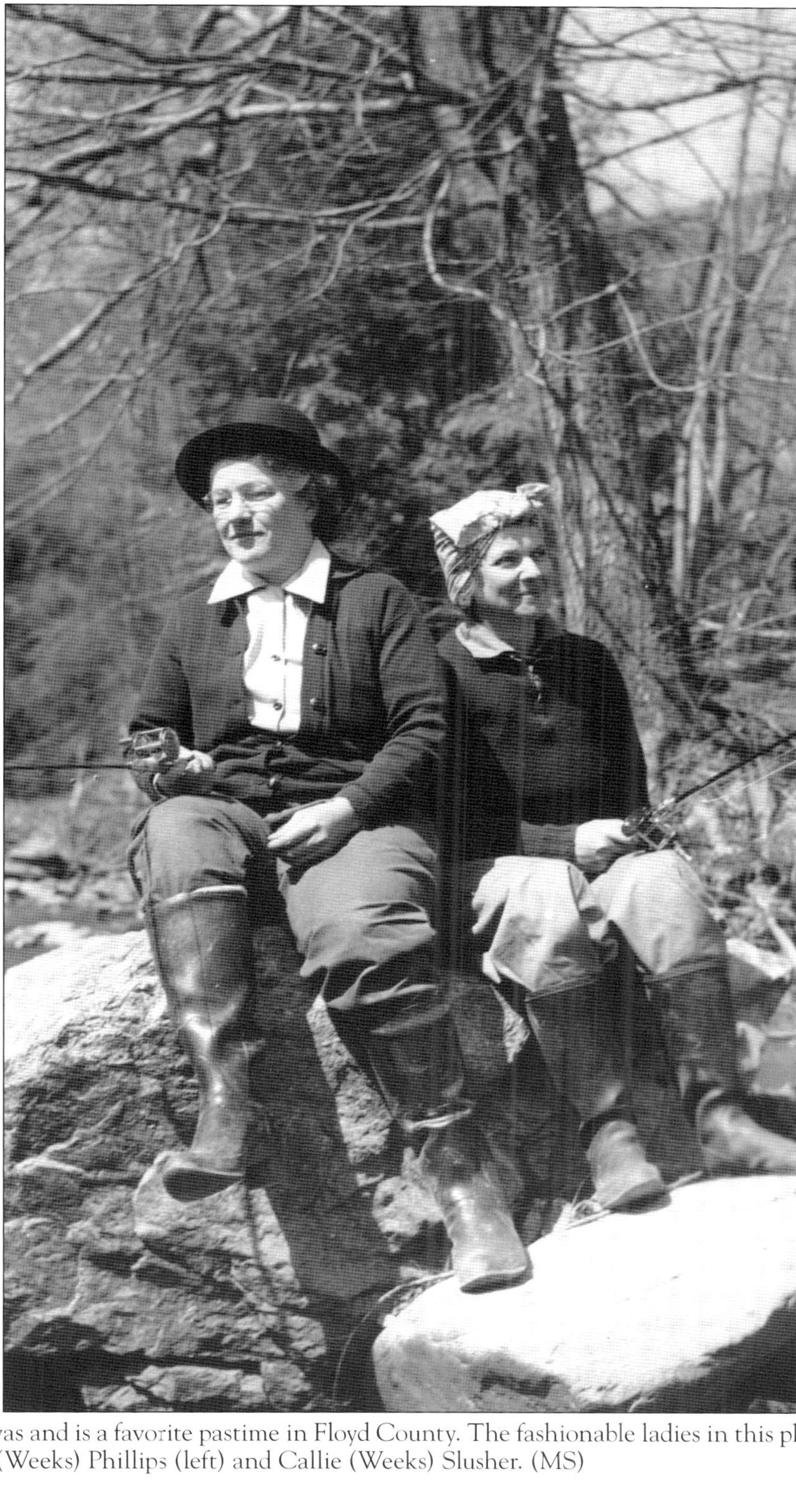

Fishing was and is a favorite pastime in Floyd County. The fashionable ladies in this photograph are Zula (Weeks) Phillips (left) and Callie (Weeks) Slusher. (MS)

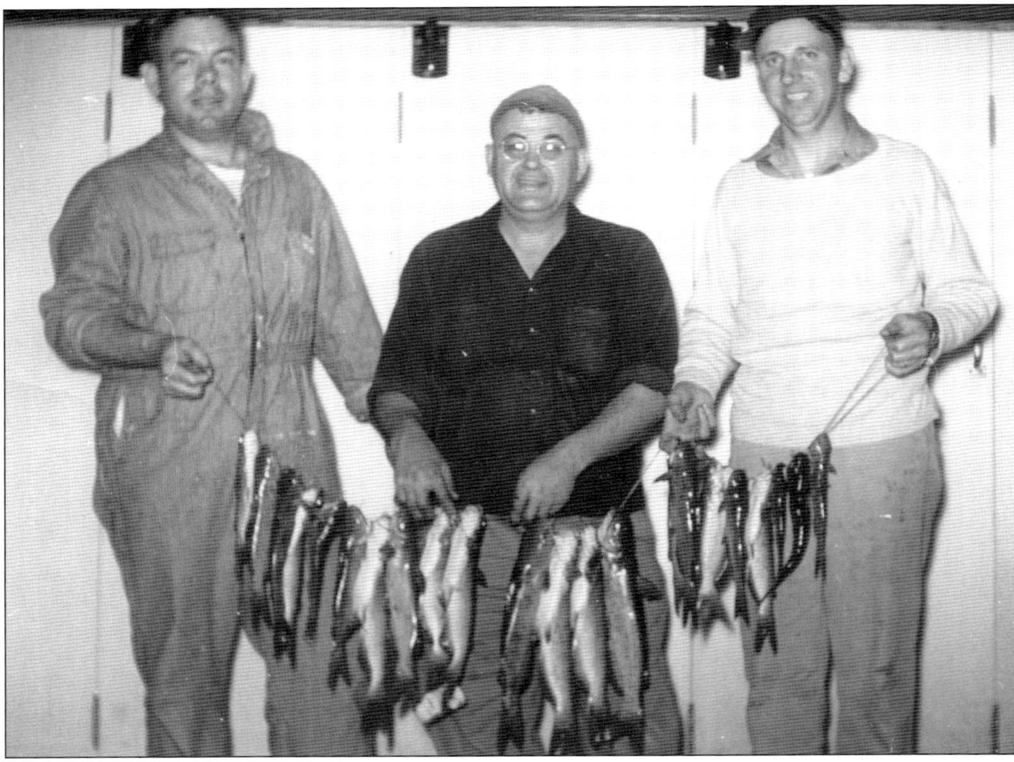

Trooper Tom Gibbs, Dinky Harris, and John R. Graham show off their catch from the Little River. (JG)

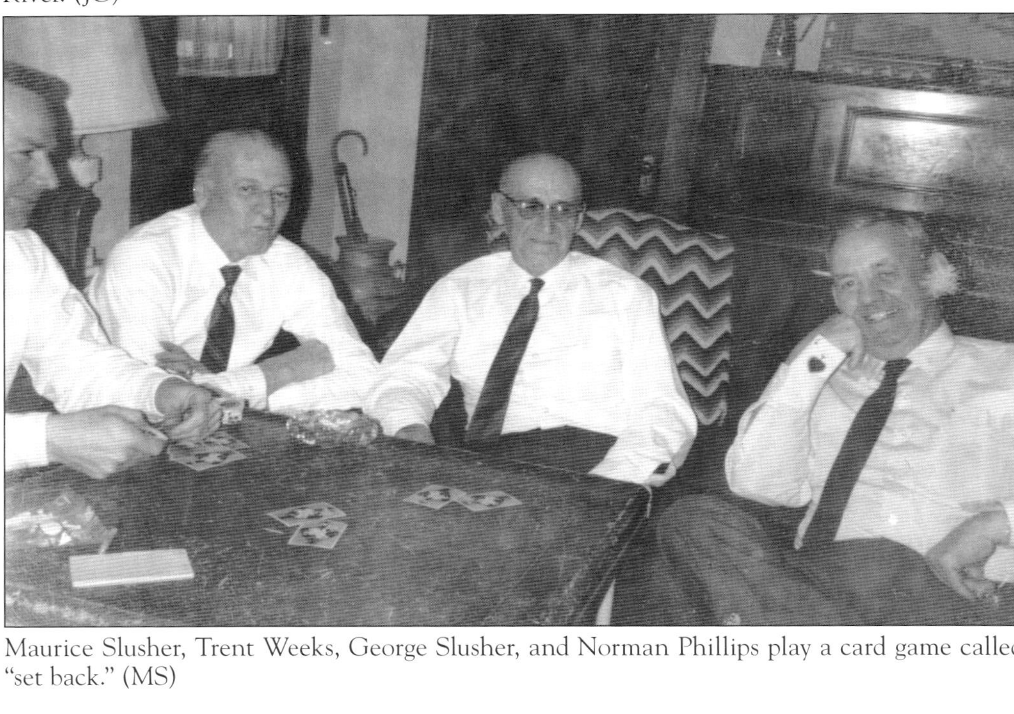

Maurice Slusher, Trent Weeks, George Slusher, and Norman Phillips play a card game called "set back." (MS)

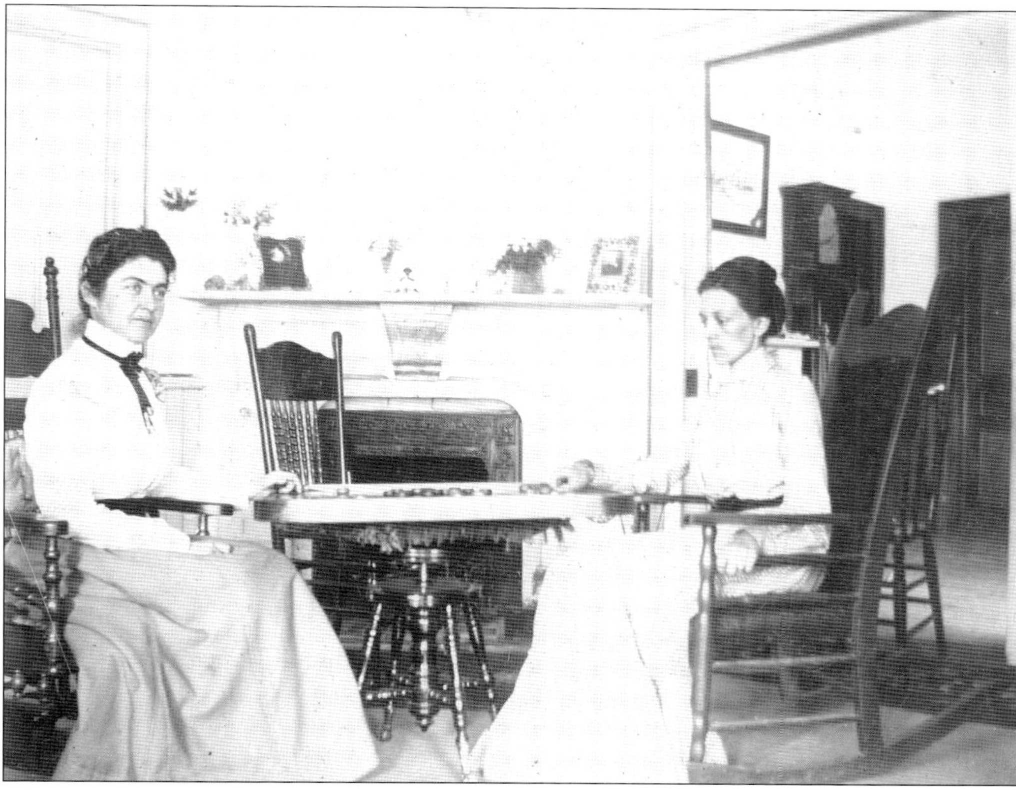

These two ladies are playing a parlor game called carrom. The board is set up on a piano stool.

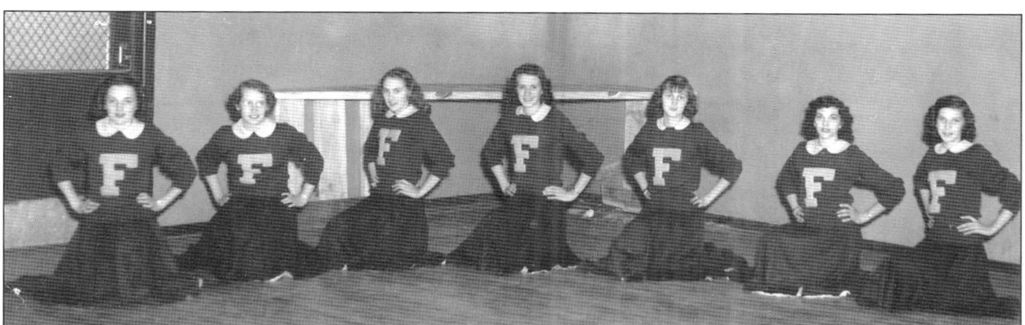

These 1950 Floyd High School cheerleaders were senior Norma Graham, senior Christene Thomas, junior Elizabeth Markle, junior Virginia Yearout, sophomore Betty Sumner, senior Susie Sweeney, and junior Margie Graham. (JG)

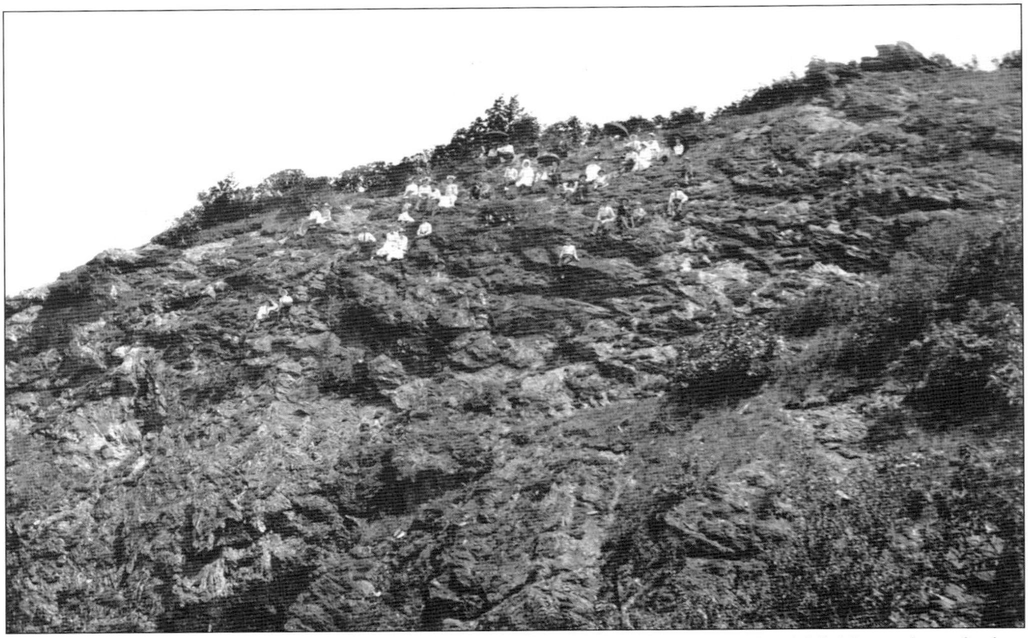

Locals climb the Buffalo, the highest peak in Floyd County, on June 23, 1905. Now identified as a natural area preserve, it continues to attract hikers and sightseers.

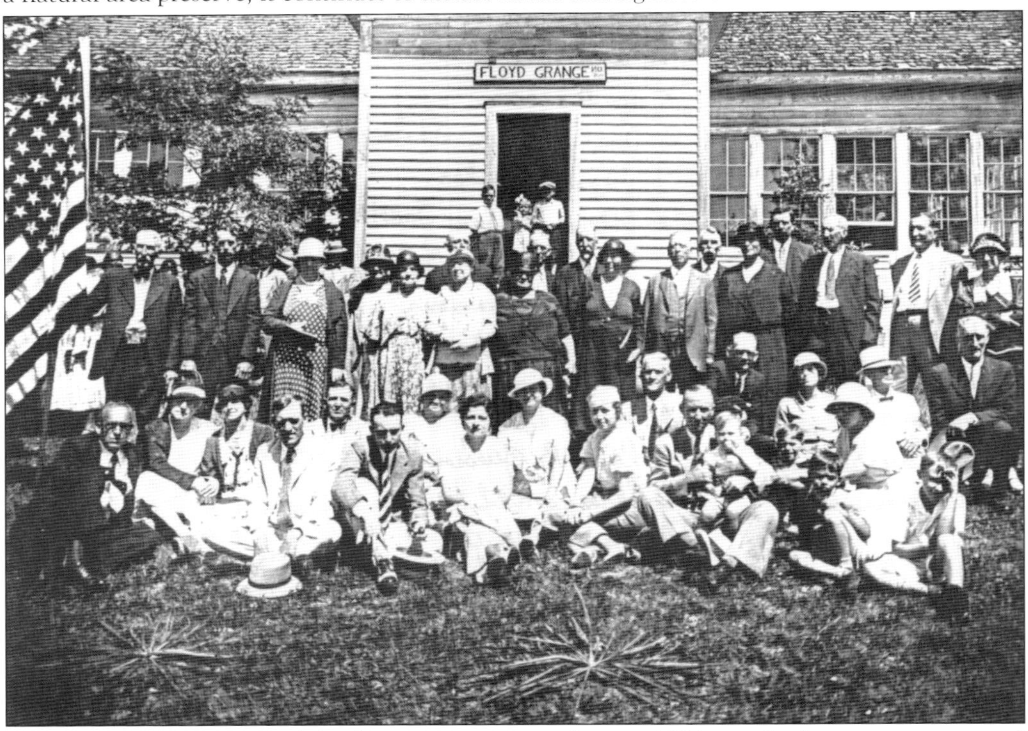

The Floyd Grange, south of Floyd on Route 221, seen here in 1937, was the first grange organized in Southwest Virginia. Many of these people have been identified as members of the Skidmore, Vaughn, Smith, Quesenberry, Via, Dillon, Howard, Shelor, and Simmons families.

Six

FARMING AND FAMILY

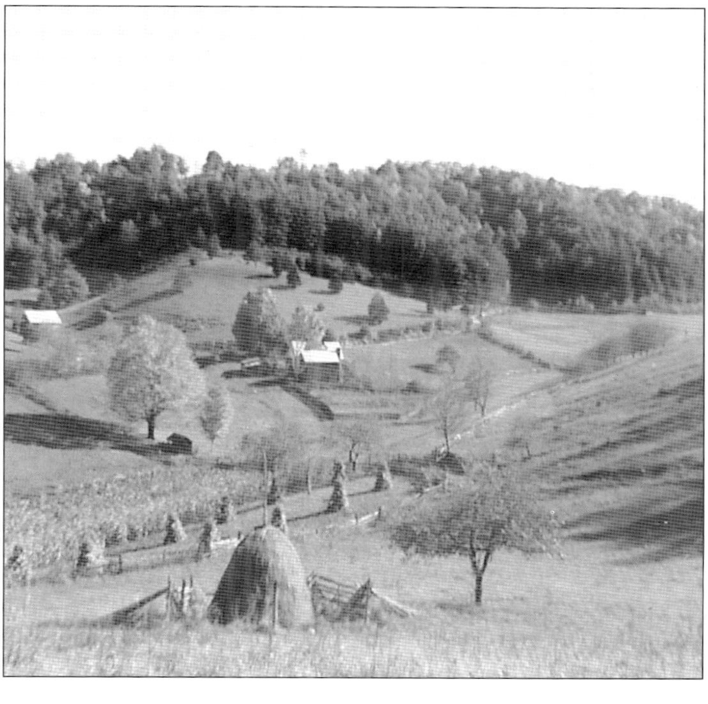

In 1838, Jacob McNeil Jr., the son of a Revolutionary War soldier, and his wife, Elizabeth Auldridge, settled their family on 1,200 acres of hilly timberland near the Locust Grove section of the county. This view of the McNeil farm in the 1940s shows the husbandry of Jacob McNeil Jr.'s grandson, Thomas Benton, and Florence Aldridge McNeil, with its fenced haystack and neat rows of fodder shocks, its shaded springhouse, the log house of McNeil's son, James Ireson McNeil, and Benton's newer house behind it. (OCG)

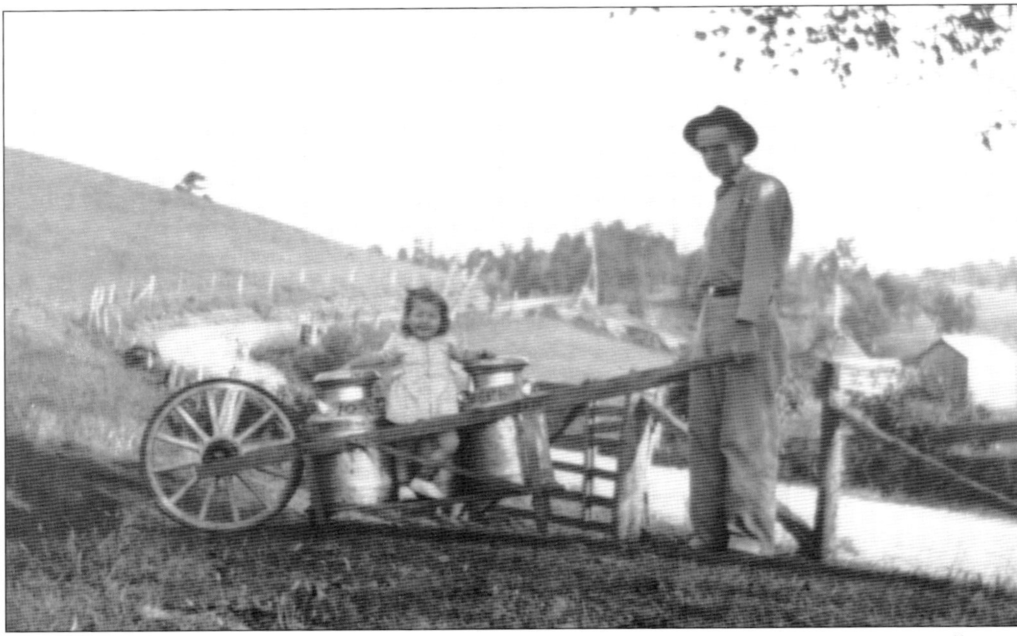

Freeman Maurice Slusher Sr., with his daughter, Nancy, uses a wheelbarrow to transport milk cans to meet the milk hauler. From 1943 to 1949, Freeman and his wife, Ruth Gardner Slusher, milked cows in an open lot and cooled milk, sold as Grade C, in cans in running spring water. (JSK)

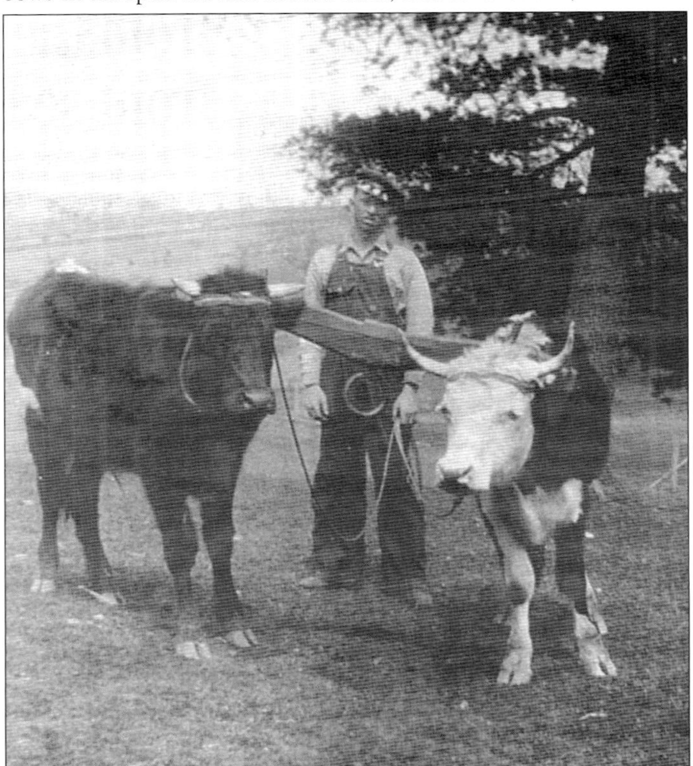

A young boy poses with a yoke of young steers whose dams were likely the family's milk cows. (JH)

Roosevelt Phillips pauses while laying off garden rows using a homemade layoff plow pulled by Hereford steers. (DDS)

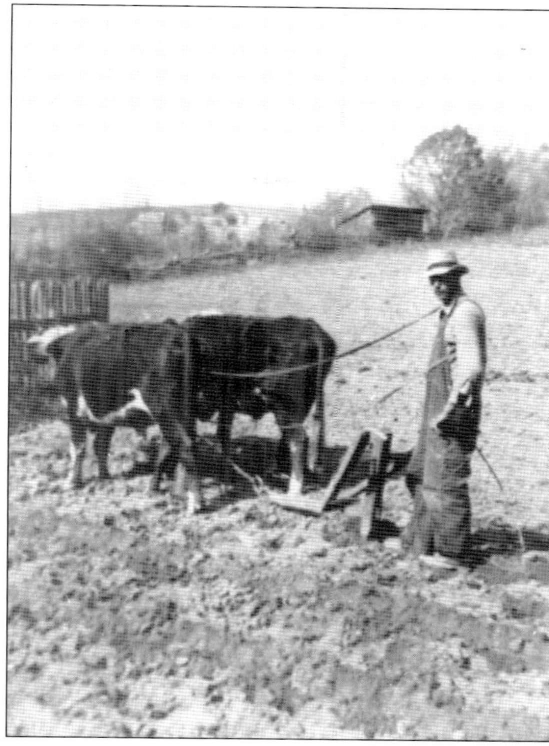

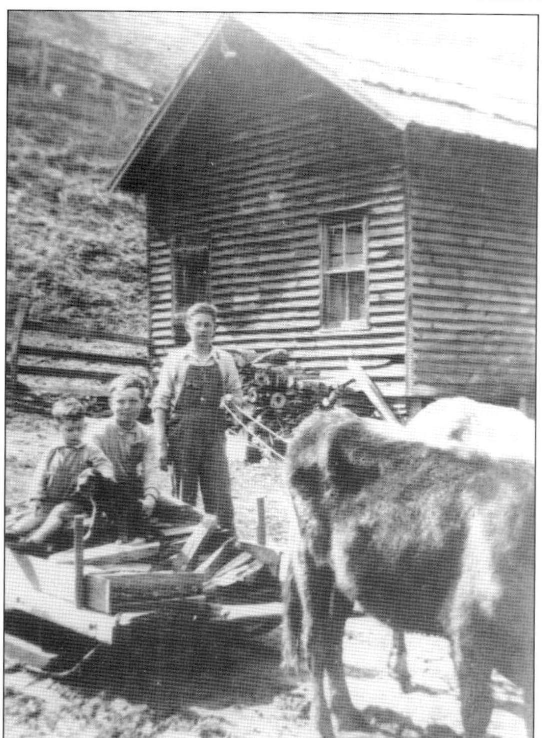

From left to right, Richard, Marvin, and Melvin Cox haul stove wood with a sled pulled by a yoke of young steers around 1937. (RC)

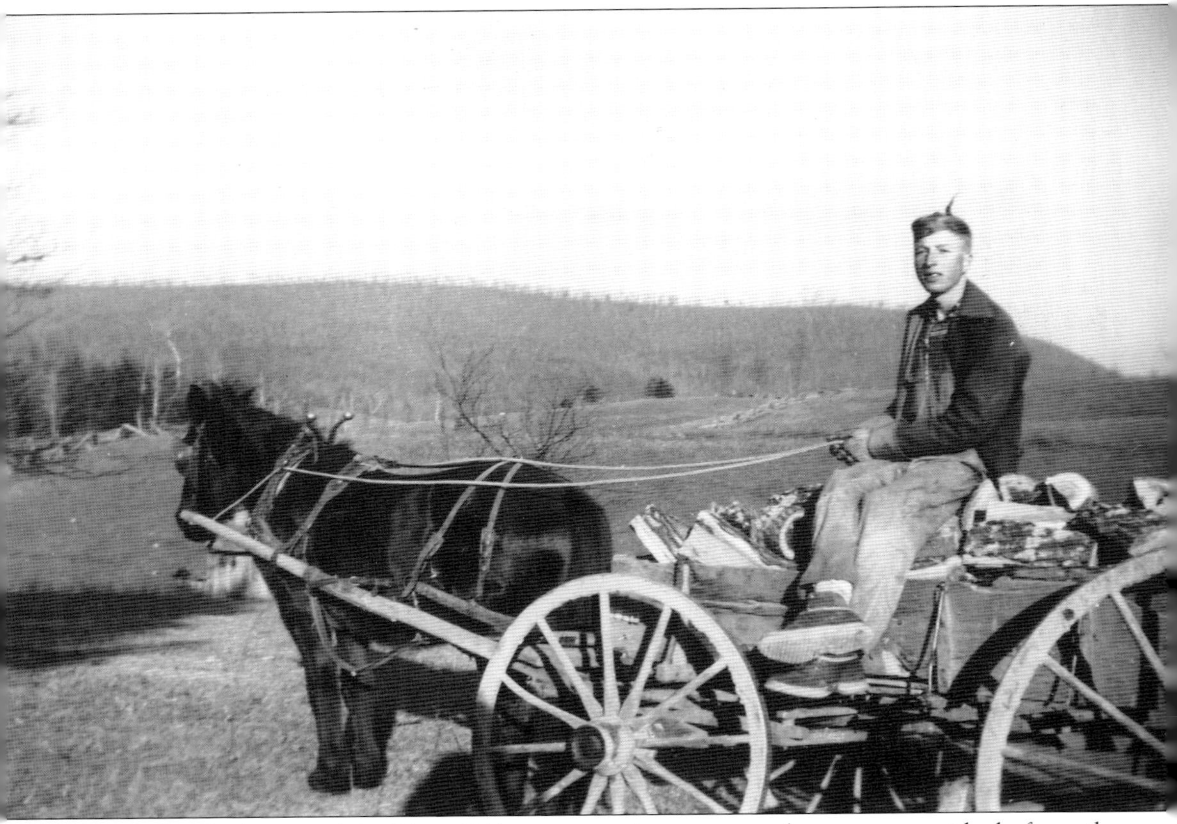

Haydon Dickerson of the Horse Ridge community uses a one-horse wagon with shafts, rather than a wagon tongue, to haul in stove wood around 1940. Owners of very small farms sometimes kept only one horse, combining with a neighbor to make a team for heavier work such as plowing crop fields. (HD)

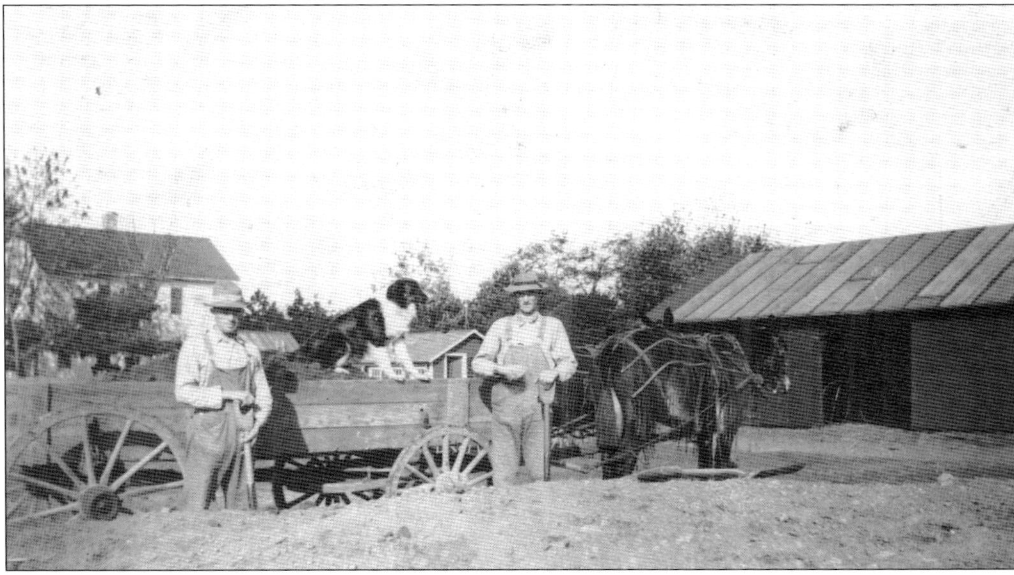

These horses and the dog patiently wait as Bruce Marshall and Peyton Reece complete the task at hand in Shady Grove. (DDS)

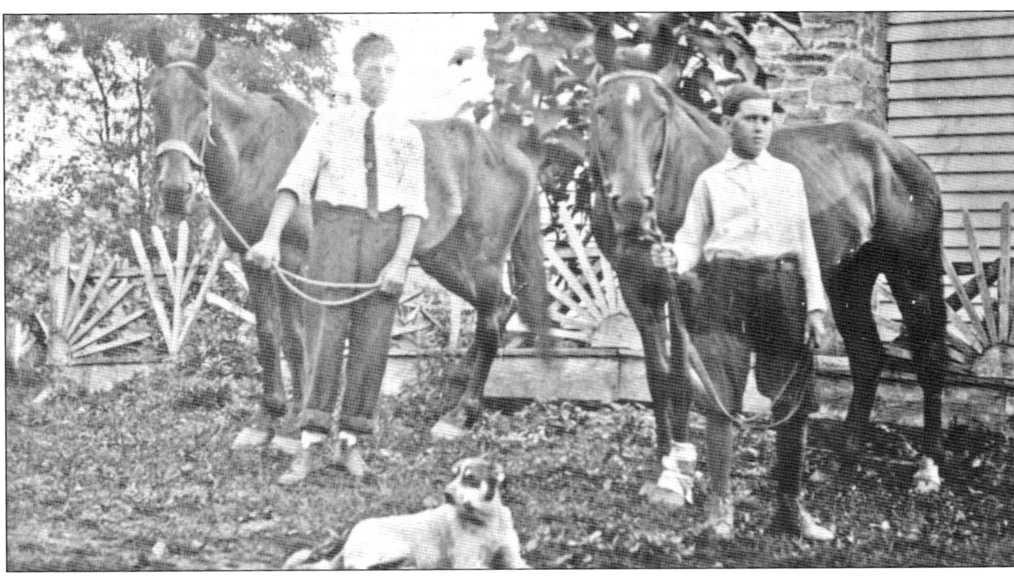

At the Reed Phillips home place, distinguished by its sunset fence, Early Phillips holds Frank, and his brother, Jett, holds Dan, who he said "could almost talk to you" and was great friends with the dog, Teddy. As Jett Phillips said, "A horse knows a dog and a dog knows a horse." (RC)

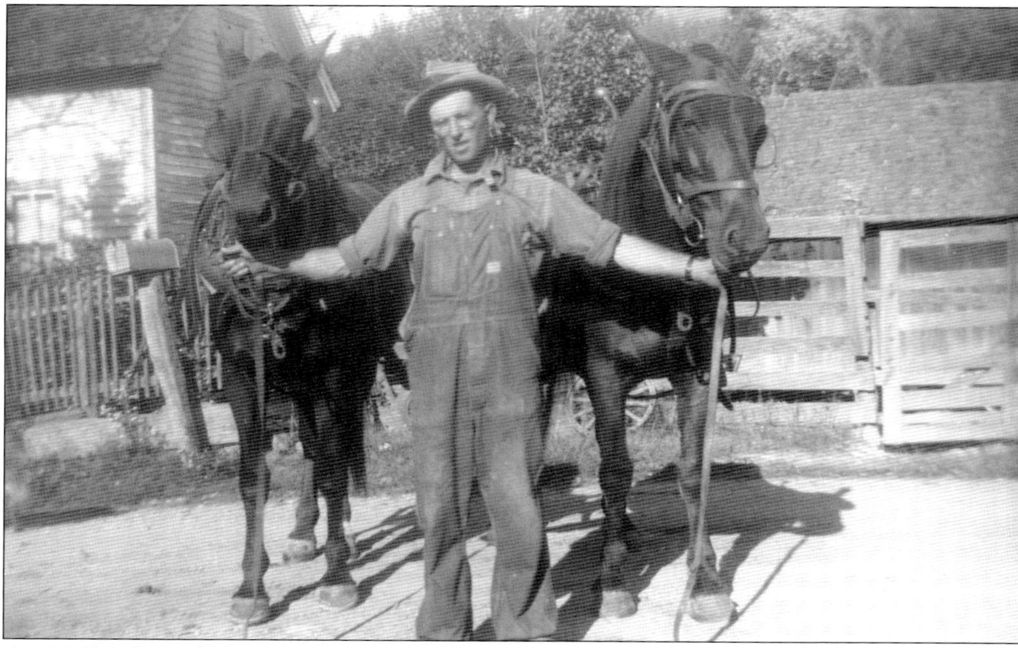

Asa Hollandsworth pauses in the late 1930s after putting work harnesses on his horses, Roy and Nell, at his Indian Valley farm. (RC)

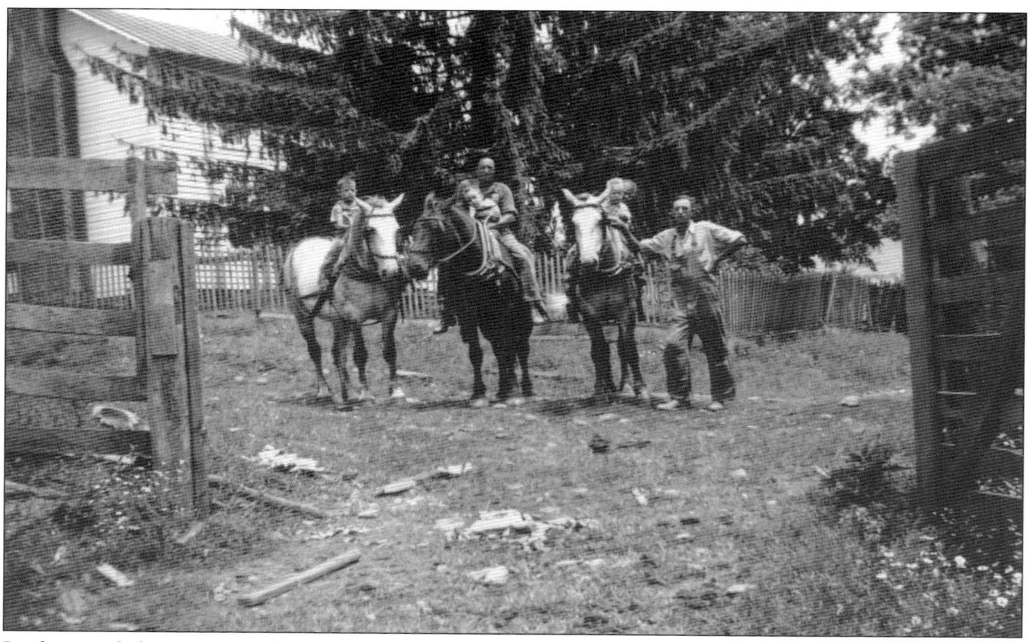

In front of their parents' home at Union around 1944, Dewey and Lemon Keith pause for a photograph with their children before beginning the day's farm work. From left to right, they are, Lemon Keith's son, John Lewis Keith, on Daisy; Dewey Keith and his son, Harold Lee Keith, on Bill; Lemon's sons, Charles Ray and Franklin Keith, on Dan; and Lemon Keith. (JSK)

This loaded wagon pulled by a mule team was likely heading to a barn to store the hay or unthreshed grain in the loft.

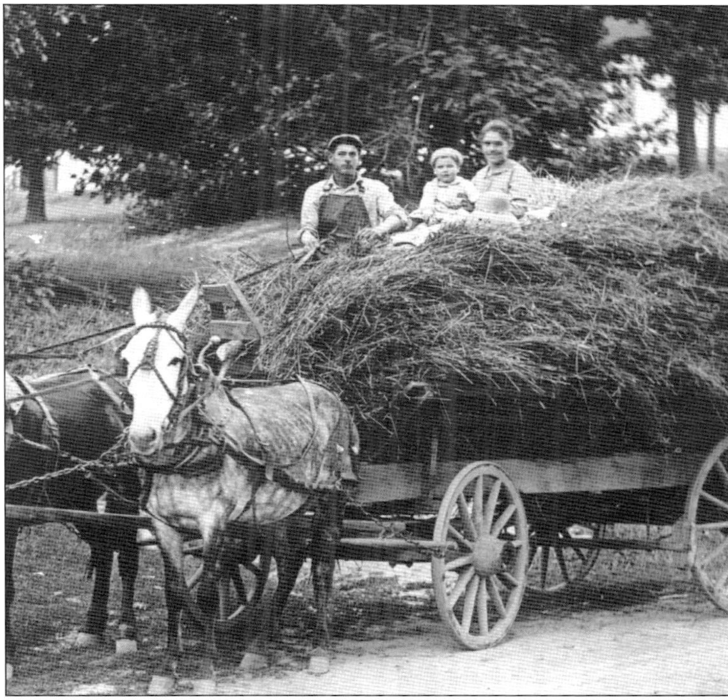

This cantilevered bank barn, built by Hardin Price Hylton, the first Hylton postmaster, on Route 221 at Route 787, is considered the oldest structure in the Willis area. It was bought in 1905 by Albert Gardner and in 1940 by Marvin Sowers. Horses would pull a loaded wagon up the bank in back and into the double-pen loft, large enough to allow horses to be unhitched there and taken out. (JSK)

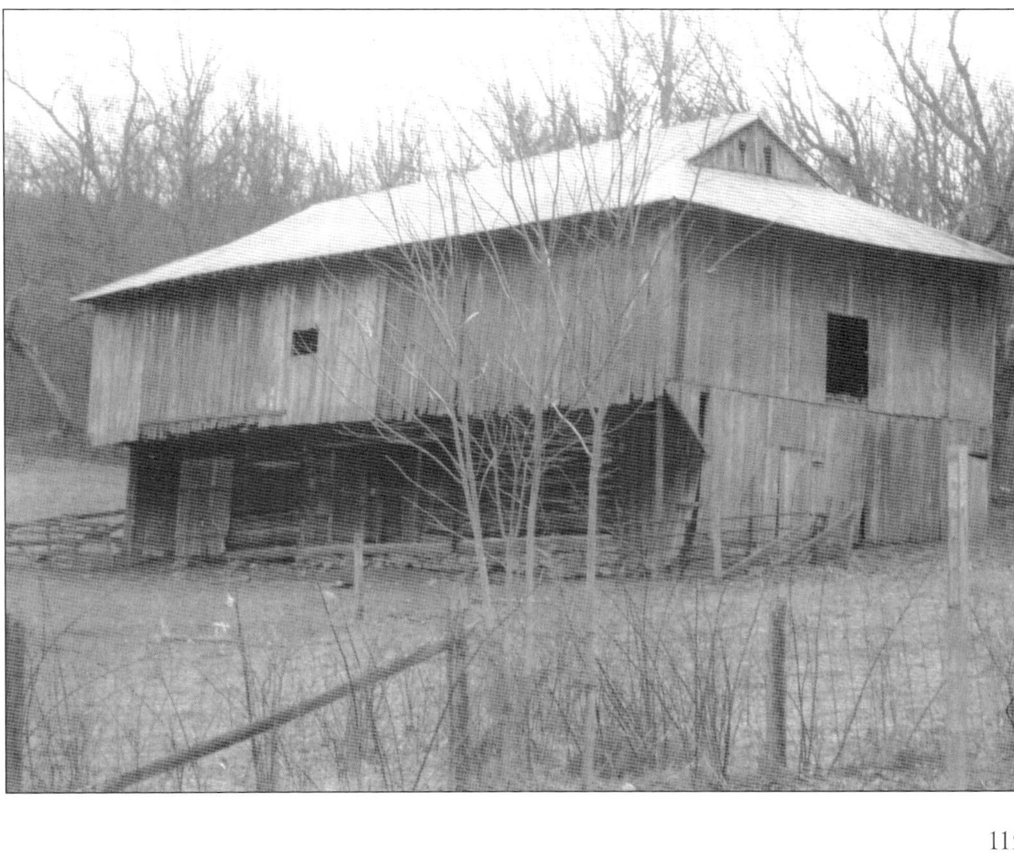

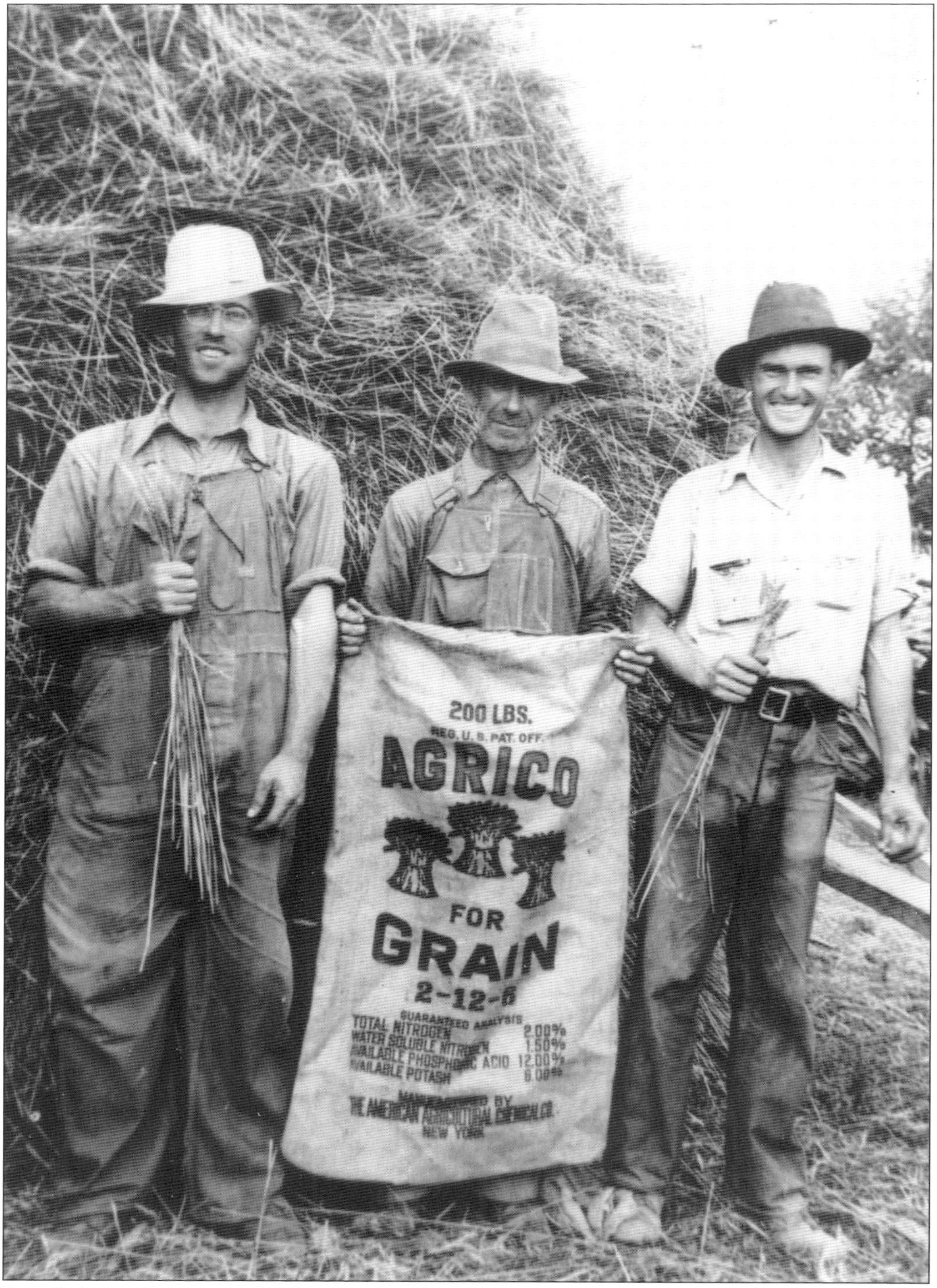

From left to right, Asa Hollandsworth, his half-brother, Sherman Hollandsworth, and Sherman's son, Martin, proudly pose for an advertisement for Agrico fertilizer, which they had used for their wheat crop around 1935. (RC)

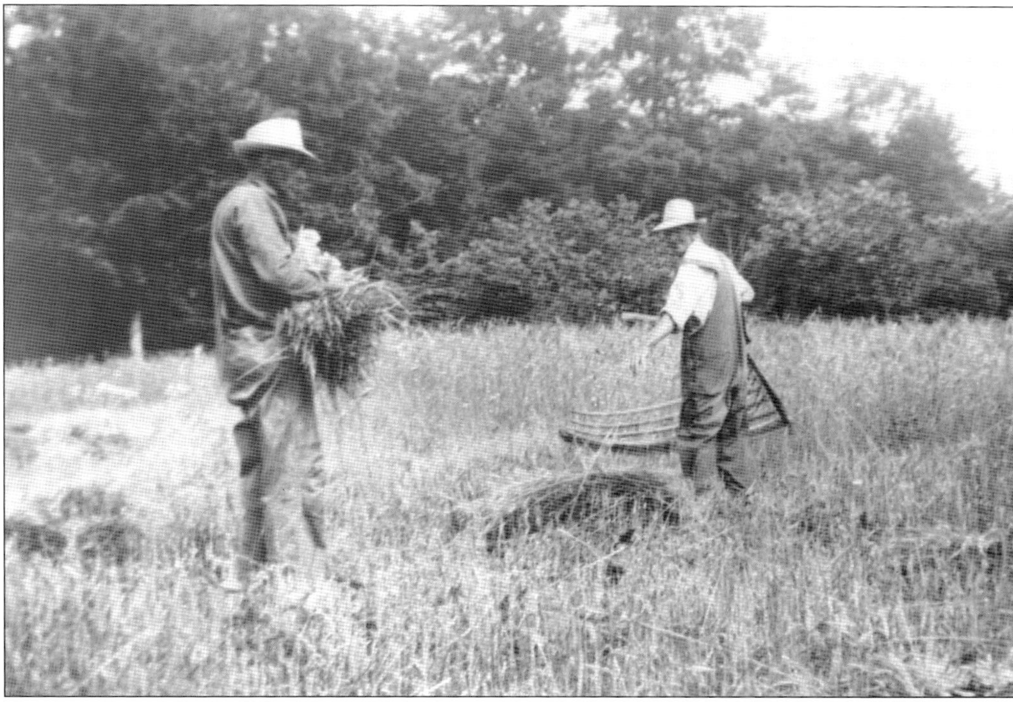

Brothers Roosevelt (left) and Wesley Phillips cradle a boundary of oats. A handful of stalks would be twisted to bind each sheaf and seven sheaves would form a shock, with stalks of the top sheaf bent to form a cap covering the heads of the other six. Once dry, they were stored in a barn loft or stacked in the field to await threshing. (DDS)

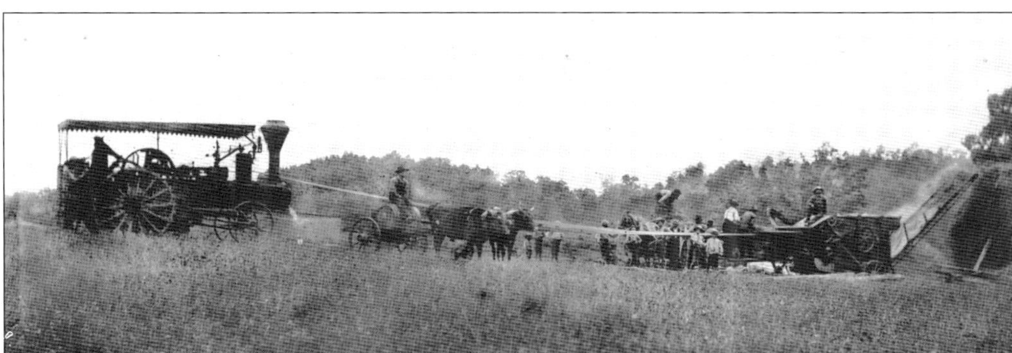

This steam engine on the James Asa Sowers farm in 1905, while remaining a safe distance from the dry straw to avoid igniting a fire, both pulled and powered—see the pulley belt—the threshing machine, which separated grain from straw and chaff. The cart, pulled by a team of oxen, transported firewood and water to fuel the steam engine. Farmers exchanged work during threshing time.

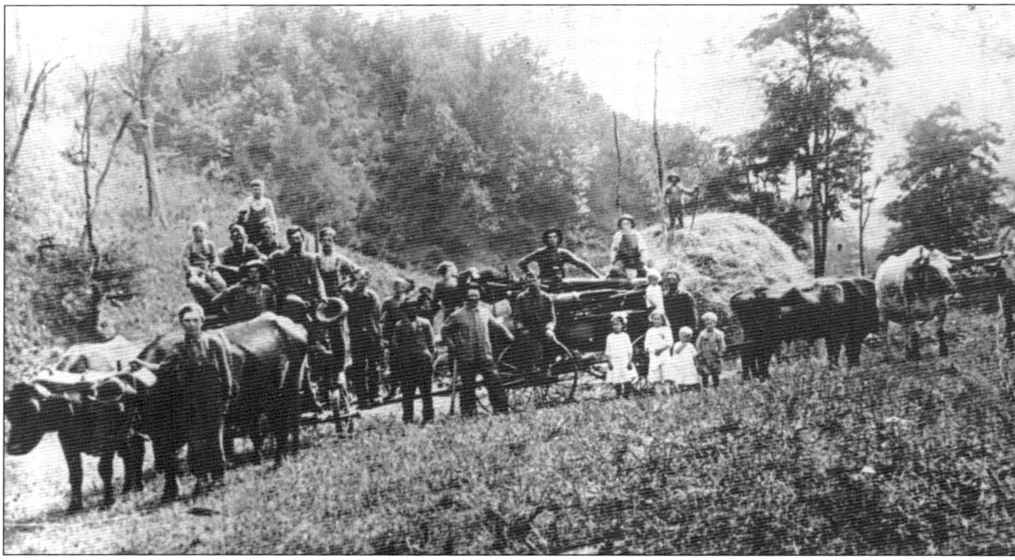

With threshing completed, the Boyd and Quesenberry families prepare to leave the Ross Hollandsworth farm. Wives prepared a meal for all who came to help, and children did age-appropriate jobs. The straw was either stacked or hauled to the barn to use for feed, cattle bedding, or filling for mattresses. (GB)

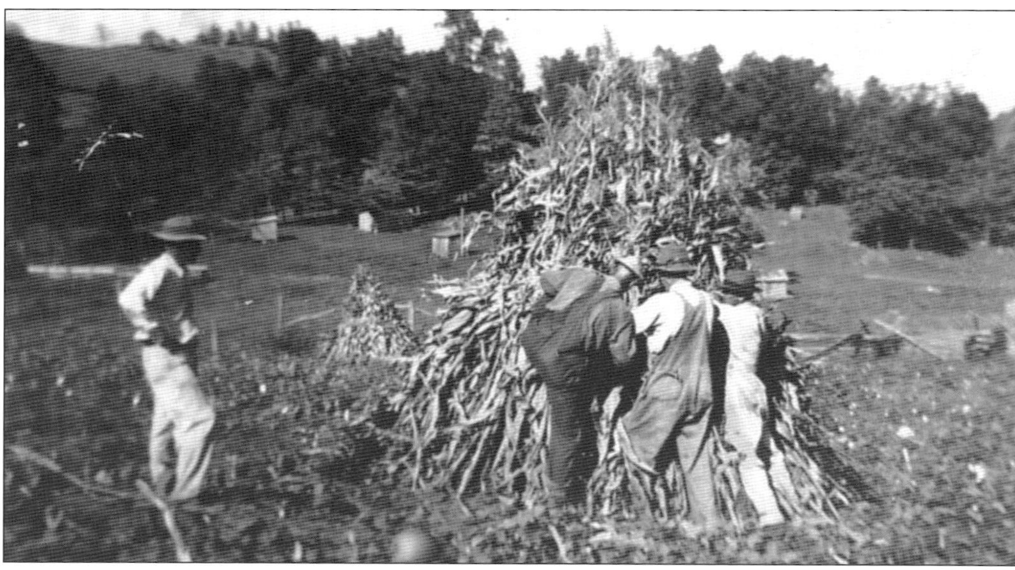

With George Slusher looking on, (from left to right) Roy Weddle, Roger Slusher, and Hugh Simmons work together using cornstalks to bind a large shock of field corn fodder, from which the corn has been shucked. On his Rush Fork farm, Roger Slusher fed the fodder to cattle as roughage to supplement hay during winter months. (APS)

The J.A.L. Sutphin family prepares to harvest apples, an important food crop. Bushels of apples were stored in cellars to be used throughout the winter. Many were preserved by drying for fried apple pies; others were cooked and canned as applesauce or apple butter. (APS)

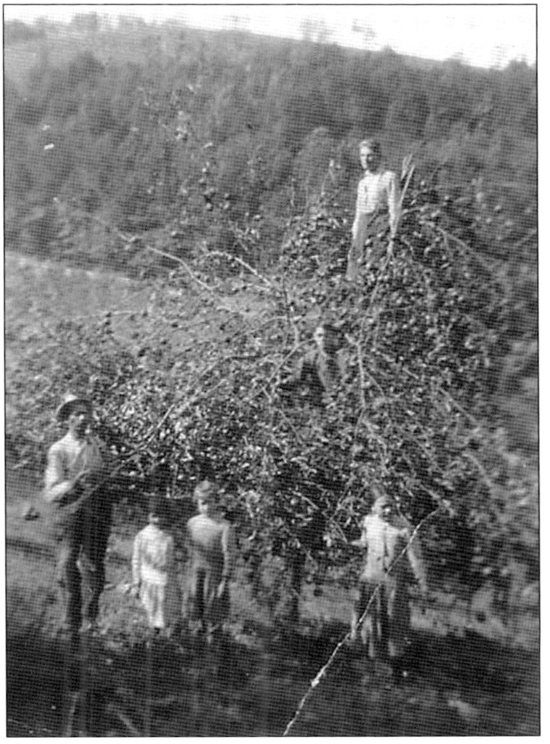

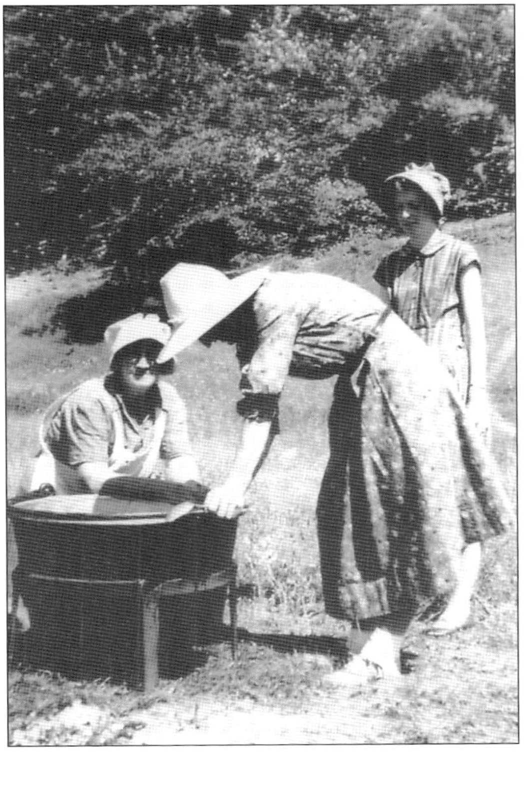

Cora Phillips (left), Dovie Phillips (center), and Dovie's daughter, Aldene Phillips, are possibly scrubbing the greenish "canker" from their copper kettle with vinegar and soda before starting a run of apple butter. But rolled-up sleeves and the lack of sweaters suggest that this is the end, rather than the beginning of a long autumn day in the southwest section of Indian Valley. (ZQ)

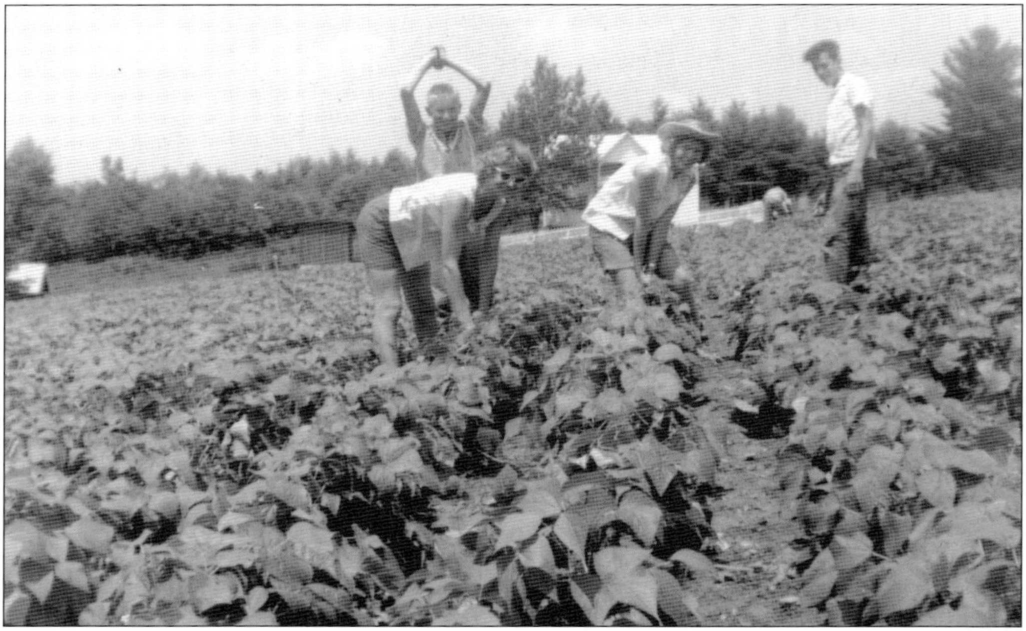

Like many others, this family in the Shady Grove community raised beans not only for their own use but also for sale as a cash crop in nearby towns or to canneries like the Huff Cannery west of Floyd. Hard at work here are, from left to right, Diane (Burnett) Phillips, Mike Branscome, Maureen (Branscome) Dalton, and Wayne Bond. (DDS)

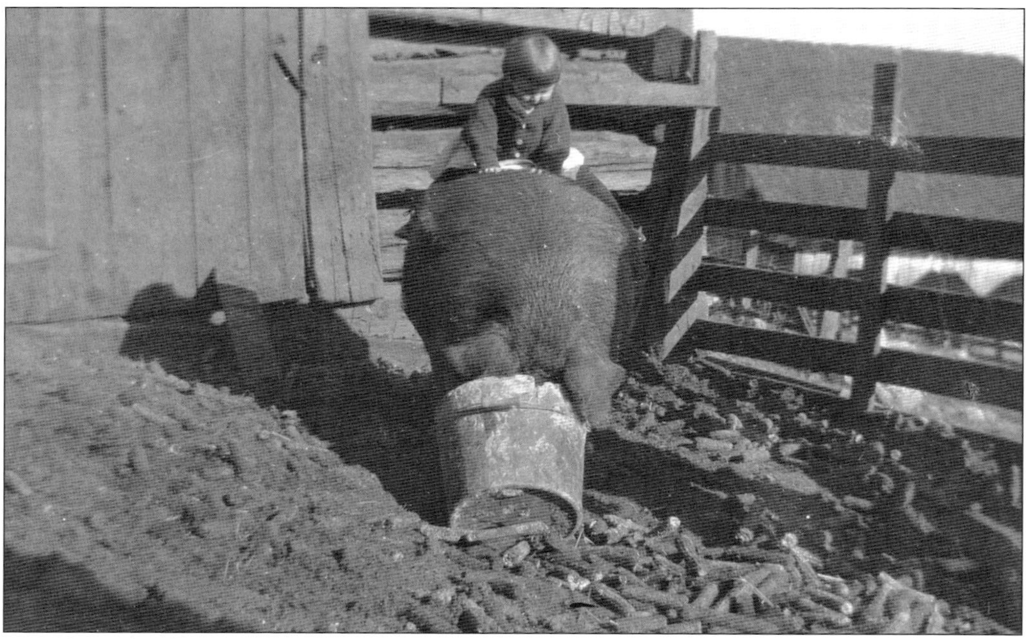

Most farm families raised hogs to have meat for their own consumption and to have salt-cured or smoke-cured hams to trade for family needs at their community store. Here, Harriet (Shank) Allen sits astride a large sow during feeding time. Note the abundance of corn cobs lining the hog lot. Later, Shank was a president of the Floyd County Historical Society. (SS)

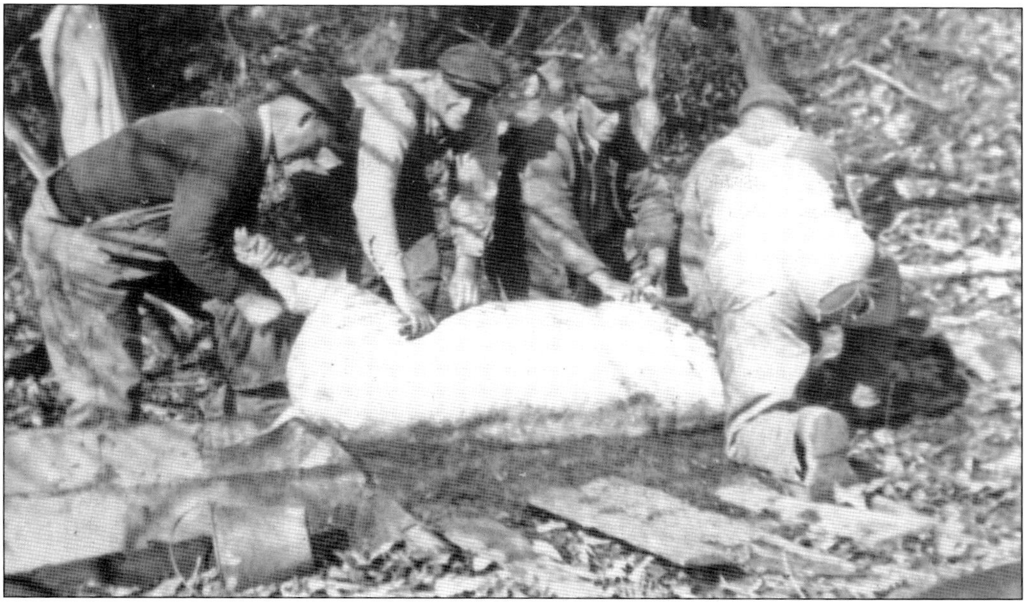

Hog-killing time was usually in late November, when the weather was cold enough for the meat not to spoil while curing and the full moon was beginning to wane—considered the best time for meat to release the most fat for lard. In 1944, Sherrod Quesenberry (far left) and Bruce Marshall (third from left) help with scraping loosened hair from a hog that has been briefly dipped in scalding water. (DDS)

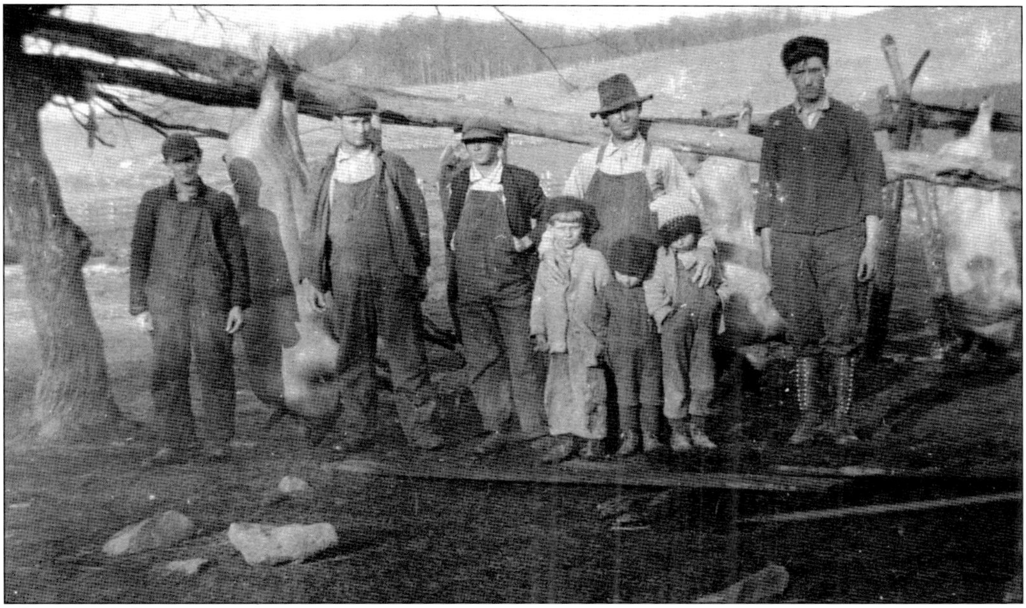

After a hog was scraped, its hamstrings in the hind legs were exposed, and a gambrel stick was inserted between the hamstrings and leg bones. The hog was then hoisted and suspended head down and the carcass was opened and cleaned out. Neighbors helped each other with the laborious tasks of butchering, preparing the meat for curing and canning, and rendering the fat for lard. (SS)

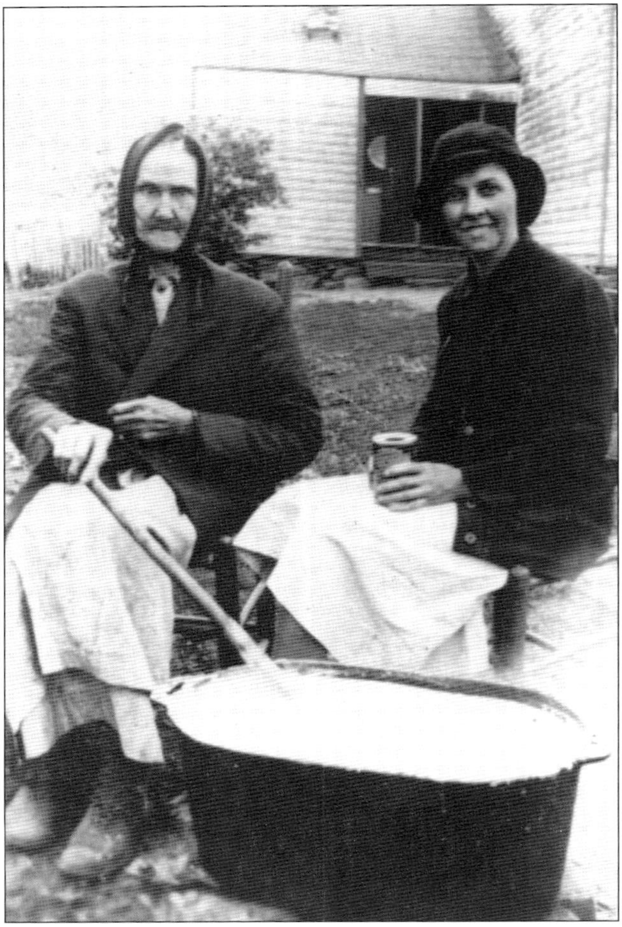

Here, soap is made from a mixture of hog lard and lye from wood ashes.

A few Floyd County farmers secured allotments to raise tobacco, a labor-intensive but profitable "money crop." Because the burley tobacco preferred in this climate is air-cured, the distinctive flue-curing barns of Southside Virginia and North Carolina were almost unknown here.

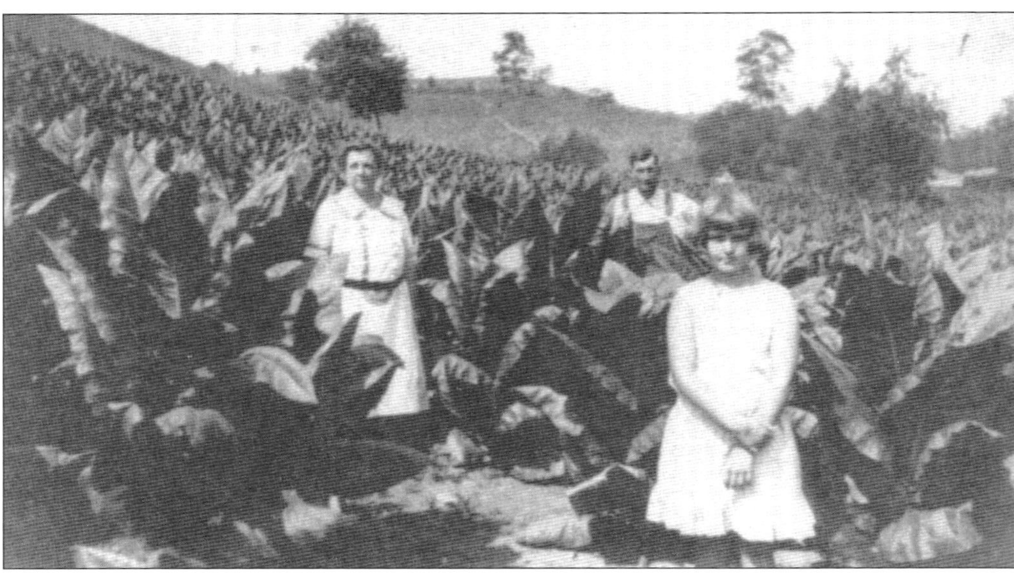

John Henry Quesenberry poses with his large flock of chickens. (DDS)

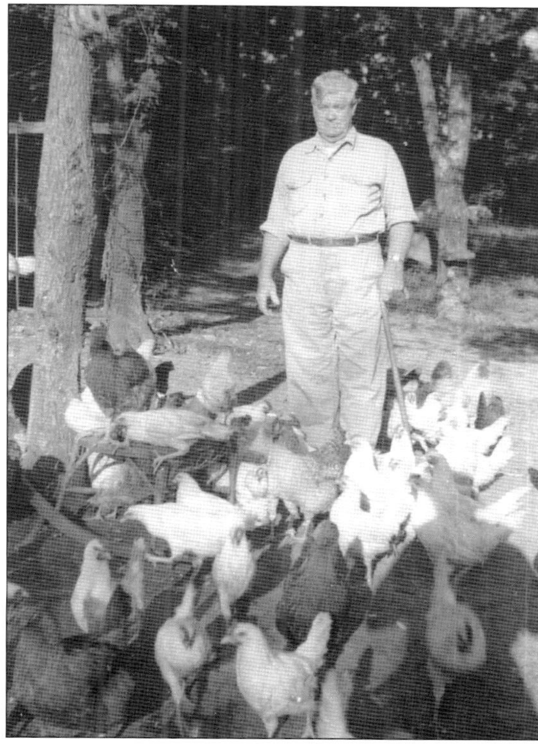

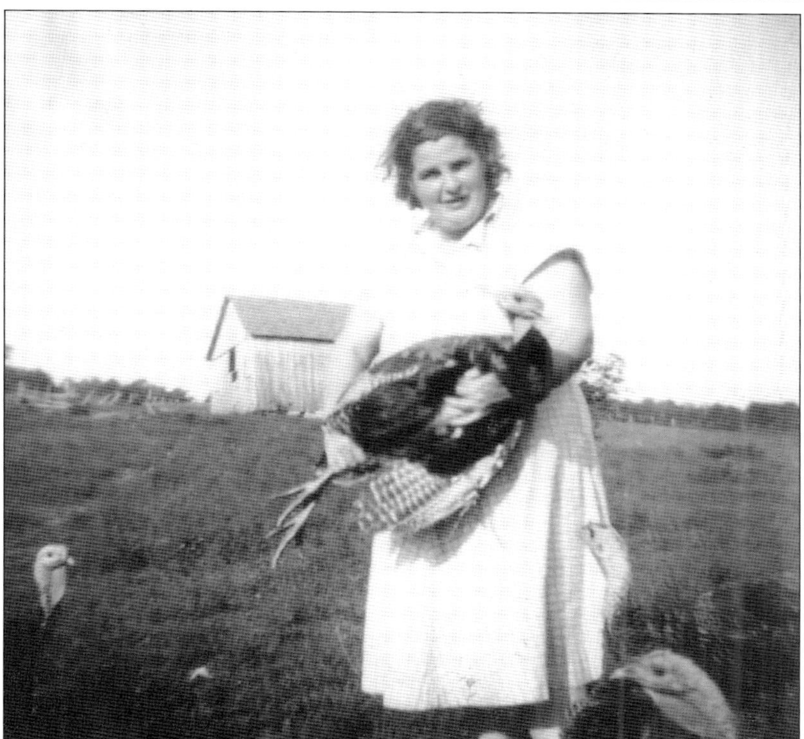

Laura Boyd of Indian Valley holds one of her turkeys. Her daughter had the job of following the turkeys to see where they laid their eggs, which was never at the same place two days in a row, and then gather the eggs for the family to eat or sell. (MMG)

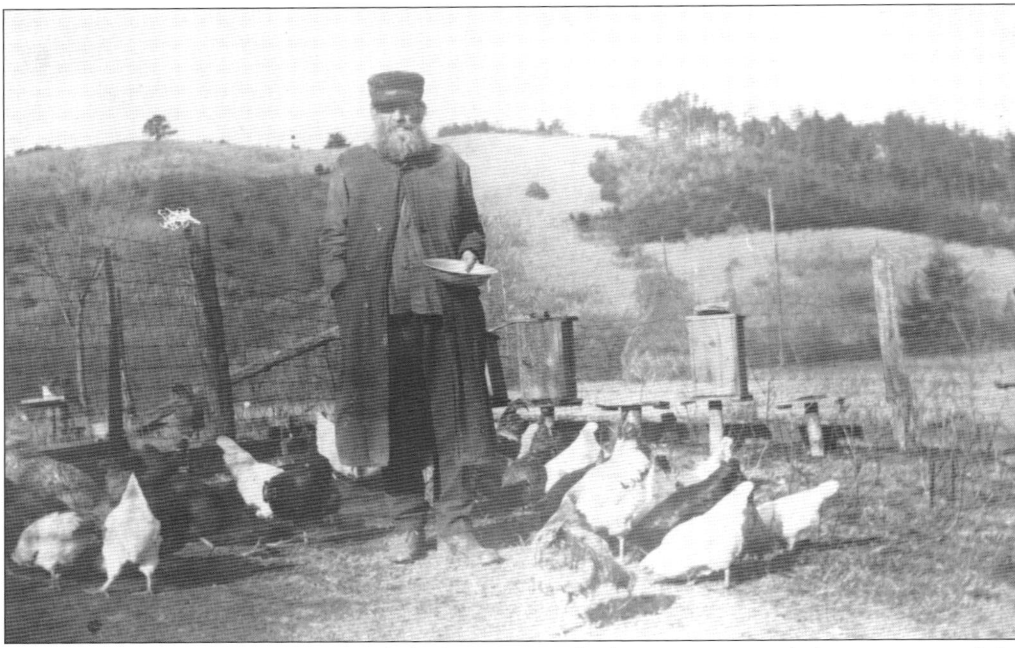

Ransles Graham raised turkeys and chickens. Note the bee gums around the perimeter of the chickens' enclosure. Honey was a valuable commodity for farm families. (OCG)

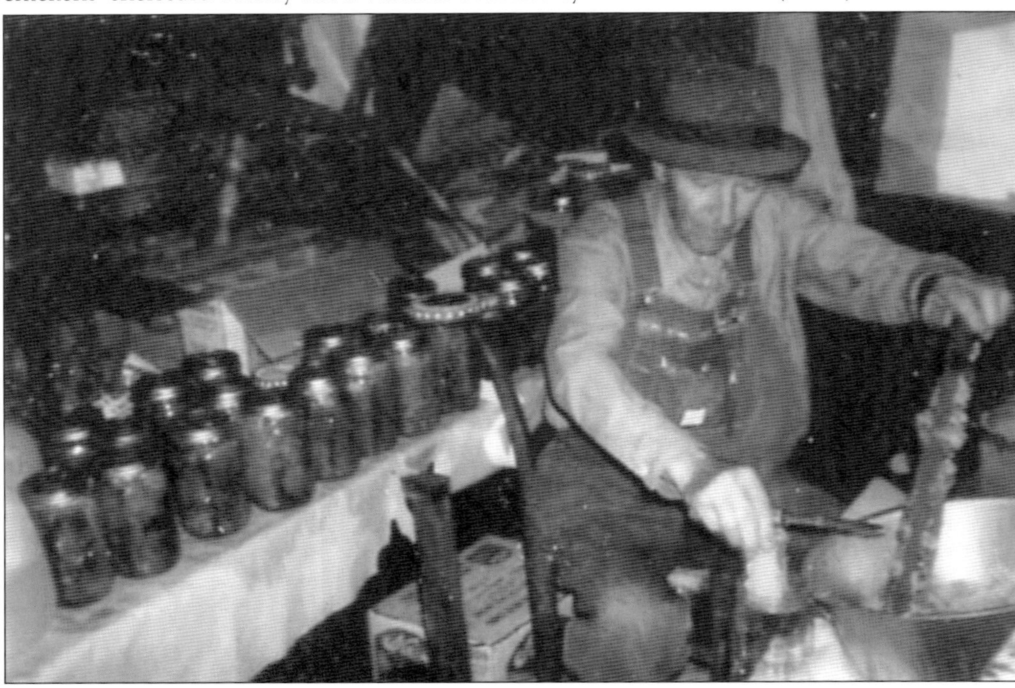

Pearl Nason Cockram cans honey and combs from his hives of bees. He is shown inside the "Honey House" cutting out the honey from frames that were placed in the bee hives. The hives were about 150 feet away from the house, located just off the Blue Ridge Parkway in the Tuggles Gap area. (DC)

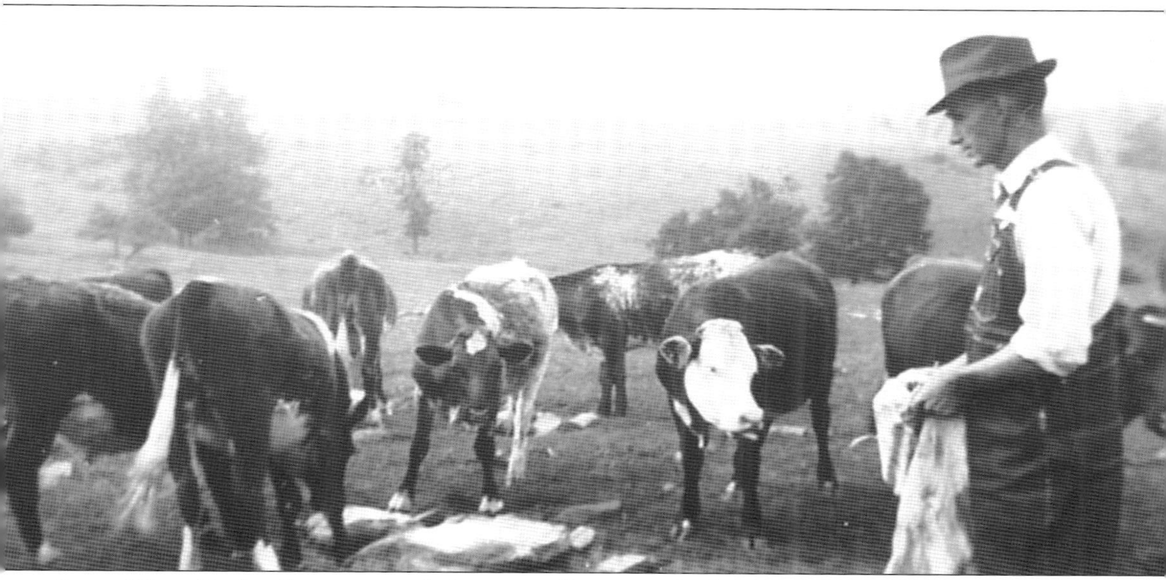

Roger Oliver Slusher Sr. puts out salt for some of his young heifers in a field on Black Ridge. Most farm families had cattle to provide milk, butter, meat, and valuable income. Many farmers used steers, or oxen, to pull farm machinery and wagons. (APS)

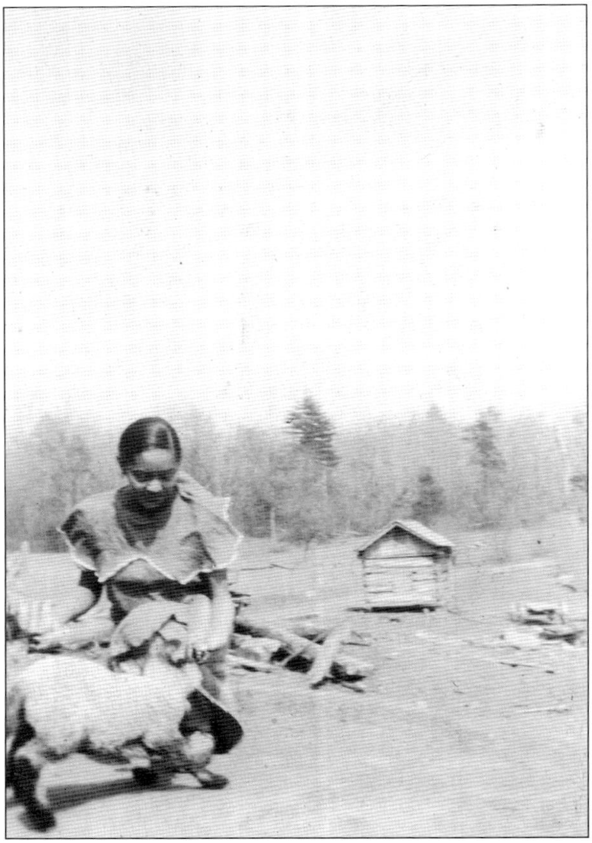

A lamb is hopeful that it is feeding time as Grace (Claytor) Beale enjoys playing with it. (WB)

From left to right, Charles K. Shelor, Floyd P. Smith, and Mary Elizabeth (Shelor) Pilson admire sheep on J.F. Smith's farm. (MAS)

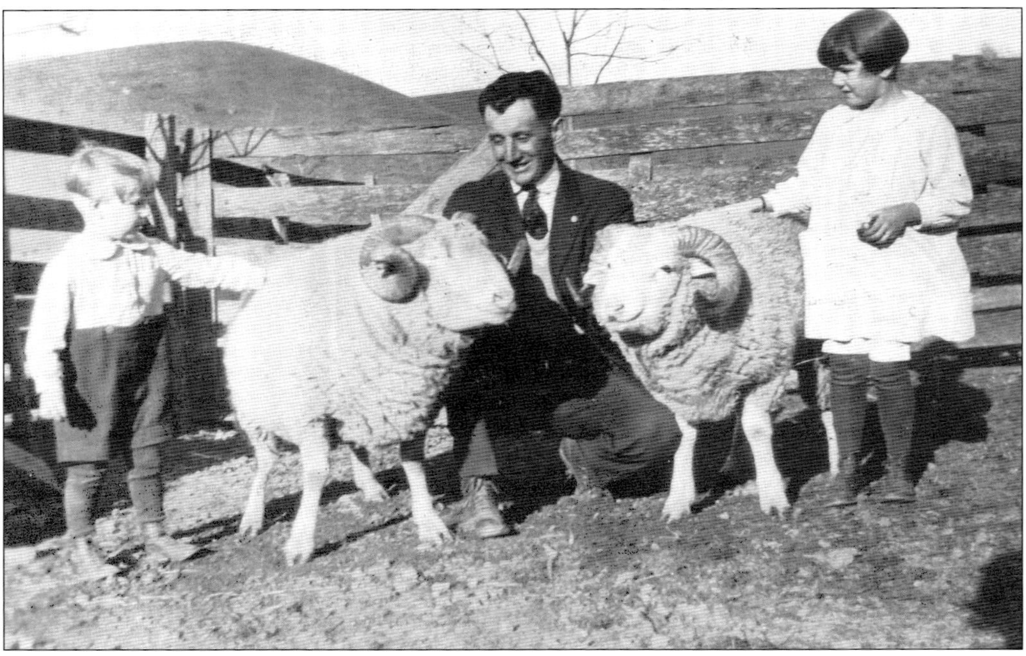

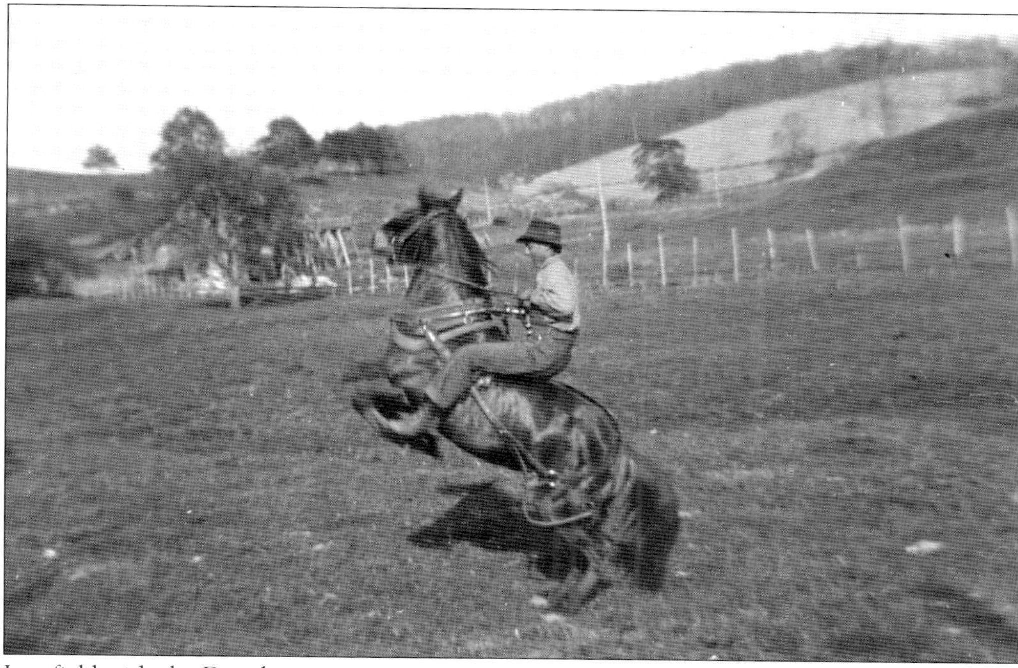

In a field with the David Vest mill in the background, a farmer and his horse, already in a work harness, enjoy showing off for the camera before the day's work begins. (SS)

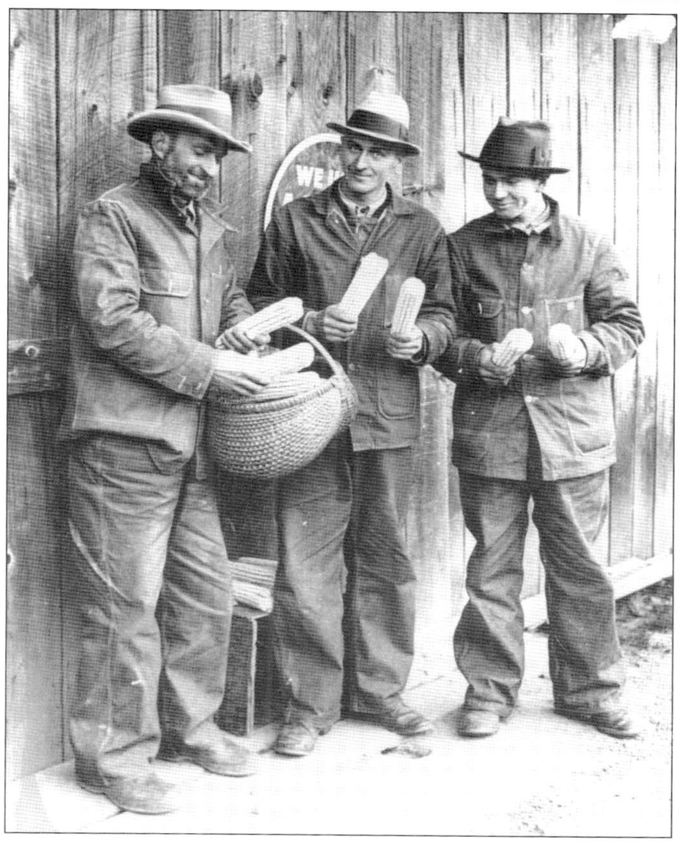

From left to right, Noah Reed and his sons, Asa and Ole Reed, admire ears of field corn from their harvest around 1940. This photograph was used as part of the seed corn provider's advertisement campaign praising the corn's size and quality. (CS)